René Girard, Theology, and Pop Culture

Theology and Pop Culture

Series Editor: Matthew Brake

The *Theology and Pop Culture* series examines the intersection of theology, religion, and popular culture, including, but not limited to television, movies, sequential art, and genre fiction. In a world plagued by rampant polarization of every kind and the decline of religious literacy in the public square, *Theology and Pop Culture* is uniquely poised to educate and entertain a diverse audience utilizing one of the few things society at large still holds in common: love for popular culture.

Titles in the series

René Girard, Theology, and Pop Culture, edited by Ryan G. Duns and T. Derrick Witherington

Theology and Horror: Explorations of the Dark Religious Imagination, edited by Brandon R. Grafius and John W. Morehead

Sports and Play in Christian Theology, edited by Philip Halstead and John Tucker

Theology and Prince, edited by Jonathan H. Harwell and Rev. Katrina E. Jenkins

Theology and the Marvel Universe, edited by Gregory Stevenson

Theology and Westworld, edited by Juli Gittinger and Shayna Sheinfeld

René Girard, Theology, and Pop Culture

Ryan G. Duns and T. Derrick Witherington

LEXINGTON BOOKS/FORTRESS ACADEMIC
Lanham • Boulder • New York • London

Published by Lexington Books/Fortress Academic
Lexington Books is an imprint of The Rowman & Littlefield Publishing Group, Inc.
4501 Forbes Boulevard, Suite 200, Lanham, Maryland 20706
www.rowman.com

6 Tinworth Street, London SE11 5AL, United Kingdom

Copyright © 2021 The Rowman & Littlefield Publishing Group, Inc.

All rights reserved. No part of this book may be reproduced in any form or by any electronic or mechanical means, including information storage and retrieval systems, without written permission from the publisher, except by a reviewer who may quote passages in a review.

British Library Cataloguing in Publication Information Available

Library of Congress Cataloging-in-Publication Data

Names: Duns, Ryan G., 1979–, editor. | Witherington, T. Derrick, 1985–, editor.
Title: René Girard, theology, and pop culture / [edited by] Ryan G. Duns and T. Derrick Witherington.
Description: Lanham : Lexington Books/Fortress Academic, [2021] | Series: Theology and pop culture | Includes bibliographical references and index. | Summary: "René Girard, Theology, and Pop Culture provides a fresh and engaging introduction to and the application of René Girard's mimetic theory. From movies to social media, television to graphic novels, the contributors explore popular culture's theological depths and challenge readers to consider what culture reveals about them"—Provided by publisher.
Identifiers: LCCN 2021015870 (print) | LCCN 2021015871 (ebook) | ISBN 9781978710085 (cloth) | ISBN 9781978710108 (pbk) | ISBN 9781978710092 (epub)
Subjects: LCSH: Girard, René, 1923–2015. | Memetics. | Popular culture. | Theology. | Popular culture—Religious aspects.
Classification: LCC B2430.G494 R53 2021 (print) | LCC B2430.G494 (ebook) | DDC 302.01—dc23
LC record available at https://lccn.loc.gov/2021015870
LC ebook record available at https://lccn.loc.gov/2021015871

Contents

Acknowledgments		vii
Introduction		ix
1	Mimesis, *Mean Girls*, and the Culture Creating Them: Tina Fey's Interrogation of the Teen Comedy *Brian Bajzek*	1
2	*Star Wars*: Between Myth and Gospel *Erik Buys*	13
3	Desire, the Scapegoated Other, and J.J. Abrams' *The Force Awakens* *John C. McDowell*	27
4	Girard's Lasso of Truth: *Wonder Woman* and the Overcoming of Satan *Stephanie Perdew*	43
5	Those Who Have Eyes to See: The Divine Origins of the Modern Plot Twist *Jordan Almanzar*	57
6	Gazing into a Mirror: Watching *Hoarders* with Girard *Ryan G. Duns*	71
7	From the Hermeneutic of Violence to Redemption: *The 100* and Mimetic Theory *Paolo Diego Bubbio*	87
8	Mercy, Honor, and Girardian Conversion in *The Karate Kid* and *Cobra Kai*	103

Ryan Smock

9 The Pleasures and Perils of Revenge: *Sons of Anarchy* and Girard   121
George A. Dunn

10 Exorcising Blame through *A Contract with God*: A Girardian Analysis of Will Eisner's Graphic Novel   141
Daniel DeForest London

11 Unmasking the Theological Shell: A Girardian Reading of Jonathan Hickman's *Secret Wars*   155
Matthew Brake

12 From Autonomy to Annihilation: The Monstrous Truth of the Romantic Lie   169
Robert Grant Price

13 Subtweeting in the End Times: Social Media and the Escalation to Extremes   185
Justin Lee

14 Starving for Beauty: On Anorexia and Mimetic Desire   203
Anna Scanlon

15 From #MeToo to #WeToo: Mimetic Ecclesiology and the Possibility of Structural Reform   217
T. Derrick Witherington

Index   231

About the Editors   235

About the Contributors   237

Acknowledgments

We would like to express our profound gratitude to Matthew Brake, series editor for Theology and Popular Culture. We are grateful that you believed in this project and that you contributed your voice to it. On behalf of all our authors, I would like to say a word of thanks to Martha Reineke and Grant Kaplan who were generous in their peer-review feedback. This volume has been made stronger by incisive comments. Finally, to our colleague Ethan Van Der Leek, who gave a thorough read of each essay and saved many of us from embarrassing gaffs: Thank you. Your enthusiasm for this project has been infections, and we are tremendously grateful to you for all of your work. A word of thanks, too, to our talented undergraduate reader, Noah Smith, who generously read through a number of essays and provided helpful feedback.

Many of the chapter revisions for this volume took place during the coronavirus pandemic of 2020. It has been a privilege to work with so many gifted scholars who manifested tremendous grace under great pressure. Derrick and I thank you for your intelligence, creativity, hard work, patience, and good humor.

We believe the Theology and Popular Culture series is poised to make a vital contribution to theological reflection. As the essays in this volume demonstrate, reading culture through a theological lens reveals hidden and neglected depths of our world. Theologians do not perceive a different world; rather, they perceive the world differently, as porous to the transcendent. With René Girard as our companion, we hope readers will be challenged to see the world with new eyes.

Introduction

René Girard and Mimetic Theory—the Devil Is in the Details... and in Prada

Ryan G. Duns

This book is a collection of essays demonstrating how the mimetic theory of the French-American thinker René Girard (1923–2015) can be used to uncover implicit and otherwise neglected theological themes present within popular culture. Each author has selected an artifact—a movie or television show, a literary or graphic novel, a social media phenomenon—and examined it through the lens of mimetic theory. As these authors show, Girard's theory makes apparent the fecundity of "popular culture" for theological reflection. "Popular culture," as we use it, refers to everyday structures, artifacts, beliefs, practices, and actions shared by a society. Our authors hail mainly from the United States, Australia, and Europe, and their contributions reflect their historical and cultural situatedness. Our task is not to offer an exhaustive treatment of all aspects of popular culture but, more humbly, to explore how widely available symbols, values, and practices can serve as a locus for theological reflection. In these exploits, the authors have expanded and enriched the burgeoning field of Girard studies and shown how rich and exciting theological reflection can be occasioned by sojourning with Girard and permitting him to help us see our culture through a new lens.

Since several introductions to Girard and his work already exist, we offer only the briefest of biographical sketches.[1] He was born on Christmas Day, 1923, in Avignon, emigrated to America in 1947, and earned a doctorate in history at Indiana University. Girard then taught at a number of colleges and universities (Duke, Bryn Mawr, Johns Hopkins, SUNY Buffalo) before assuming the Andrew B. Hammond Professorship at Stanford University, a post he held from 1981 until retiring in 1995. In 2005 his intellectual achievements were honored with his election to the *Académie française*. When he died in 2015, he had authored at least eighteen books and inspired research in fields ranging from philosophy to economics, literary criticism to gender studies, theology to neuroscience. Thanks to the work of the Colloquium on Violence and Religion (COV&R), *Imitatio*, the Raven Foundation, and a worldwide network of researchers, interest in Girard's work continues to grow.

To acquaint newcomers with the contours of mimetic theory our introduction uses the 2006 film *The Devil Wears Prada* to illustrate three of Girard's key insights: the nature of mimetic desire, the scapegoat, and the effect of religious conversion inspired by the Judeo-Christian Scriptures. Although they develop and mature over the course of his career, these three "planks" recur throughout Girard's *oeuvre*. A fourth "apocalyptic" plank seems to have been added toward the end of his life. Several authors in this collection address Girard's apocalypticism so, given limited space and the constraints of the movie, this introduction will only surface and lightly engage the topic.

In what follows, we examine four scenes to put cinematic skin on what may seem like an abstract theory. We hope this exercise will familiarize readers with key vocabulary and concepts such as mimetic desire, external and internal mediation, the scapegoat, mythology, and the Judeo-Christian breakthrough, all while showing how Girard helps us to perceive otherwise concealed dimensions of our culture. After beating the bounds of mimetic theory, we conclude this introduction by providing a brief overview of the book's plan and contents.

MIMETIC DESIRE: THE CASE OF THE CERULEAN SWEATER

The Devil Wears Prada tracks the career of an aspiring journalist Andy (Anne Hathaway) who takes a job as the second-assistant to powerful fashion editor Miranda Priestly (Meryl Streep). Andy arrives into the high-pressure, high-fashion world of *Runway* magazine as a frumpily dressed outsider. Over the course of the film, however, viewers watch her evolution. Under the guidance of Nigel (Stanley Tucci), she adopts the fashions—inner *and* outer—of those around her. Predictably, her transformation strains her relationship with boyfriend Nate (Adrian Grenier), who increasingly resents Miranda. This comes to a head when Miranda decides to bring Andy to Paris for fashion week. Nate perceives what Andy cannot: as she is swept up *in* and *by* fashion, her life transforms. "You used to make fun of the *Runway* girls," he says, "now you've become one of them." They decide to break up but, as Nate walks away, Andy speaks his name and he turns. Just then, her phone rings. "I'm sorry," she says, fumbling to answer the call. An incredulous Nate departs: "You know, in case you were wondering, the person whose calls you always take, that's the relationship you're in. I hope you two are very happy together." A touch of melodrama, but viewers can appreciate how much Andy has changed, physically and affectively, and now appears to be a different person from the character we met at the movie's beginning. In fact, one way to interpret the film is as a cinematic chronicle of Andy's pilgrimage *in* and *of* mimetic desire, both in its good and bad forms.

Girard's mimetic theory sheds light on Andy's transformation. In *Deceit, Desire, and the Novel* (1965), Girard articulates an insight into the nature of desire through readings of Cervantes, Proust, Dostoevsky, and Shakespeare. The book opens with a passage from *Don Quixote* where Quixote praises Amadis of Gaul as "the most perfect knight," the "pole, the star, the sun for brave and amorous knights." Quixote concludes his paean: "Thus, my friend Sancho, I reckon that whoever imitates him best will come closest to perfect chivalry."[2] His insight: human desire is imitative or mimetic. This may sound strange, given that we tend to think of desire as being linear. *I* desire *that object*, my desire proceeding outward from me to the thing desired, A to B. Girard's study of literature, however, led him to reject such linearity. Rather than a straight line, Girard saw desire as having a triangular structure. *I* desire *that object* because my role model desires it. Desire, on Girard's account, is mediated. Or, in a formula familiar to Girardians, "I desire according to the desire of another." The desire of another endows an object with an aura of desirability. Marketers know this, and commercials make use of beautiful people to sell products. A campaign, however, aims to do more than sell *things*. A celebrity endorsement, a depiction of famous people enjoying *this* car or *that* beverage, sells a way of life. "If you buy this," we are implicitly told, "you can have this kind of life." We "borrow" our desires from our models because we sense that if we comport ourselves as they do, we can have and enjoy the lifestyle they possess.

The "cerulean sweater" scene in *The Devil Wears Prada* serves as a handy way of grasping this truth. First, some context: Miranda and her staff are preparing a fashion shoot. One attendant presents two cerulean belts for consideration and laments them for being "so different." Andy snickers. When queried she admits, "both those belts look exactly the same to me, you know, I'm still learning about this stuff." This elicits Miranda's devastating response:

> This . . . stuff? Oh, OK. I see. You think this has nothing to do with you. You go to your closet and you select, I don't know, that lumpy blue sweater, for

instance, because you're trying to tell the world that you take yourself too seriously to care about what you put on your back. But what you don't know is that that sweater is not just blue, it's not turquoise, it's not lapis. It's actually cerulean. You're also blindly unaware of the fact that in 2002, Oscar de la Renta did a collection of cerulean gowns. And then I think it was Yves St. Laurent—wasn't it?—who showed cerulean military jackets. And then cerulean quickly showed up in the collections of eight different designers. Then it filtered down into some tragic casual corner where you, no doubt, fished it out of some clearance bin. However, that blue represents millions of dollars and countless jobs and so it's sort of comical how you think that you've made a choice that exempts you from the fashion industry when, in fact, you're wearing the sweater that was selected for you by the people in this room. From a pile of stuff.[3]

Embedded within this trickle-down theory we find Girard's insight into our "borrowed" desires, desires loaned to us—quite literally—by models. Miranda understands how desire is contagious and passes from person to person, how a single designer's choice can influence an industry. She knows, too, how to manipulate it. As we see later in the movie, by the mere dint of a gesture—a head nod, a smile—she can ensure a designer's success; a head shake, or her pursed lips, can spell career catastrophe. Not unlike Sarah's laugh in Genesis 18, Andy's snicker betrays her ignorance to dynamics already at play within history.

Girard would have us note at least two dynamics. Andy laughs because she suffers from the illusion of autonomous or nondirected desire. She believes herself to be aloof from and outside the influence of the fashion industry. This, Girard contends, is the "romantic lie" which gives subjects a false sense of independence. Indeed, Girard might endorse Miranda's monologue as a *genealogy* of mimetic desire, one attentive to how we imitate the desires of others. Miranda dispels the romantic lie by disclosing what Girard calls the "novelistic truth" which lays bare how our desires are interconnected. Because we borrow our desires from others, often multiple others, we are not monadic individuals but intersubjective "interdividuals," a concept Girard develops in *Things Hidden Since the Foundation of the World*. As Miranda icily recounts, we cannot extricate ourselves from the web of human desire, for even Andy's nonchoice of her sweater bears the trace of others' desires. In her attempt to stand aloof from the industry, she remains ignorant of its role in forming her choices. Paradoxically, Girard would insist, authentic autonomy comes not by rejecting the influence of others upon our desire but through recognizing it. We are, all of us, bearers of second-hand desires.

Some critics balk at this claim. Joshua Landy, for instance, fears that Girard's theory leaves no room for innovation. If Girard is right, if all desires are borrowed, where does this regress stop? Surely there must be an *Ur*-model who set everything in motion. But, should this be the case, then how do we ever desire anything novel? Does not the history of fads—Tulip Bulbs to Tamagotchi, Beanie Babies to Bedazzling—give lie to Girard's grand theory?[4] Pushing Girard's insight to its logical conclusion would radicalize Qoheleth's observation, for there could be "nothing new under the sun" (1:9). Landy's critique does not, however, deliver a death-stroke to mimetic theory. Later in life, Girard nuanced his claim about mimetic desire and admitted that there were some phenomena that were not covered by his theory: "For example, I believe in the love that parents have for their children, and I don't see how you could interpret that love in a mimetic fashion."[5] Here, it seems, he distinguishes natural appetites—for food or knowledge—from desires elicited by our models for *this* or *that* object. Novelty occurs when agents bring together and creatively combine the various desires mediated through our relational nexuses. The innovator does not create desire *ex nihilo* but discerns a sympathetic resonance within extant desires and brings them together in a novel way. For Girard, desire is directed, but not wholly determined, by others.

The second issue Girard would have us note in Miranda's speech would be the *metaphysical* insight that "all desire is a desire for being."[6] Desire, for Girard, is less about having *this* or *that* than about being. As mentioned, in addition to selling us objects, marketers pitch us an *ontology* or a way of life. Our deepest desire is not simply to *have* but *to be*. This desire *to be* plays out in two ways. In "external" mediation, the subject and the model never overlap or conflict. The model—living or deceased, real or imaginary—conveys a mode of being through speech, or dress, or lifestyle. So long as supplies last, we can all wear the same type of jeans or buy the same cars. In instances of "internal" mediation, by contrast, this distance between the subject and the model collapses and they fall into conflict. Vying for the same object or professional position, two friends can become rivals as they compete. In instances of internal mediation, the more my model desires something, the more intense my desire will grow, which only magnifies my model's desire in a reciprocal cycle. Left unchecked and unchallenged, this cycle can escalate to the point that the object ceases to be important because what matters most is defeating the opponent. Political debates seem increasingly to manifest this dynamic, as delivering devastating one-liners and "taking down" an opponent appears more important at points than attaining the desired elected office.

We find elements of external and internal mediation in the belt scene. On the surface, the genealogy concerns external mediation: creative designers and their models endow certain fashions with a halo of desirability, one that expands as the color or design diffuses into the broader public. This scene, though, captures the first stirrings of internal mediation. After Miranda humiliates her, Andy seeks Nigel's counsel. He remonstrates her for not appreciating *Runway*'s history and significance and, grudgingly, agrees to tutor her in style. While we do not see her makeover, we do see its effect when she walks into the office and Emily, Miranda's other assistant, sees her. Garbed in the latest fashion, Andy "looks good" on the outside. But her transformation is hardly cosmetic, for she seems now possessed of confidence and style. Fashion becomes her, you might say. Subtly at work, however, is the reality that she becomes fashion because she is beginning to view Miranda not as an obstacle but as her own "lodestar" and guide. She is gradually changing into "the people in this room" she had earlier derided.

The movie shows how the gravitational pull of internal mediation draws Andy into its field. Increasingly oriented by Miranda, she begins to desire according to the *haute couture* other. More than changing her taste in fashion, Andy's taking Miranda as her model results in her transformation. Externally, her metamorphosis is guided by Miranda's favorable gaze, the admiration of colleagues, and the desire of the handsome journalist Christian Thompson. Her intimate friends, while noting the external makeover, also sense an internal disintegration. Increasingly hallowed by fashion's gods, Andy appears increasingly hollow and superficial. Girard would quickly identify Andy's devolution as an instance of her becoming Miranda's mimetic double or twin: as Amadis for Don Quixote, and Jesus for saints, so Miranda for Andy, her "star" and "sun" telling her not only *what* to desire but, more fundamentally, *who* to become.[7]

So far, we have seen how *The Devil Wears Prada* possesses both the genealogical and ontological dimensions of mimetic theory. Genealogically, we do not conjure desire out of thin air because we "desire according to the desire of others." In place of a hermetically sealed-off *ego*, Girard offers a vision of an interdividual subject who "borrows" her desires from the social other. Ontologically, furthermore, we desire more than *this* or *that*. All desire is a desire for being. Drawn into Miranda's orbit and modeling her desires, Andy grows ever more into the image and likeness of Miranda. Let us now consider the effect of internal mediation by turning to a second scene to get a sense of how desire can lead to rivalries and how rivalries can be resolved through the use of a scapegoat.

"EVERYBODY WANTS TO BE US"

All desire, for Girard, is a desire for being. When this desire is externally mediated—by a fashion model, for instance—there is little risk of the subject interfering with the model. Internal mediation, on the other hand, can lead to subject and mediator converging upon and feuding over an object. We see this in children: a child, surrounded by many toys, will suddenly want the toy selected by another child. Occupying the same orbit, the tykes go from playmates to antagonists. One of the subplots in *The Devil Wears Prada* illustrates this potential for rivalry and the scapegoat's role in diffusing crises fueled by internally mediated desire.

Let us examine the rivalry between Miranda and Jacqueline Follet, the editor of the French edition of *Runway*. After Andy spends a night with Christian Thompson, Andy inadvertently discovers a mock-up of a *Runway* cover listing Jacqueline as editor-in-chief. Christian confirms the plan to replace Miranda with Jacqueline: "You're really surprised? Jacqueline's a lot younger than Miranda. She has a fresher take on things. Not to mention that American *Runway* is one of the most expensive books in the business. Jacqueline does the same thing for a lot less money." Already we find the elements of internal mediation: two similar subjects—beautiful, successful, and ambitious woman—converge on one desired object (editor). Miranda-as-model struggles to retain control while Jacqueline emerges as a rival. All the rouge in Paris cannot conceal the revolt orchestrated to promote Jacqueline, to advance Christian Thompson's career, to save *Runway*'s publisher Irv Ravitz money, and to sideline Miranda. To all appearances, it certainly appears as though Jacqueline has outmaneuvered her opponent. After Christian divulges their machination, Andy springs into action and struggles to alert Miranda to the conspiracy. Her efforts, though, seem fruitless. Try as she might, she cannot manage to inform her boss of the plot against her.

Were this an Aaron Spelling production, Jacqueline and Miranda would duke it out in a water fountain. Yet Miranda, the doyenne of desire, employs a far subtler and ultimately more devastating tactic. Instead of fisticuffs, she averts professional crisis and personal catastrophe by sacrificing Nigel's career. Although she had supported Nigel for the presidency of the newly-launched James Holt International, she undermines him by engineering it so that Jacqueline is offered the position. Nigel, Miranda's loyal "insider," suddenly becomes an "outsider" whose expulsion preserves corporate peace. In effect, Nigel unknowingly absorbs the energy from Miranda and Jacqueline's escalating conflict; he is, in a sense, nonviolently "scapegoated." The future of the magazine, as Miranda sees it, must be built on the grave of Nigel's aspirations.

Viewers can begin to appreciate the nature and scope of this scapegoating only in the wake of Nigel's betrayal when, in the back of a sedan, Miranda and Andy have an exchange. Miranda:

> You thought I didn't know. I've known what was happening for quite some time. It just took me a little while to find a suitable alternative for Jacqueline. And that James Holt job was just so absurdly overpaid that of course she jumped at it. So I just had to tell Irv that Jacqueline was unavailable. Truth is, there's no one that

can do what I do. Including her. Any of the other choices would have found that job impossible and the magazine would have suffered.

Like Girard, Miranda intuits how unrestrained rivalry proves deleterious to the social order and how a "release" of the tension is required. So, to prevent *Runway*'s collapse, she sacrifices Nigel in order to redirect Jacqueline toward the position he was meant to occupy. After her backseat revelation, the hollowness of Miranda's earlier reference to Jacqueline as "my friend and longtime esteemed colleague" is apparent. Her decision, albeit loathsome, hardly lacks precedent, for she follows the lead of Caiphas who, learning of the plot to kill Jesus, admitted, "It is better for you to have one man die for the people than to have the whole nation destroyed" (John 11:50).

Of course, this bourgeois scapegoating is a far cry from the sacrificial immolations Girard explores in *Violence and the Sacred*. For starters, Miranda deliberately manipulates a process which, Girard contends, generally operates unbeknownst to participants. It is not that a group decides to find a scapegoat. Instead, in times of unrest and chaos, the scapegoat "emerges" and acts as a figure to galvanize the fragmenting group over and against the scapegoat. One needs to look no further than the political and social landscape to see this process in play. How easily we blame social and economic unrest upon a surrogate figure—often "the Other" embodied in the racial, ethnic, or sexual minority. The scapegoat provides a common enemy (or, in the film, a common victim) to sate warring factions. Perhaps a handy encapsulation for the logic of scapegoating: the many become one by the expulsion of one. In the throes of chaos and disorder—whether it be civil unrest, economic uncertainty, or the imminent changeover in editorial leadership—and as unity fragments and dissolves, a tried-and-true measure to restore order is to galvanize the group against a common target.

If we look at the rest of their exchange, we see further how the first two planks of mimetic theory—internally mediated desire and scapegoating—interpenetrate.

> **Miranda:** I never thought I would say this, Andrea, but I really, I see a great deal of myself in you. You can see beyond what people want, and what they need and you can choose for yourself.
>
> **Andy:** I don't think I'm like that. I couldn't do what you did to Nigel, Miranda. I couldn't do something like that.
>
> **Miranda:** You already did. To Emily.
>
> **Andy:** That's not what I . . . no, that was different. I didn't have a choice.
>
> **Miranda:** No, no, you chose. You chose to get ahead. You want this life. Those choices are necessary.

Andy: But what if this isn't what I want? I mean what if I don't want to live the way you live?

Miranda: Oh, don't be ridiculous. Everybody wants this. Everybody wants to be us.

With that, Miranda dons her sunglasses, smiles, and goes out to meet reporters jockeying to photograph her. Andy sits, speechless, as she finally realizes how deeply she has been influenced by her mentor. As though all at once, everything becomes clear and she perceives the rot beneath the glamour and glitz. A moment of reckoning arises as she must now weigh Miranda's words: Is this what *everybody* wants? Is this what *she* desires? Is this *who* she wants to be?

Miranda Priestly: a truly Luciferian character, casting light in two directions. First, *toward* a way of life Andy had previously thought shallow and superficial; Miranda's desire is contagious and infects all who fall into her orbit. Her vision penetrates the deepest recesses of the human heart, exposing to Andy and to viewers the dynamics of mimetic desire. Girard, we suspect, would smile wryly at her name, for she enacts a "priestly" or hieratic role in sacrificing everything and everyone in order to ensure the prosperity of *Runway* and to retain her position. With eyes newly opened, Andy must confront whether this is *who* she is—Miranda's monstrous double—or whether there might still be a chance to turn away from this glittering path. It is this moment of decision that leads us to our third and final scene.

THE REDEMPTION OF DESIRE

Mimetic theory's third "plank" involves the revelatory power of the Judeo-Christian Scriptures. Because this volume focuses upon Girard's ability to uncover and illuminate the theological dimensions of popular culture, let me give a definition of "theology." Theology is the intellectual effort to reflect on and present truths revealed by God. Theologians reflect on what believers believe about God, how God has been made known to believers, and how these beliefs shape believers' lives. Even though Christian theologians do not all agree about what "counts" as material for theological reflection, they do agree that Scripture is central. As readers will see throughout the volume, Girard deeply appreciated the revelatory power of the Scriptures. So much so, in fact, that we begin our discussion of this "third plank" by noting the vital difference between "myths" and Scripture.[8]

Myths, for Girard, are not innocuous tales but narrative attempts to conceal acts of real violence. They "incorporate the point of view of the community that has been reconciled to itself by the collective murder [scapegoat] and is unanimously convinced that this event was a legitimate and sacred action, desired by God himself, which could not conceivably be repudiated, criticized, or analyzed."[9] Real victims, scapegoats, are entombed in myths which are stories told *by* the crowd *about* the crowd to affirm their innocence and the victim's guilt. Myths "work" by narratively concealing the violent foundations of human culture. Cultures do not carry their victims around in tumbrels but, rather, preserve them in mythic amber. In *Violence and the Sacred*, *Things Hidden Since the Foundation of the World*, and *The Scapegoat*, Girard advances this controversial claim.

What warrants Girard to make this claim? When he turned to the Judeo-Christian Scriptures, he discovered a countermythical narrative. Ancient myths, he argues, were told from the side of the victor (Romulus versus Remus), whereas biblical stories take the side of the victim. God stands on the side of Abel, not Cain; God exercises a preferential option for the poor and downcast, not the mighty and powerful; the Psalms and Isaiah take the side of the victim; in the Gospels it is Jesus, the "Lamb of God who takes away the sin of the world" (John 1:29), who is the innocent one vindicated by God through the Resurrection. The Gospel, as Girard sees it, is the myth that exposes and vitiates the myths that perpetuate sacred violence. What myth conceals, the Gospel reveals as the Biblical revelation which exposes culture's bloody foundations and implicates us in scapegoating violence. Christianity, in this way, destroys mythology. Thus the Gospel must not be approached timidly as one story among others, it cannot be regarded as but one counternarrative among an array of others. The Gospel needs to be lived out as a countermovement that looks to Jesus as providing the pattern of an authentically human life. Theology and anthropology intertwine and illuminate one another. Christianity is not merely a *gnosis* or "way of thinking" but a *praxis* or "way of life." To live *imitatio Christi* is to live according to God's desires as disclosed through Jesus. Christians receive the Good News as a message of being liberated from mythic darkness into the light of the Risen Christ whose Spirit draws us into communion with the Holy Other who redeems and fulfills our deepest desires.

Central to Girard's claim is what he regards as the "Triumph of the Cross." As the apostle Paul saw, the Cross is a *skandalon* or stumbling block: "The message of the cross is foolishness to those who are perishing, but to us who are being saved it is the power of God" (1 Corinthians 1:18). For those mired in a violent ethos where "might makes right," Christ's crucifixion is absurd. But Girard offers a way of beholding the Cross as "a kind of divine trap."[10] The wheel of violence that for centuries had turned effortlessly seemed once more to claim another victim at Calvary. The Cross, however, dupes Satan and exposes the mechanism that had hitherto operated in the darkness. What seemed "business as usual" ground to a halt:

> By nailing Christ to the Cross, the powers believed they were doing what they ordinarily did in unleashing the single victim mechanism. They thought they were avoiding the danger of disclosure. They did not suspect that in the end they would be doing just the opposite: they would be contributing to their own annihilation, nailing themselves to the Cross, so to speak. They did not and could not suspect the revelatory power of the Cross.[11]

By exposing the victim-making mechanism that subtends and perpetuates the old order, the Cross pierces the mythic mantle and pours light into its sacred darkness. The Cross capacitates us to see what myth works to conceal. The "foolishness" of the Cross proclaims a logic, indeed a *Logos*, wholly at odds with the order of violence to which we have been accustomed. To those with ears to hear, the word of the Cross proclaims victory over the old order and makes possible a new way of life.

In the final sentence of *The Girard Reader*, Girard makes clear the centrality of the Cross within his thinking. He concludes an extensive interview with James Williams by claiming that his mimetic anthropology has roots in Christian orthodoxy: "Mine is a search for the anthropology of the Cross, which turns out to rehabilitate orthodox theology."[12] His search, you might say, succeeds in two ways. In his critique of mythology, Girard offers an account of being human that leads to and depends on the Cross. The Cross, in this case, can function as a synecdoche for every means of preserving the extant social order through violence. This anthropology is not, though, a gnostic indictment of the material world. On the contrary, the Cross exposes humanity's dependence on and addiction to its violent scapegoating tendencies; instead of indicting the material world, the Cross reveals how we live within it in a distorted manner. When contemplated from the side of history, from Calvary on Good Friday, the Cross reveals the extent to which fallen humanity has been entranced by the gods of violence and seduced into securing and maintaining its peace through violence. The Cross, in this way, reads us and reveals us to ourselves. But with Easter's dawn, the Cross takes on new significance and manifests the consequence of being fully human in a sinful and broken world. The Resurrection's ratifying "Yes" to Jesus Christ's identity is simultaneously a "No" to humanity's mendacity and violence. The Crucified and Risen *Logos* shows us who, and how, we are to be according to God's design. Instead of reviling the material world and trying to deliver us from it, the Resurrection indicts its sinful history and reforms how we live within it. We, too, can live according to the Spirit that raised Jesus from the dead and empowers us to live "as if death were not" as we participate in the unfolding of God's new creation.[13]

When watched alongside Girard, we can discern traces of these anthropological insights in *The Devil Wears Prada*. Certainly, the movie can be viewed as an ostentatious display of desire's distortions and its insatiable desire *to be* in vogue. Astute viewers may detect, with Girard's assistance, intimations of desire's potential for redemption. We see a hint of this moment of grace toward the film's end when Andy exits Miranda's car and walks toward a fountain. Noticing her absence, Miranda calls her. Andy looks, sees Miranda's number, and throws her phone into the *Fontaines de la Concorde*. A fitting, if secular, baptism as the phone sinks into a fountain whose name means "one heart." The instrument of her captivity, the digital chain binding Andy to Miranda, becomes through its immersion into the water the means of liberation. Having faced the "romantic lie" and accepted the "novelistic truth," Andy is freed to choose who to be. She forsakes Miranda's promises, rebuffs the enticement of prestige and power, and embarks upon an unknown path into a future she cannot foresee. Although religion plays no role in the film, it is hard to miss the theological symbolism. For, as Girard writes, "repudiation of a human mediator and renunciation of deviated transcendency inevitably call for symbols of vertical transcendency whether the author is Christian or not. All the great novelists respond to this fundamental appeal but sometimes they manage to hide from themselves the meaning of their response."[14] Regardless of director David Frankel's religious commitments, he makes recourse to deeply symbolic elements to convey Andy's conversion from a deviated pattern of desire to a desire negotiated in freedom. The novelistic truth, the revelation of our interdependent desire, graces Andy with painfully-won wisdom. For all her faults and superficialities, Emily *was* right: Andy sold her soul the first time she "put on that first pair of Jimmy Choo's." Nate was right, too. And Miranda, who saw better than anyone the mechanism of mimetic desire, astutely noticed in Andy her own likeness. In casting her phone into a watery grave, Andy enacts a quasi-baptism of her own desire and passes from the death of deviated desire to a new life negotiated with eyes now opened to mimetic desire. The phone's symbolic descent (*katabasis*) into the fountain's watery depth marks a sacramental moment of ascent (*anabasis*) and rebirth to a new mode of life.

Viewers do not learn if Andy succeeds as a journalist or if she lives happily ever after with Nate. We know only that her conversion in Paris makes possible a new mode of life. Girard, in fact, would appreciate the ending because, as he noted, every novelistic conclusion is a new beginning.[15] Of endings, Girard writes:

The conclusions of all the novels are reminiscent of an oriental tale in which the hero is clinging by his finger-tips to the edge of a cliff; exhausted, the hero finally lets himself fall into the abyss. He expects to smash against the rocks below but instead he is supported by the air: the law of gravity is annulled.[16]

Not quite as dramatically, the film ends with Andy expecting her demise but finding herself unexpectedly buoyed:

Andy: Learned a lot. In the end, though, I kind of screwed it up.

Editor: I called over there for a reference. . . . Next thing you know, I get a fax from Miranda Priestly herself, saying that of all the assistants she's ever had . . . you were, by far, her biggest disappointment. And, if I don't hire you, I am an idiot.

Symbolized by the cellphone's immersion in water, desire's baptism and redemption from disoriented patterns and its recreation by grace does not annul the yearning *to be*. It reorients it and makes possible relationships negotiated not over and against but in solidarity with others. The grace of the novelistic truth releases one not to live a different life but to live life differently, to live as one attuned to the dynamics and potential disorders of mimetic desire.

Let us conclude this first foray into Girard's thought by mentioning the apocalyptic tenor of his later writings. Girard introduces *Battling to the End* with a lapidary admission: "This is an apocalyptic book."[17] To imaginations nursed on Hollywood special effects, "apocalyptic" may evoke images of cataclysmic asteroid showers or zombie hordes. This is not Girard's intent. Rather, "apocalypse" describes the revelation of the violent scapegoating mechanism at the heart of culture. For Girard, the mythic veil has been pulled back and divine light has dispelled sacred darkness. Revelation, on this score, is less a discrete proposition than a historical process of confronting and embracing the truth of our origins. As Girard puts it in *Battling to the End*, "The truth about violence has been stated once and for all. Christ revealed the truth that the prophets announced, namely, that of the violent foundation of all cultures. The refusal to listen to this essential truth exposes us to the return of an archaic world that will no longer have the face of Dionysus, as Nietzsche hoped."[18] Because the old ways of dealing with violence—scapegoating and myth-making—have been exposed, they can no longer preserve our social order. Human culture faces a choice: acknowledge Christ's call to repent of our violent ways *or* rush headlong toward mutually assured destruction.

We can no longer live cocooned by our old myths and must face the truth of human violence. The Cross has created a definitive breach in the mythic order and exposed an opening to an ethos configured according to the Gospel.

This "revelation," then, is simultaneously informative and formative. For the Gospel both conveys saving knowledge about the dark origins of our culture and graciously capacitates us to live according to the divinely disclosed logic of the Scriptures. Grant Kaplan describes Girard's understanding of revelation as occurring "not so much in the suddenness of an event, but in the slow and painful coming-to-understand that unifies being forgiven with becoming conscious of one's sinfulness. The revelation transforms what it means to understand: not so much to conceive but to undergo change. . . ."[19] Revelation, Jesuit theologian Raymund Schwager held, implicates its addressees in a formative process. In the Old Testament, he writes, "When Yahweh reveals himself as the Lord, he does not grant humans additional knowledge. He unmasks their latent violence and shows them that they can live peacefully and truthfully in his name only. Through his self-revelation God founds a new community among men and women."[20] Thus, in the breakdown of the old mythic order built on victims we are forced to confront the breakthrough of the Gospel. We face, consequently, a choice between Dionysus and the Crucified, a way that perpetuates violence or a style of life lived out under the suasion of the Holy Spirit that guides followers along Christ's way of peace. Herein rests the apocalyptic choice: either continue perpetuating our violent ways and bring about our own demise *or* repent of our violence and embrace a new way of being in communion with one another.

With ears attuned by Girard, we may discern in the final scene of *The Devil Wears Prada* intimations of this apocalypse. After Andy lands the job at the newspaper, she walks out of the building and espies Miranda getting into a car. She waves to her former boss, but the gesture is unreturned. From behind a window, Miranda watches Andy walk off into her post-*Runway* future. A new way, uncertain and unknown, opens before Andy. Her time under Miranda's tutelage has informed and formed her and, having seen for herself the ugly side of the beauty industry, Andy embraces a new pathway. A smile plays on Miranda's face and she chuckles. This glimpse of humanity evanesces when her gaze turns to her driver and she orders him: "Go." Cinematically and existentially, the two characters move apart, each having opted for a different trajectory. Miranda remains within a system where her will is law, a Dionysian order where even her closest ally might be sacrificed to preserve her power or augment her prestige. Having seen the shadow beneath the sequins, Andy balks and withdraws. She has lifted fashion's mythic veil and refuses to wear it, so she renounces Miranda's ways—foolish as it may seem to those beguiled by the industry—and walks out of *Runway* and into the future.

RENÉ GIRARD, THEOLOGY, AND POPULAR CULTURE

Since 2006, viewers have delighted in the glamour, excess, and intrigue depicted in *The Devil Wears Prada*. When watched in Girard's company, however, it becomes both entertaining and instructive. The film portrays the peril and the potential of mimetic desire. When misdirected and caught in the throes of rivalry, it becomes distorted by what Girard calls "ontological sickness." Misdirected desire can deform us into pusillanimous, narcissistic, and self-aggrandizing beings. Desires formed in relationships with role models who show us how *to be* in nonrivalrous ways, by contrast, testify to mimetic desire's goodness. Again, and contrary to his critics, Girard insisted upon mimetic desire's goodness. "If our desires were not mimetic, they would be forever fixed on predetermined objects; they would be a particular form of instinct. Human beings could no more change their desire than cows their appetite for grass. Without mimetic desire there would be neither freedom nor humanity."[21] We discover our freedom not in spite of our longings, but through them.

The authors in this volume believe viewing culture through the lens of mimetic theory to be an instructive exercise. As I have suggested in this introduction, and as each of our authors have endeavored to demonstrate, even a date-night movie can, when watched with Girard, yield a suggestive *tableau vivant* or "living picture" of desire and its movements. Eyes attuned to mimetic theory readily detect triangular patterns of desire, instances of external and internal mediation, myths and scapegoating, and in the case of our authors, the presence of the divine in the everyday. We hope this volume works like Wittgenstein's ladder: once you ascend its rungs, it ceases to be necessary and can be kicked away. Without desiring obsolescence, we seek to encourage readers to take Jesus' mimetic exhortation to "go and do likewise" (Luke 10:37) seriously and to examine our culture to see how they, too, can glimpse hints and traces of a God who abides in all things, a God who enkindles and animates desire in a quest to find, as the Song of Solomon puts it, "the one whom my soul loves" (3:4).

OVERVIEW OF ESSAYS

The theological tenor of these essays largely reflects the Judeo-Christian tradition. This is as much a consequence of Girard's own Christian commitment as to the parameters set out in the initial call for papers. In our invitation to contribute chapters, each author was asked to consider how Girard's thought could be used to read and interpret popular culture. So, instead of a "Theology *of* René Girard" we assay to offer something more akin to "René Girard *and* Theology." The copula is crucial, for we are not so much concerned with exegeting Girard's work as we are committed to using Girard to probe popular culture. This volume, drawing together the work both of well-known and emerging Girard scholars, represents how widely and richly Girard can help us see all things anew. We hope the diversity of offerings and each author's creativity will be a spur to future reflection. Indeed, it is our hope that this project spurs further explorations into how Girard's mimetic theory can help readers to discover "things hidden" within their cultures.

We have organized the volume into four categories. The first group of essays by Brian Bajzek, Erik Buys, John McDowell, Jordan Almanzar, and Stephanie VanSlyke invite Girard to the movies. From a high school's hallways to a galaxy far, far away, each author engages Girard to show how mimetic theory furnishes a viable and illuminating lens through which to view *Mean Girls*, *Fight Club*, *Wonder Woman*, and the *Star Wars* saga.

The next four authors turn to the small-screen as they invite Girard to watch television with them. Essays from Paolo Diego Bubbio, George A. Dunn, Ryan Smock, and Ryan Duns probe the ways in which watching television through a Girardian lens allows the shows to "watch" us. The television's faint light can, with Girard's assistance, illuminate the dynamics of human desire that we would otherwise not perceive. Moreover, the authors scrutinize the ethical and theological significance of contemporary television, at times exploring the dark recesses of the entertainment industry.

With Girard at their side, the next three authors venture into the library to "take up and read." Matthew Brake, Daniel London, and Robert Price take Girard as a co-reader of classic texts and contemporary graphic novels. Their investigations into these texts illustrate further how Girard's theory exposes the too easily underappreciated depths of these texts. With Girard's aid, readers can better appreciate how these fantastic stories are, in a sense, very much *our* stories and revelatory of the way human desire can be deformed and, by divine grace, transformed.

Finally, we offer three essays exploring how Girard illuminates current social and cultural events. Justin Dean Lee, Anna Scanlon, and Derrick Witherington apply the mimetic theory to social media, anorexia, and ecclesial reform. These authors masterfully demonstrate how a theory born from Girard's understanding of literature can be applied to a wide array of social issues. These chapters underscore the way Girard's theory can be diversely applied and how illuminating it can be in many circumstances.

Derrick and I have enjoyed working with each of the authors who have contributed essays. We have learned a great deal from each author's creative appropriation and application of mimetic theory. Even though we all approached our pop culture artifacts with different theological sensibilities, the ecumenical approach taken in this volume demonstrates how fecund and versatile Girard's thought can be. We hope readers will be intrigued by these essays, excited by the theological depths they uncover, and inspired to "Go and do likewise" (Luke 10:37) by using Girard's work to illuminate, and to envision the ongoing transformation of, popular culture.

NOTES

1. Michael Kirwan, *Discovering Girard* (Darton, Longman, and Todd: London, 2004); Scott Cowdell, *René Girard and the Nonviolent God* (Notre Dame: Notre Dame Press, 2018); Cynthia Haven, *Evolution of Desire* (East Lansing: MSU Press, 2018); Gil Baile, *Violence Unveiled* (New York: Crossroad, 2002).
2. René Girard, *Deceit, Desire & the Novel*, trans. Yvonne Freccero (Baltimore: Johns Hopkins, 1961), 1.
3. Wendy Fineman et al. *The Devil Wears Prada* (Twentieth Century Fox, 2006), DVD
4. Joshua Landy, "Deceit, Desire, and the Literature Professor: Why Girardians Exist," *Republics of Letters: A* Journal for the Study of Knowledge, Politics, and the Arts 3, no 1. (September 15, 2012): 1–21 at 7.
5. René Girard, *When These Things Begin: Conversations with Michael Treguer,* trans. Trevor Cribben Merrill (East Lansing: MSU Press, 2014), 12.
6. Ibid.
7. I explore this dynamic in my "Desire and Conversion in*The Death of Ivan Ilyich*," *Contagion: Journal of Violence, Mimesis, and Culture*, 27 (2020): 215–238.
8. For a recent effort to show how Girard's work can contribute to the task of theological reflection, see Ryan Duns, "'In Despair, Despair Not': Ways to God for a Secular Age," *Theological Studies* 82, no. 2 (2020): 348–369.
9. René Girard, *Things Hidden Since the Foundation of the World*, trans. Stephen Bann and Michael Metteer (Stanford: Stanford University Press, 1978), 148.
10. René Girard, *I See Satan Fall Like Lightning*, trans. James Williams (Maryknoll: New York, 2001), 149.
11. Ibid., 142.
12. René Girard, *The Girard Reader*, ed. James Williams (New York: Crossroad, 2001), 288.
13. James Alison, *Raising Abel* (New York: Crossroad, 1996), 110–111.
14. Girard, *Deceit, Desire & the Novel*, 312.
15. Ibid., 297.
16. Ibid., 294.
17. René Girard, *Battling to the End: Conversations with Benoit Chantre*, trans. Mary Baker (Lansing: Michigan State University Press, 2010), ix.
18. Ibid., 104.

19. Grant Kaplan, *René Girard, Unlikely Apologist* (Notre Dame: Notre Dame Press, 2016), 94.
20. Raymund Schwager, *Must There Be Scapegoats?* Trans. Maria Assad (New York: Crossroad, 2000)
21. Girard, *I See Satan Fall Like Lightning*, 15.

BIBLIOGRAPHY

Alison, James. *Raising Abel: The Recovery of the Eschatological Imagination.* New York: Crossroad, 1996.

Duns, Ryan. "Desire and Conversion in *The Death of Ivan Ilyich.*" *Contagion: Journal of Violence, Mimesis, and Culture* 27 (2020): 215–238.

———. "'In Despair, Despair Not': Ways to God for a Secular Age." *Theological Studies* 82, no. 2 (2020): 348–369.

Finerman, Wendy, et al. *The Devil Wears Prada.* Beverly Hills, California: 20th Century Fox Home Entertainment, 2006.

Girard, René. *Battling to the End: Conversations with Benoît Chantre.* East Lansing: Michigan State University Press, 2010.

———. *Deceit, Desire, and the Novel: Self and Other in Literary Structure.* Translated by Yvonne Freccero. Baltimore: Johns Hopkins University Press, 1976.

———. *The Girard Reader.* Edited by James Williams. New York: Crossroad, 2001.

———. *I See Satan Fall Like Lightning.* Translated by James Williams. New York: Maryknoll, 2001.

———. *Things Hidden Since the Foundation of the World.* Translated by Stephen Bann and Michael Metteer. Stanford: Stanford University Press, 2014.

———. *When These Things Begin: Conversations with Michael Treguer.* Translated by Trevor Cribben Merrill. East Lansing: Michigan State University Press, 2014.

Kaplan, Grant. *René Girard, Unlikely Apologist.* Notre Dame: Notre Dame Press, 2016.

Kirwan, Michael. *Discovering Girard.* London: Darton, Longman, and Todd, 2004.

Landy, Joshua. "Deceit, Desire, and the Literature Professor: Why Girardians Exist." *Republics of Letters: A Journal for the Study of Knowledge, Politics, and the Arts* 3, no. 1 (September 2012): 1–21.

Schwager, Raymund. *Must There Be Scapegoats? Violence and Redemption in the Bible.* Translated by Maria Assad. New York: Crossroad, 2000.

Chapter 1

Mimesis, Mean Girls, and the Culture Creating Them

Tina Fey's Interrogation of the Teen Comedy

Brian Bajzek

A startling number of teen comedies seem to hate teenagers. Despite being marketed toward and plotted around adolescents, most movies involving teenagers present the same pessimistic premise: high school is a terrible time. The storylines of countless teen comedies highlight how stereotyping, shaming, and ostracization run rampant in classrooms and cafeterias. Although these films often identify social injustice, they also reinforce roles like "the jock," "the nerd," and "the prom queen," inadvertently furthering constructs they appear to satirize. This reinforcement is especially problematic in its impact upon teenage girls, whom popular culture tends to portray as naturally, even self-evidently red in tooth, claw, and designer lipstick. By elevating juvenile labels like "mean girl" to the level of archetypes, filmmakers codify them, tacitly teaching teenagers that inauthenticity is innate or inevitable.

Unlike the typical teen comedy, productive Girardian analysis must provide more than a list of examples acknowledging inauthenticity. Girard's work calls for vocal critique, subversion, and constructive response. This paper argues that, with her film *Mean Girls*, Tina Fey accomplishes these tasks, building a Trojan horse out of the tropes and expectations her narrative gleefully tears open from the inside.[1] *Mean Girls* is an amusing send-up of high school cliques, an examination of female "frenemies," and an unmasking of mimetic rivalry and scapegoating. It also transcends each of these categories, confronting broader societal sins, especially those perpetuated by popular culture. From its first frame, the film indicts the artifice and inauthenticity inherent in its genre, contemporary American pop culture, and even viewers' expectations regarding "queen bees," "wannabes," and their cinematic counterparts.

Analyzing *Mean Girls* through the lens of mimetic theory, I explore how we identify and view "mean girls" onscreen, and what repercussions this might have for our treatment of women offscreen. Implicit in these analyses is a series of questions: Why is high school automatically understood as a popularity contest? Why does popular culture revel in creating conflict between teenagers, and especially *female* teenagers? Are the viewers of teen comedies themselves complicit in teaching girls that infecting others with insecurity is always "*so* fetch"? After exploring these questions' connections to the filmmakers' artistic decisions, I will suggest that mimetic theory can uncover unexpectedly theological resonances in the film's denouement. Like Girard's work, *Mean Girls* suggests that we can respond to unjust social structures with more than resignation or anger, cooperating with unexpected grace in the face of culturally ingrained mimesis and violence.

MEAN GIRLS: A BRIEF SYNOPSIS

Mean Girls begins by introducing its viewers to the protagonist: Cady Heron. Instead of seeing Cady, however, we see from her vantage point.[2] The camera frames her parents' faces as they prepare to send her off for her first day of school: "This is your lunch, OK? Now, I put a dollar in there so you can buy some milk. You can ask one of the big kids where to do that." Surprisingly, the camera tilts upward from what previously seemed to be a small child's height, cutting to reveal that the recipient of this pep talk is sixteen years old. In many ways, Cady is even more of a blank slate than the preschoolers for whom such an address is typically prepared. Unlike most American teenagers, she is entirely unfamiliar with the rhythms and rituals of high school life. This is because Cady's parents are research zoologists, and the Heron family has spent twelve years living in Africa.

Enrolled for the first time in public high school, Cady is ill-suited to her new social setting. After spending her first day in varying degrees of uncomfortableness and isolation, she befriends two self-identified outcasts: Janis and Damian. They inform Cady about the school's complex hierarchy of cliques, warning her to avoid its "teen royalty": the Plastics. This trifecta—Karen ("one of the dumbest girls you will ever meet"), "totally rich" Gretchen, and Regina George—are presented with a mixture of wonder and hatred. Janis and Damian are especially damning in their introduction to

Regina: "She may seem like your typical selfish, backstabbing, slut-faced ho-bag. But in reality, she is so much more than that. She's the queen bee. The star." Cady is surprised, therefore, when the Plastics invite her to sit with them at lunch. Despite her obvious hatred of Regina, Janis is thrilled by this development. She encourages Cady to befriend the Plastics, treating Cady as a spy. During a trip to Regina's opulent home, Cady learns about Regina's "Burn Book," a journal the Plastics fill with insults about their classmates. Cady tells Janis about the book, and Janis suggests they publish it to expose the Plastics' cruelty. Cady refuses.

This situation changes dramatically after Regina learns that Cady has developed a crush on Regina's ex-boyfriend, Aaron. Although Regina offers to talk to Aaron on Cady's behalf, she kisses him in front of Cady at a Halloween party. Regina and Aaron begin dating again. Cady is heartbroken. She, Janis, and Damian decide to destroy Regina's "resources" for popularity: her romantic relationship, her physique, and her friendships. This process involves breaking Regina and Aaron up, tricking Regina into eating weight-gain bars, and turning the Plastics against each other. In the process, Cady inadvertently reinvents herself in Regina's image, taking on her speech affectations, her fashion preferences, and her penchant for manipulation. Ms. Norbury, Cady's math teacher, expresses frustration with Cady's declining grades, but this does little to distract Cady from her goal: she must destroy Regina.

When Regina realizes what Cady has done, she lashes out in an act of social sabotage. Regina copies and distributes the contents of the Burn Book throughout the school, inserting a page about herself to shift the blame to Karen, Gretchen, and Cady. The book's contents spark schoolwide fistfights and chaos. The principal eventually corrals all junior girls in the gym, and Ms. Norbury forces them to acknowledge their mutual backstabbing and manipulation. Many of the girls offer emotional apologies, but Regina, Gretchen, and Cady do not. After Janis proudly admits to her and Cady's plan to sabotage Regina, Regina furiously flees the school, and Cady follows in tears. In response to Cady's pursuit, Regina screams that everyone thinks of Cady as "a less-hot version of [Regina]." Her tirade is cut short, however, as she absentmindedly steps into the road and is struck by a school bus. Her spine is broken, and the film's second act ends.

Left to deal with the aftermath of her actions, Cady is grounded by her parents, ostracized at school, and rejected by Aaron. In a moment of remorse, she takes full responsibility for the Burn Book, then apologizes to Regina and Ms. Norbury. Ms. Norbury makes Cady compete in the state Mathlete finals (an act earlier described as "social suicide"), and Cady correctly answers the competition's final question, winning her team the championship. Later that evening, Cady is elected Queen of the Spring Fling dance. During her impromptu acceptance speech, Cady apologizes for her actions, declares that all of her classmates "look like royalty," and snaps her plastic tiara. Cady then redistributes the crown's pieces to other girls in the crowd, including Gretchen, Janis, and Regina. She reconciles with Janis and Damien and rekindles her relationship with Aaron.

The film's epilogue picks up after summer vacation. The Plastics have gone their separate ways. Aaron attends Northwestern University, and he and Cady see each other on weekends. *Mean Girls* ends with its characters interacting peacefully, and Cady reflects upon her experiences. As the students enjoy this idyllic scene, Damian points out a new group of "Junior Plastics," and Cady imagines them being hit by a bus, joking, "If any freshmen tried to disturb that peace . . . well, let's just say we knew how to take care of it . . . just kidding." The film ends with a shot of Cady's face, clearly grateful to have grown beyond the past year's difficulties.

MIMESIS AND MEAN GIRLS

Pivoting to a basic Girardian reading of *Mean Girls*, several layers of inter-teen inauthenticity offer themselves as candidates for critique. Girard's work is rooted in the observation that human beings are innately imitative. Other animals mimic the behaviors of one another to acquire and develop skills, but human beings' mimetic capacities run deeper.[3] According to Girard, our desires are mediated to us through those we seek to imitate. This mediation of desire is largely unthematized, but it permeates all human activities, even constituting the process by which human culture originally emerged.[4] This primordial social scaffolding shaped humanity relationally, and the mediation of desire is just as impactful today as it was at the dawn of hominization. Modern cultures distract from this basic truth by rewarding autonomy and praising the pursuit of self-sufficiency.[5] In contrast, great artists are able to unmask the real truth of human life: we are radically dependent upon others, and our desires are mediated interdividually.[6] This mediation gives our desires a "triangular" character, as those things we desire are primarily attractive because of our deep yearning to be like those we hold up as models.[7]

In instances of what Girard refers to as "external mediation," the model serving as mediator occupies a social sphere beyond that of the imitator.[8] The aspirational quality of externally mediated desire informs the emergence of social classes, as illustrated in Janis' overview of the school's various cliques and their places in the pecking order. This social ladder impacts all students, regardless of the rung they occupy. Despite their outcast status, Janis and Damian are also implicated in the perpetuation of the school's social order.

Janis presents it as self-evidently important and inescapable. What keeps this engine of inauthenticity running is everyone's imitation of and obsession over the Plastics, especially Regina.

Regina's relationship with others is one of external mediation. Her fabulousness is perceived as an unattainable goal, driven home during Janis and Damian's introduction of the Plastics, one of the movie's many instances of heightened reality and surrealism. When we first see Regina, five boys are carrying her onto the field at gym class, fawning over her like a contemporary Cleopatra. A series of fourth-wall breaking asides from Regina's classmates highlights their obsession with her: "Regina George is flawless. She has two Fendi purses and a silver Lexus. I hear her hair's insured for $10,000. I hear she does car commercials. In Japan. . . . One time, she punched me in the face. It was awesome." Regina's name means "the queen" in Latin. By the end of her introductory sequence, the film has made its point: this queen's subjects regard her with admiration, fear, love, and loathing, and they are all talking about her constantly.

The potential dangers of external mediation are nothing, however, compared to those opened by internal mediation. In instances of internal mediation, the imitator has a much more realistic possibility of attaining the status of the one being imitated. While there is some degree of internal mediation and rivalry between the Plastics (as evidenced especially in Gretchen's rant comparing herself to Brutus and Regina to Caesar), Cady's conflict with Regina provides *Mean Girls'* clearest example of internal acquisitive mimesis. This conflict is also the movie's most destructive.

There are many modes of internal mediation, but all of them are rooted in a toxic social proximity between imitator, imitated, and object(s) of desire.[9] The imitator may, for example, desire the respect or attention enjoyed by the model. Cady's conflict with Regina clearly exemplifies an element of this, as Cady increasingly covets Regina's sex appeal, popularity, and power over others. The object of desire can also be a person, over whom the imitator and imitated find themselves competing. In *Mean Girls*, Aaron becomes the object of a triangular rivalry the moment Regina learns of Cady's desire to date him. This desire inspires Regina to use him as a tool to hurt Cady. This only escalates Cady's desire for Aaron, who has now become desirable primarily as a weapon by which Cady and Regina might supplant each other. In even more extreme instances, the lines between object, imitation, and desire blur further, especially when the imitator develops desire for one who is indifferent to admiration (or—as is more often the case—one who *feigns* such indifference).

Eventually, internal mediation can become something more sinister, as the imitator seeks to *become* the model of imitation. This metaphysical desire betrays the imitator's basic dissatisfaction with herself or himself.[10] In Cady's case, this dissatisfaction stems from her unfamiliarity with American culture. Prior to her integration into the Plastics, Cady's personality is very vaguely defined. Regina is not entirely incorrect when she exclaims, "I, like invented her!" Soon, the model becomes the thing that defines the imitator. At the height of Cady's obsession with destroying Regina, she describes herself as "a woman possessed. I spent about 80 percent of my time talking about Regina. And the other 20 percent of the time, I was praying for someone else to bring her up so I could talk about her more."

In such situations, the existential malaise of the imitator escalates their imitation. Cady's relationship with Regina exemplifies the mimetic mirroring that results from such intensification: "As the rivalry itself effaces what differences remain, [they] are finally no more than each other's *doubles*."[11] Aaron's disgust at Cady's transformation perfectly encapsulates this doubling effect: "You are just like a clone of Regina." The core of such mimetic desire is "a radical ontological sickness," the desire to fill a void deep within oneself by seeking out a mediator deemed capable of overcoming the emptiness and lack of meaning.[12]

Once the imitator and the model become practically indistinguishable, the desire to supplant the model becomes all-consuming. This devolves into self-perpetuating cycles of violence that culminate in paroxysm (e.g., the rioting after the distribution of the Burn Book) and the transference of blame to a scapegoat (who is eventually ostracized).[13] This burst of violence provides a temporary release to the communal tension built up by interdividuation.[14] In *Mean Girls*, this scapegoating falls on both Regina and Cady, but—as I argue below—its impact and importance are transformed by Cady's actions.

On a basic Girardian read, *Mean Girls* is an indictment of how mimetic mechanisms take hold of high schoolers, and it critiques the inauthenticity underpinning teen cliques. However, the Girardian impact of Fey's film extends beyond a basic unmasking. By engaging unjust sociocultural mechanisms beyond the confines of its high school setting, *Mean Girls* deconstructs and redeems the very genre it exemplifies.

FEY'S VÉRITÉ FILMIQUE

By broadening its scope beyond inter-teen inauthenticity, *Mean Girls* takes aim at the multifaceted mechanisms that reduce high schools to petri dishes for radical ontological sickness. The most basic and straightforward of these targets is the negative impact adults have had on the film's teenagers. The adults in *Mean Girls* are either resignedly frustrated with the problems of the school (e.g., the school principal; Cady's parents), hypocritical (Coach Carr, who tells students that teen sex leads to pregnancy and death, then proceeds to sleep with a number of them), or enabling (Regina's mother). Although each of these attitudes perpetuates the problems at North Shore High School, the latter is particularly dangerous.

Mrs. George's introduction is equally comical and disturbing. As Cady marvels at the opulence of Regina's house, Gretchen encourages her to "check out" Mrs. George's breast implants, which are "hard as rocks." After greeting the Plastics (her "best girlfriends"), Mrs. George excitedly informs Cady, "There are no rules in this house. I'm not like a regular mom. I'm a cool mom. Right, Regina?" Regina sarcastically responds, "Please stop talking!" After winkingly offering Cady alcohol, Mrs. George manically asks the girls for updates on high school gossip, relationship statuses, etc., noting, "You girls keep me young." No parent should so desperately seek the approval of teenagers. Here, Fey is overtly lampooning America's obsession with (and enabling of) attractive teenage girls. Standard social norms do not apply to the Plastics. Adults treat them with the same reverence and desire as their peers do. As we will see below, Ms. Norbury is a notable and necessary exception to this rule. For the moment, however, the impact of people like Mrs. George provides a perfect pivot to Fey's primary object of criticism: American pop culture.

Mean Girls takes place at the height of MTV's early-aughts heyday, a time when teenagers obsessed over the social machinations and backstabbing on "reality" TV like *The Real World*, *Laguna Beach*, *The Hills*, and the celebrity fetishization of *Cribs*. This period witnessed the ascendance of Paris Hilton and the other lifestyle celebrities prefiguring the "influencers" soon to rise through YouTube, Instagram, etc. Regina George's life is essentially an extended episode of *My Super Sweet 16*, which premiered shortly after *Mean Girls'* release, shifting the voyeuristic lens of MTV *Cribs* to nonfamous teens who happened to be wealthy and entitled. In an era that idolatrized extravagant spending and teen tantrums, Regina George is the ideal queen.

The aforementioned trends also tended to sexualize and exploit teenage girls, and *Mean Girls* makes an explicit target out of one of the era's more controversial phenomena: *Girls Gone Wild*. Where exploitation on MTV was (and still is) largely passive, *Girls Gone Wild* turned teen partying into a breast-baring, inhibition-eschewing spectacle. Fey uses Regina's young sister, Kylie, to draw an explicit connection between other forms of pop culture's sexualized mimesis and spring breakers exposing themselves on camera. When we first encounter Kylie, she is imitating the dancing she sees in the music video for Kelis's extremely suggestive "Milkshake." Later, she mimics girls flashing their breasts on camera. Fey's point is clear: this behavior is *learned*. The toxicity of such exploitative pop cultural mimesis speaks for itself, but no one around Kylie seems to care.

In addition to these and other instances of overt critique, *Mean Girls* employs a subtler form of cultural subversion, using the tropes of the teen comedy itself to critique *viewers'* complicity in acquisitive, mimetic modeling and scapegoating. Fey and director Mark Waters use the aesthetic maximalism of the aughts to their advantage, giving *Mean Girls'* middle stretch the guise of a straightforward teen comedy. The film's opening and closing sections offer significantly more fourth wall breaking, surrealist touches, and deconstructive asides. In the film's middle third, however, these metatextual tendencies recede into more predictable deception, rivalry, and revenge. Why? *Mean Girls* is indicting the viewer's participation in the conventions of the teen comedy. As the plot ramps up, we become caught up in the fun of Cady's plan to destroy Regina. We are complicit in the mechanisms driving the film's characters to manipulate, shame, and ostracize one another. By the time the girls begin rioting, viewers are nearly as engaged in the acquisitive-mimetic cycles of the scapegoating mechanism as the characters are. We want to see Regina get what she deserves. This heightens the impact when the scales finally fall from Cady's—and, therefore, the viewers'—eyes. When Cady recognizes her actions as those of "a mean girl," viewers are indirectly implicated, both as participating in the "fun" of mimetic rivalry, and in the broader cultural frameworks that make, encourage imitation of, and then indict "mean girls."

Fittingly, Fey's own character in the film, Ms. Norbury, is her mouthpiece for calling out culturally inculcated inauthenticity. As she addresses the girls of North Shore's junior class, she forces them to recognize that none of them are innocent bystanders. For example, *Mean Girls'* characters constantly exchange insults as if they were terms of endearment (e.g., "Boo. You whore."; "Slut" and other shaming name-calling; "Get in, loser. We're going shopping."). In one scene, the Plastics ceremonially insult their own flaws in the mirror, then turn to Cady expectantly, waiting for her to do the same. These slights are symptomatic of subtle hierarchical subjugation and self-hatred, even among close "friends." Ms. Norbury presents the class with a simple truth: "You all have got to stop calling each other sluts and whores. It just makes it OK for guys to call you sluts and whores." Fey is delivering one of the film's central arguments, and its implications extend far beyond any given high school. Contemporary American culture and the film's viewers are complicit in the creation of "mean girls," which is itself a harmful, reductive label.

Fey wants to dissect the broader cultural mechanisms that lead to the codification and acceptance of labels like "mean girl," and that prompt teenagers like Regina and Cady to develop such toxic identities. She also wants to examine why anyone would indulge or emulate someone like Regina George. She comes to a simple conclusion: we have *all* been taught to act this way, and popular culture perpetuates the cycle. In its outright assault on the *mensonge romantique* underpinning the genre of the teen comedy and the culture(s) from which it originates, *Mean Girls* provides a constructive *vérité filmique*. One question remains, however: If we agree with Fey's critiques, what resources can theologically minded readers of Girard draw from her interrogation of the teen comedy?

TEEN QUEENS AND TRANSFORMATIVE GRACE: A THEOLOGICAL CONCLUSION

To explore the unexpectedly theological themes in *Mean Girl*'s conclusion, one further facet of Girard's theory must be unpacked: the theological solution to scapegoating. Girard finds a hopeful alternative to scapegoating in the Bible's siding with the victims of mimetic violence, presenting injustice through the eyes of the marginalized (Abel's murder, Joseph's being sold into slavery, etc.).[15] The Judeo-Christian scriptures name, decry, and seek to overcome these injustices. This reversal reaches its zenith in the person of Christ, as God enters into the drama of history in an unprecedented sense, incarnate as the perfectly blameless victim who is slaughtered nonetheless.[16] Christ's life, death, and resurrection unmask and defeat the evil of the scapegoating mechanism, inaugurating a community rooted in the reversal of mimetic violence.[17] Is *Mean Girls* an overtly Christian film? No. Or, as its characters would probably put it, "No. Duh." This does not mean, however, that its insights are not theologically relevant or exemplary of cooperation with the divinely inaugurated reversal of the scapegoating mechanism. How, then, does *Mean Girls* offer a burst of theologically resonant hope in the cacophony of culturally ingrained violence? By breaking a plastic tiara.

Cady's actions in the film's final act incarnate what Bernard Lonergan calls "the Law of the Cross": the love that returns good in the face of evil.[18] Drawing from Girard and Lonergan, Doran stresses that although this law of love is most fully incarnate in the person and actions of Jesus of Nazareth, it is exemplified by more than just those that call themselves 'Christians.'[19] This law is operative when anyone—regardless of religious affiliation, cultural context, or previous conduct—responds to inauthenticity and injustice with actions that performatively speak the words, 'I love you, hate does not get the final say.' Whether thematized as Christian or not, this love participates in Jesus' love, the only thing capable of overcoming and soteriologically subverting the mimetic mechanism and its cycles of scapegoating. It is also the conduct encouraged by those works of art presenting the *vérité romanesque*. It is cooperation with the grace that can transform the most broken social situations (even if it is not thematized in any religious sense).

Just as many of the novels Girard identifies as unmasking acquisitive mimesis are not explicitly religious stories, the *vérité filmique* offered by Tina Fey can take part in a theologically illuminative exploration of authentic relationality. This cruciform relationality uncovers previously unimaginable possibilities, overcoming evil and reversing relational decline through self-emptying love. From the moment she takes the blame for the Burn Book, Cady's actions are purgative ("When you get bit by a snake, you're supposed to suck the poison out. That's what I had to do: suck all the poison out of my life."), even self-emptying. She owns her culpability and loses all her social status, while also taking on the consequences of the Plastics' actions. This is cooperation with grace. It transfigures the situation in her school.

This transformation reaches its apex in her redistribution of the Spring Fling crown. Cady renounces both the object of her mimetic clashes with Regina (the popularity and social acceptance for which the crown is metonymic symbol), and the inauthentic cultural framework that dictated that conflict. She rejects the idea that high school ought to be automatically understood as a popularity contest. She abdicates a crown symbolizing conflict between girls taught to mistrust and manipulate each other to gain approval. By extension, Tina Fey rejects the presumption that a character in a teen comedy can only "win" by ensuring that her rivals "lose." Instead, Fey's protagonist shares her victory with all the girls pop culture would consider her enemies. *Mean Girls* gives its viewers a model worth imitating: one who destroys acquisitive mimetic modeling by giving away her crown. Although it may initially seem like an odd choice for theological analysis, *Mean Girls* offers its viewers a surprisingly powerful primer on cruciform love in the face of culturally conditioned mimesis and violence.

It seems fitting to conclude this essay by reflecting upon *Mean Girls'* final shot, an image that inverts the movie's first frame. As I noted at the outset of the chapter, *Mean Girls* opens through Cady's eyes. She begins the film as a blank slate sent into a frightening new world, and her perspective gives viewers the chance to see a familiar setting and genre through a decentering, deconstructive lens. By the time the film reaches its moment of crisis, Cady and the viewers have been immersed in the mechanisms of mimetic rivalry, obsessing over an identity and conflict rooted in desire gone awry. Then, in a moment of unexpected grace, Cady speaks the truth, regardless of the consequences. She gives away her crown and sees the beauty in others as cause for celebration, not cattiness. Once the chaos has subsided, Cady reflects upon the past year: "I had gone from home-schooled jungle freak to shiny Plastic to most hated person in the world to actual human being." Viewers have undergone this same journey as observers, seeing her and her peers through the lenses of labeling, an instinct ingrained in us by the genre *Mean Girls* deconstructs. In the film's final frame, we see Cady, front and center, and the responsibility now falls on the viewers. We must celebrate her and other teenagers as more than reducible to labels like "freak," "Plastic," or even "mean girl." We must recognize them as human beings, deserving of more than mimetic rivalry and cultural violence.

NOTES

1. Tina Fey, *Mean Girls* (USA: Paramount, 2004). Directed by Mark Waters. http://www.script-o-rama.com/movie_scripts/mean-girls-movie-transcript.html. Accessed December 5, 2019. All quotes from the film are from this transcript.

2. Fey subtly shifts both Cady's and the viewer's perspectives over the course of the film. At the start, Cady's naivety serves as a tool for helping viewers see the strangeness of an all-too-familiar setting (and, in doing so, establishes her as a sympathetic, easily manipulated *tabula rasa*).

3. René Girard, *Things Hidden Since the Foundation of the World*, trans. Stephen Bann and Michael Metteer, first edition (Stanford, Calif.: Stanford University Press, 1987), 84–104. Girard understands mimetic desire to be one of the positive differences leading human beings to advance beyond other animals, so mimetic desire should not be considered inherently evil (cf., *I See Satan Fall Like Lightning*, 15–16). Instead, the problems of sin, scandal, and victimization warp an innately good element of human identity, distorting desire (Ibid., 16–18).

4. James Alison, *The Joy of Being Wrong: Original Sin through Easter Eyes* (New York: Crossroad, 1998), 16–17.

5. *Things Hidden Since the Foundation of the World*, 7. Girard refers to this distraction as the *mensonge romantique*, the romantic lie.

6. This is a central argument of Girard's *Deceit, Desire, and the Novel: Self and Other in Literary Structure*, trans. Yvonne Freccero (Baltimore: Johns Hopkins University Press, 1976). Girard refers to this artistically unmasked truth as the *vérité romanesque*, the truth of the novel. The heroes of the great novels are only able to come to some healing or resolution to the extent they renounce their self-centeredness and egoism. This parallels Cady's character arc.

7. *Deceit, Desire, and the Novel*, 2.

8. Ibid., 9.

9. Ibid., 10.

10. Ibid., 66.

11. René Girard, *Violence and the Sacred*, trans. Patrick Gregory (Baltimore: Johns Hopkins University Press, 1977), 159, emphasis Girard's. See also *Deceit, Desire, and the Novel*, 99–100, 105–106.

12. Robert M. Doran, *The Trinity in History: A Theology of the Divine Missions, Volume One: Missions and Processions* (Toronto: University of Toronto Press, 2012), 210. Both Doran and Alison assert that identification of the malformed metaphysical desire at the root of acquisitive mimesis is one of Girard's primary contributions to

theological anthropology. See *Trinity in History, Vol. 1* and *The Joy of Being Wrong* for their respective (and complementary) applications of this insight.

13. René Girard, *The Scapegoat*, trans. Yvonne Freccero (Baltimore: Johns Hopkins University Press, 1989), 15–16. For a fuller account of this process' codification in culture, myth, and religion, see *Violence and the Sacred*, 89–118.

14. *Violence and the Sacred*, 101.

15. *Things Hidden Since the Foundation of the World*, 144–79.

16. Ibid., 167–70.

17. *The Scapegoat*, 206–12.

18. *The Trinity in History, Vol. 1*, 205–26.

19. Ibid., 227–57.

BIBLIOGRAPHY

Alison, James. *The Joy of Being Wrong: Original Sin through Easter Eyes*. New York: Crossroad, 1998.

Doran, Robert M. *The Trinity in History: A Theology of the Divine Missions, Volume One: Missions and Processions*. Toronto: University of Toronto Press, 2012.

Fey, Tina. *Mean Girls*. Directed by Mark Waters. USA: Paramount, 2004. http://www.script-o-rama.com/movie_scripts/mean-girls-movie-transcript.html.

Girard, René. *Deceit, Desire, and the Novel: Self and Other in Literary Structure*. Translated by Yvonne Freccero. Baltimore: Johns Hopkins University Press, 1976.

———. *The Scapegoat*. Translated by Yvonne Freccero. Baltimore: Johns Hopkins University Press, 1989.

———. *Things Hidden Since the Foundation of the World*. Translated by Stephen Bann and Michael Metteer. Stanford: Stanford University Press, 1987.

———. *Violence and the Sacred*. Translated by Patrick Gregory. Baltimore: Johns Hopkins University Press, 1977.

Chapter 2

Star Wars
Between Myth and Gospel

Erik Buys

This chapter deals with the first six episodes of the *Star Wars* film saga. It explores how George Lucas translated the work on mythology of his mentor Joseph Campbell into the space adventures of his alternative universe.[1] It also shows how this approach to mythology is challenged by René Girard in light of the Gospel.

Campbell points out that mythical narratives, despite surface differences, basically have the same shape. His concept of the monomyth summarizes the structural similarities between myths from around the world.[2] The monomyth represents the supposedly one (hence "mono") story (hence "myth"), told repeatedly in many cultural guises. It is a container of the narratives people rely on to make sense of their experiences. Essentially, the monomyth proclaims that members of a society must be prepared to make individual or collective sacrifices to establish a cultural identity. Individuals who redeem society by making those sacrifices become heroes. The monomyth is a hero myth.[3]

Girard agrees with Campbell that a mythical narrative about the redemptive violence of heroic sacrifice lies at the heart of cultural identity formation. Unlike Campbell, however, he does not consider that ever-present narrative as a mere expression of human self-understanding, but as a persistent untruth. Moreover, for Girard, Christ's Passion does not endorse the myth of redemptive sacrificial violence, but instead reveals the divine grace of a redemptive non-violent love.[4] The Gospel uncovers the lies behind the ever-recurring mythical imagination and liberates individuals and communities from a deceptive sacrificial self-understanding.[5] As the following analysis makes clear, the first two *Star Wars* trilogies form a tragedy that situates itself between the deceitful mythical justification of sacrifice and the Gospel revelation of the scapegoat mechanism.

THE HERO MYTH OF REDEMPTIVE VIOLENCE

Mythical narratives reflect the difference between what a culture deems "good" (heroic, constructive) violence and "bad" (monstrous, destructive) violence. All cultural distinctions arise from this distinction. Like destructive violence itself, all acts, objects, or subjects associated with that violence are taboo. However, if ritual allows them in a structured way, they are deemed beneficial. When read with Girard, sacrifice can be understood as a *vaccine* of controlled violence that redeems communities from the *epidemic disease* of uncontrollable violence.

Myths recount how any transgression of taboos outside of a ritual context leads to disasters. By evoking the fear of these disasters, myths not only encourage respect for cultural prohibitions, but also encourage active participation in acts of sacrificial violence as a means to preserve social order. In short, myths provide the cultural imagination that coordinates the maintenance of human communities.[6]

One of the stories that inspired *Star Wars*, the well-known Oedipus myth, illustrates the basic features of stories about redemptive violence.[7] In this narrative, Oedipus represents the ironic, almost comic, paradox at the heart of tragedy. Despite efforts to avoid the prophecy that he will kill his father and marry his mother, he cannot evade his fate. In fact, his transgressions unleash a plague, transforming Oedipus into the monstrous vector of violent disaster. However, by "dying" to himself and by removing himself as the monster of violence, Oedipus becomes the community's redeemer.

Girard accurately summarizes the ambiguous depiction of mythical heroes like Oedipus:

> A source of violence and disorder during his sojourn among men, the hero appears as a redeemer as soon as he has been eliminated, invariably by violent means. It also happens that the hero, while remaining a transgressor, is cast primarily as a destroyer of monsters.... The hero draws to himself a violent reaction, whose effects are felt throughout the community. He unwittingly conjures up a baleful, infectious force that his own death—or triumph—transforms into a guarantee of order and tranquility.... There are stories of collective salvation, in which the death of a single victim serves to appease the anger of some god or spirit. A lone individual, who may or may not have been guilty of some past

crime, is offered up to a ferocious monster or demon to appease him, and he ends up killing that monster as he is killed by him.[8]

Campbell concurs. He considers myths and the sacrificial rites they sustain as attempts to reconcile the human mind with the apparent inevitability of death to create life.[9] According to him, we are governed by an endless sacred cycle of destruction and creation. At the heart of this transcendent system lies heroic sacrifice, which transforms the cosmic forces of disorder into a force for order and harmony. For Campbell, the ambiguity of mythical creatures metaphorically expresses the human awareness of the ambiguous nature of these cosmic energies. Divine heroes or heroic gods are at once responsible for crisis and order.[10] Hence Campbell claims: "Whether you call someone a hero or a monster is all relative to where the focus of your consciousness may be."[11] In short, the mythical hero balances the two sides of the sacred by bringing so-called necessary sacrifices and thus sets an example. Following the scenario of their particular hero myths, communities all over the world attempt to redeem themselves from crises through sacrifice.

GLIMPSES OF THE SCAPEGOAT REALITY

Tempting as the universal myth of redemptive violence may be because of its promise of peace, there is something fishy about the picture reflected in the Oedipus myth. Apparently, the force embodied by Oedipus causes the chaos of a *natural* disaster as the consequence of a transgression of *social* taboos. Yet there is no causal relationship between killing your father and marrying your mother on the one hand, and the outbreak of the plague on the other. Oedipus is a *scapegoat*, in other words, one who is accused of causing an epidemic for which he bears no responsibility.

Girard's mimetic theory uncovers the role of the scapegoat mechanism at the foundation of our cultures and our myths. Girard suggests that the mythical narrative of our community obscures three truths.[12] First, it blurs the imitative or "mimetic" aspect of our desires. Second, it distorts the similarities between ourselves and our enemies. Third, it hides the arbitrariness of the deadly violence we ultimately use to redeem our community from disasters. Girard puts it succinctly: "In myth, violent death is always justified."[13]

Tragedy hints at the true origin of social chaos, namely our tendency to imitate each other's desire. If we cannot or do not want to share the object of that mimetic desire, rivalry turns us into enemy doubles. Girard writes: "[The tragic poet] whistles up a storm of violent reciprocity, and differences are swept away in this storm . . ."[14] As different competitors find social unity by imitating each other's enmity against one of the rivaling parties (the "scapegoat"), the collective elimination of the latter is easily experienced as a fateful outcome of the whole process. Tragedy articulates this experience of so-called necessary violence. Instead of acknowledging that the reunited community and its victims had an equal share in the violence, tragedy reintroduces a radical difference between the community and its victims. Instead of disclosing the role of mimetic dynamics on all sides, tragedy convinces its audience that those who died were responsible for disorder in the first place, which makes their death inevitable to establish order. In short, tragedy ultimately *reflects* the working of the scapegoat mechanism, instead of *revealing* it. It resorts to the mythical justification of sacrifice.[15]

A closer look at the story of Anakin Skywalker in *Star Wars* makes clear in what sense it is a tragedy as Girard understands it.

THE TRAGIC REFLECTION OF MYTHICAL LIES IN STAR WARS

"The original idea was a story, ultimately of salvation, of revealing that the villain is actually the hero."[16] These words of George Lucas about his story's leading character recall the ambiguity of Oedipus. *Star Wars* also reflects a belief in a Janus-faced sacred force. This "Force" has a life of its own. It permeates all that is. The "dark side of the Force" is responsible for violent disorder and breeds rivalry. The "light side of the Force" is responsible for peaceful order; it eliminates violent threats. Thus, the Force animates acts of destructive and redemptive violence. The Jedi Knights are guardians of peace in the Galactic Republic. They are locked, however, in a seemingly endless battle with the Dark Lords of the Sith.

A PSYCHOSOCIAL CRISIS

According to Lucas, "if you see all six films, then you realize the story is really about [Anakin Skywalker]."[17] There are many parallels between Anakin's tragic story and the Oedipus myth. Anakin is considered by some as the "Chosen One," foretold in a prophecy as "the One who will bring balance to the Force." He seems to originate partly from the Force itself, both because of his great control over it and because he has no biological father. He is a promising apprentice to Obi-Wan Kenobi, his Jedi Master, who trains him to let go of his emotional attachments. However, traumatized by the loss of his mother, Anakin is overwhelmed by a nightmare. He dreams that his pregnant wife, Padmé Amidala, might die in childbirth. Padmé has been Anakin's caregiver. By secretly marrying this mother figure, Anakin fails to respect the Jedi prohibition on attachments. Thus, like Oedipus, Anakin becomes a transgressor of taboos.

The Grand Master Yoda tries to restrain Anakin from taking the path of the dark side. "Attachment leads to jealousy. The shadow of greed, that is," Yoda observes, and commands Anakin: "Train yourself to let go of everything you fear to lose."[18] Yoda's advice is in vain. Anakin more eagerly listens to the Sith tragedy of Darth Plagueis, told to him by Senator Palpatine. According to Palpatine, Plagueis was such a powerful Sith Lord that he could create life and keep his beloved ones from dying. However, by not completely sharing his power with his apprentice, Plagueis provoked the latter's rivalry. Finishing the story, Palpatine paints Anakin a picture of Masters who lose their power by withholding it from their apprentices:

> Darth Plagueis became so powerful . . . the only thing he was afraid of was losing his power, which eventually, of course, he did. Unfortunately, he taught his apprentice everything he knew, then his apprentice killed him in his sleep. Plagueis never saw it coming. It's ironic he could save others from death, but not himself.[19]

Plagueis is what Girard calls a model-obstacle, a role model in a paradoxical double-bind. On the one hand, he commands his apprentice to imitate his desire. On the other hand, he possesses the object of desire and so becomes an obstacle to his apprentice's desire. The apprentice is simultaneously enticed—*imitate me*—and rebuffed—*imitate me not*. Also, the more Plagueis holds on to the power desired by his apprentice, the more he in his turn imitates the desire of his apprentice, which arouses the latter's desire even more—and *vice versa*. Girard:

> In giving my model a rival I return to him, in a way, the gift of the desire that he just gave to me. I give a model to my own model. The spectacle of my desire reinforces his at the precise moment when, in confronting me, he reinforces mine.[20]

For instance, when a toddler notices the interest of a playmate for a toy he had forgotten about, his desire for the toy might be aroused. Instead of enjoying whatever he was doing, he will likely claim the toy as being his and insist that he was "the first" to want it. Often, the playmate will mirror the toddler's behavior. For each one of them, remaining blind to the mimetic nature of their own desire, their violence is a defensive response to the other's so-called first aggression. Girard notices that

> The more the antagonists desire to become different from each other, the more they become identical. Identity is realized in the hatred of the identical. This is

the climactic moment that twins embody, or the enemy brothers of mythology such as Romulus and Remus. It is what I call a confrontation of *doubles*.[21]

The rivalry between doubles contagiously spreads, until a society finds itself in a crisis. Palpatine tricks Anakin into rivalry with the Jedi. He is the secret mastermind of a civil war, yet manages to present himself as the solution to the crisis he actually organized himself. The mimetic dynamic embodied by Palpatine is the Biblical Satan. Girard clarifies:

> Satan . . . is a kind of personification of "bad contagion" just as much in its conflictive and disintegrative aspects as in its reconciling and unifying aspects. . . . Satan . . . is the one who foments disorder, the one who sows scandals, and then at the height of the crises that he himself provokes, Satan suddenly brings them to an end by expelling the disorder.[22]

Palpatine establishes the first Galactic Empire. As a dictatorial "false Messiah" Emperor Palpatine sows the very fear from which he promises to save the Republic. He turns out to be Darth Sidious, a Sith Lord. Anakin becomes his apprentice, Darth Vader.

Seduced by the dark side of the Force, Vader tragically loses his future with Padmé in his attempts to save it. His rage against the Jedi causes her death. Moreover, Vader himself ends up being dismembered as he tries to slay his "brother" Obi-Wan. The Emperor saves Vader, but the cost of this salvation is steep, for Vader is entombed in black machine armor to keep him alive. Jesus describes how "those who want to save their life will lose it" (Mark 8:35a). The price Vader pays to gain power over the Empire indeed seems a Pyrrhic victory. Additionally, Vader's twin son and daughter, who already lost their mother Padmé in childbirth, will end up rivaling the monstrous twin Sidious and Vader.

A POLITICAL SOLUTION

Mimetic rivalry ends when one of the fighting parties either surrenders, is banned, or is eliminated. Of course, the one with the most allies usually has a better chance at emerging victorious. "Majority rule" enables victors to depict the enemy's violence as a "monstrous" attack and their own violence as a "noble" act of self-defense.

A tragedy like *Star Wars*, however, reveals that the rulers and their enemies are two sides of the same coin of mimetic rivalry: they are essentially the *same*. In fact, *Star Wars* suggests that power is inherently mimetic: power results from a *comparison with* (sometimes imagined) competitors (be it natural or social forces). Without the threat of its loss, a sense of power doesn't exist at all. Power only exists as an endless reaffirmation of the victory over, and thus rivalry with, that threat. This is the inescapable law of the Force in *Star Wars*. Palpatine makes clear that both the Sith and the Jedi are subjected to a rivalry over power in a conversation with Anakin: "The Sith and the Jedi are similar in almost every way, including their quest for greater power.... The fear of losing power is a weakness of both the Jedi and the Sith."[23] By comparing the Jedi with the Sith, Palpatine articulates Campbell's idea of the mythical consciousness, which expresses an amoral—or at least morally relative—universe: "Good is a point of view, Anakin. And the Jedi point of view isn't the only valid one. The Dark Lords of the Sith believe in security and justice also, yet they are considered by the Jedi to be evil."[24]

Yoda and Palpatine, the respective leaders of the Jedi and the Sith, believe peace can only be established by the elimination of the enemy. They present their own policy to solve the crisis as a matter of self-defense.[25] Palpatine: "The Jedi are relentless; if they are not all destroyed, it will be civil war without end.... Once more, the Sith will rule the galaxy, and we shall have peace." The Jedi Council echoes this sentiment: "I sense a plot to destroy the Jedi.... Destroy the Sith, we must."

The first victory goes to the Sith. The Jedi are nearly extinguished, children included. Palpatine, personifying the temptation to disintegrating rivalry, resembles Satan even more in the way he deceivingly renews order: "Satan expels Satan," Girard writes, "by means of innocent victims whom he succeeds in having condemned."[26]

A NEW CRISIS AND A NEW SOLUTION YET THE SAME OLD STORY

In the years after Palpatine's rise to power, Padmé's twin children lead separate lives. Luke Skywalker grows up on a remote planet as the sole child of his adoptive parents. Like Oedipus, he doesn't know his father. Nevertheless, like Anakin, he sets out to become a Jedi. He, too, is trained by Obi-Wan and Yoda. Eventually, Luke finds out Leia is his sister. He also learns that the Jedi's sworn enemy, Darth Vader, is his father.

In Luke's final confrontation with Vader, the father finds himself on the losing side. Luke, poised to vanquish his father, receives encouragement from the Emperor. In conquering the father, the son can become the father. Luke, however, contemplates his robotic hand and empathizes with his father, who has the same lost appendage. When Luke refuses to kill Vader, the Emperor violently unleashes the Force against Luke. Father and son seem lost. Until, that is, Vader gathers his strength and vanquishes the Emperor.

Thus, as in the legend of Darth Plagueis, Sidious is fought by an apprentice who is his equal. Vader kills Sidious, but is mortally wounded during the fight. The rivalry between these monstrous doubles dies as they kill each other. In their deaths, the plague of violence abates. Moreover, having destroyed their common enemy, Vader and his son find themselves reconciled before Vader dies.

In other words, the crisis comes to a halt through the mimetic bonding against a common enemy, who is eventually eliminated. Myths, however, obscure the mimetic origin of both crisis and new unity by wrongfully depicting the victim as the origin of both crisis and order. Although *Star Wars* at some point evokes the violent reciprocity between the Jedi and the Sith, the story ultimately blames the Sith for the crisis in the Galaxy and justifies their expulsion to restore peace. Anakin fulfills the prophecy of the One who brings balance to the Force. According to the logic of the story, this is a fate he cannot escape. Anakin follows the trajectory of the mythical hero. A *monster*, responsible for destructive violence while alive, Anakin becomes the *hero* who performs an act of redemptive violence in sacrificing the monster—himself! He is at once the embodiment of the dark and light side of the Force.

A CULTURAL COMMEMORATION

In the first six episodes of *Star Wars*, the epidemic of violence provisionally ends with the Sith's elimination. It allows the Jedi to re-imagine themselves as defenders of peace and to interpret their own violence as "necessary, good violence." They preserve the taboo on a vengeful return of the Sith by imitating the founding redemptive violence of Vader. Each sacrifice of so-called violent threats is a re-enactment of Vader's *salvific dead presence*. It is believed to keep the haunting violence of his former *evil living presence* outside the community.[27]

Interestingly, during the victory festivities of the Jedi, the ghost of Anakin is depicted alongside the ghosts of Yoda and Obi-Wan. Anakin has become godlike, keeping watch over the Galaxy. Girard observes that this process characterizes myths in general:

> The transformation of the evildoer into a divine benefactor is a phenomenon simultaneously marvelous and routine. . . . All this is explicable if we see that by the end of these myths unanimous violence has reconciled the community and the reconciling power is attributed to the victim, who is already "guilty," already "responsible" for the crisis. The victim is thus transfigured twice: the first time in a negative, evil fashion; the second time in a positive, beneficial fashion. Everyone thought this victim had perished, but it turns out he or she

must be alive since this very one reconstructs the community immediately after destroying it. He or she is clearly immortal and thus divine.[28]

In light of the Gospel, *Star Wars* reflects the mythical lie about violence. Anakin, like other mythical victims, seems to possess a transcendent "Force" that is responsible for destructive and redemptive violence. Hence Girard writes: "The peoples of the world do not invent their gods. They deify their victims."[29]

In reality, however, there are no inevitable forces to blame for an ever-recurring cycle of violence, and which decide who is "fittest" to survive. The Gospel revelation of this truth destroys every "mythical" justification— be it religious, political or pseudoscientific ("neo-Darwinian")—for violence. Girard stresses the Gospel's subversive power:

> The word of the Gospel is unique in really problematizing human violence. All other sources on humankind resolve the question of violence before it is even asked. Either the violence is considered divine (myths), or it is attributed to human nature (biology), or it is restricted to certain people or types of persons only (who then make excellent scapegoats), and these are ideologies.[30]

To justify violence by referring to a non-existent decisive transcendence, is thus to use an ultimate scapegoat. Violence and its sacrificial outcomes are mimetic, human realities. The Gospel proclaims the model of a non-violent God who frees us to a non-rivalrous new life.

THE GOSPEL REVELATION OF REDEMPTIVE GRACE

Asked what the most important commandment is, Jesus answers: *"Love God, and your neighbor as yourself"* (Mark 12:28–31). "To love God" is, in a Jewish sense, the prohibition on idolatry (Exodus 20:3–4). It is the prohibition to deify anything, including your own identity. Since your basic identity results from the mythical imagination of the community you belong to, the dynamic of love proposed by Jesus challenges the deification of that community and its attitude towards external enemies. For instance, a member of a girl clique may very well believe that a smart girl is excluded because she is a "slut" who "spoils group atmosphere." It's the kind of deceptive gossip myth that differentiates a group from an external enemy. It provides internal uniformity. *Star Wars* illustrates this by the "robotic" sameness of the Imperial Storm Troopers. "Otherness" in such groups is merely a difference of hierarchical position, since every member is expected to accept the same "truth" (of the leader).

Jesus points to the sameness between a group and its external enemy to enable neighborly love (Matthew 5:44), which ends the differentiating exclusion of the other and paradoxically allows for internal diversity and integrity (Matthew 10:34–36). Jesus challenges the violent peace of any sacrificial order (John 14:27) and enables the peace of non-violent internal conflict. A girl who criticizes her clique's depiction of an excluded so-called slut causes inner debates, which might result in the inclusion of the latter. The "other" turns out not to be that different from "us" after all. This dynamic goes against the one articulated by Palpatine, who also points to sameness, but only to provoke rivalry. Jesus transforms the mimesis of a desire for power into a mimesis of withdrawal from rivalry over power—grace!

The creativity of the love that is Jesus' God, is not easily grasped. When the Pharisees ask Jesus whether it is lawful to pay taxes to the emperor (Matthew 22:15–22), they are amazed by his answer: "Give to the emperor the things that are the emperor's, and to God the things that are God's." Instead of becoming a collaborator with the Roman oppressor, or an ally of the Jewish insurgents, Jesus reveals love as a dynamic that does not take part in a competition over power. Hence, Jesus is neither for nor against any given rule. For him the question is whether policy contributes to neighborly love or not. His peace does not depend on the abolishment of any cultural order (Matthew 5:17), but on a transformation of existing laws from the perspective of neighborly love. Therefore he says: "The sabbath was made for humankind, and not humankind for the sabbath" (Mark 2:27). Thus, although the love of Jesus is universalist and transcultural (since it challenges every culture to rethink itself), it is not totalitarian. Indeed, the mutual withdrawal between cultures from rivalry over power creates the space for a multicultural society.

Like the Sith and the Jedi, Caiaphas presents the age-old solution of sacrifice to save the community from a so-called looming civil war wherein Jesus would be one of the leaders: "It is better for you to have one man die for the people than to have the whole nation destroyed" (John 11:50). After Jesus is arrested, the promised sacrificial peace seems imminent: even the Roman governor Pilate and the Galilean ruler Herod become friends at the expense of a tortured Jesus (Luke 23:12).

As the leaders mimetically hold on to their power, they can only conceive of Jesus as a rival. The Gospel reveals this jealousy as the true cause of their desire to eliminate Jesus (Matthew 27:18). Despite the vehemence of the violence used against him, Jesus never succumbs to the temptation to answer violence with violence, which he uncovers as the dynamic of Satan (Matthew 4:10; 16:23). The imprisoned Jesus withstands the satanic, mimetic cycle of rivalry and its provisional sacrificial peace. Even Pilate concludes that Jesus is innocent of the charges against him (John 18:38). The power that needs the lie of an outside threat to justify its myths of self-defense cannot stand this truth about the scapegoat in its midst. This is why Jesus is crucified.

CONCLUSION

To his opponents, the crucified Jesus seems to have lost. "He saved others, he cannot save himself" (Matthew 27:42). Although these words seem to characterize the self-sacrifice of Darth Vader, Jesus' death differs radically from Vader's. Vader dies to himself and becomes the embodiment of a redeeming violence. The cultural order of the Jedi continues to exist thanks to the violent elimination of enemy threats. The death of Jesus, however, does not transform Jesus into a ghostly ruler of this world, who is imitated in further acts of violence. Contrary to Vader, Jesus saves others by refusing to kill. When Jesus dies, further attempts to draw him into the world of violence become impossible. The violent logic that needs its victim's involvement in violence to justify itself utterly fails. What dies on the cross is the foundation of violence. This is why Jesus proclaims, right before dying: "It is finished" (John 19:30). The universal lie of the scapegoat mechanism behind the ever-recurring myths of redemptive violence is revealed. In that sense, Jesus is: "The Lamb of God who takes away the sin of the world" (John 1:29). Girard writes:

> By nailing Christ to the Cross, the powers believed they were doing what they ordinarily did in unleashing the single victim mechanism. They thought they were avoiding the danger of disclosure. They did not suspect that in the end they would be doing just the opposite: they would be contributing to their own annihilation, nailing themselves to the Cross, so to speak. They did not and could not suspect the revelatory power of the Cross. . . . The powers are not put on display because they are defeated, but they are defeated because they are put on display.[31]

Easter Sunday reveals the crucified Jesus as the living incarnation of the non-violent Love that redeemed the lives of "friends" and "enemies" from a potential civil war.[32] Therefore, the Eucharistic commemoration of Jesus' death is not the repetition of deadly violence to establish peace. It is the sacramental presence of Jesus as Risen Christ and true Messiah, who does not feed on violence to become a so-called savior, but who invites us to imagine ever new ways of sharing his forgiving withdrawal from violence. Imitating Jesus' "Father" means imitating a grace that wants us to be fully alive in reconciling with each other. Imitating "Vader" means imitating a rivalry that demands our death, and/or the death of our neighbor.

Star Wars does not imagine the full potential of forgiveness, as it remains enmeshed in a fateful cycle of retaliatory violence.[33] Hence, for instance, the titles *Revenge of the Sith* and *Return of the Jedi* for episodes III and VI, respectively. However, the saga does evoke a sense of compassion for those who commit evil while they are desperately trying to do good. As Luke Skywalker discovers, there is a Darth Vader in all of us. Compassion for our own dark side may become compassion for the dark side of others as well, until there is only the life-giving space of mutual forgiveness: the space opened up by the *Resurrection of the Christ*.

NOTES

1. Bill Moyers, "The Mythology of 'Star Wars' with George Lucas," *Bill Moyers*, June 18, 1999, https://billmoyers.com/content/mythology-of-star-wars-george-lucas/.
2. Joseph Campbell, *The Hero with a Thousand Faces* (Novato: New World Library, 2008), 1–37.
3. Joseph Campbell, *The Power of Myth* (New York: Doubleday, 1991), 151–206.
4. Chris Fleming, *René Girard: Violence and Mimesis* (Cambridge: Polity Press, 2004), 115–124; Gil Bailie, *Violence Unveiled: Humanity at the Crossroads* (New York: The Crossroad Publishing Company, 1995), 128–132.
5. René Girard, *Things Hidden Since the Foundation of the World* (London: Bloomsbury, 2016), 135–172.
6. Yuval Noah Harari, *Sapiens: A Brief History of Humankind* (London: Vintage, 2015), 27–28; 35–36.
7. René Girard, *Violence and the Sacred* (London: Bloomsbury, 2013), 77–99.
8. Ibid., 97–98.
9. Campbell, *The Power of Myth*, 50.
10. Ibid., 137.
11. Ibid., 156.
12. René Girard, *The Scapegoat* (Baltimore: The Johns Hopkins University Press, 1986), 24–44; René Girard, *Evolution and Conversion: Dialogues on the Origins of Culture* (London: Continuum International Publishing, 2007), 81–88.
13. René Girard, "Are the Gospels Mythical?," *First Things* (April 1996). https://www.firstthings.com/article/1996/04/are-the-gospels-mythical.
14. Girard, *Violence and the Sacred*, 71.
15. Ibid., 88–90.
16. George Lucas, in *AFI Life Achievement Award: A Tribute to George Lucas*, written by Bob Gazzale, directed by Louis J. Horvitz (Los Angeles: AFI, 2005).
17. George Lucas, commentary scene 44, *Star Wars: Episode VI—Return of the Jedi*, screenplay by George Lucas and Lawrence Kasdan, directed by Richard Marquand (1983; San Francisco: Lucasfilm/20th Century Fox, 2015), Blu-ray Disc.
18. *Star Wars: Episode III—Revenge of the Sith*, written and directed by George Lucas (2005; San Francisco: Lucasfilm/20th Century Fox, 2015), Blu-ray Disc.

19. Ibid.
20. René Girard, *I See Satan Fall Like Lightning* (Maryknoll: Orbis Books, 2001), 10.
21. Ibid., 20.
22. Ibid., 87.
23. *Star Wars: Episode III—Revenge of the Sith*.
24. Ibid.
25. Ibid.
26. Girard, *I See Satan Fall Like Lightning*, 87.
27. Campbell, *The Power of Myth*, 50.
René Girard, *Battling to the End* (East Lansing: Michigan State University Press, 2010), ix.
28. Girard, *I See Satan Fall Like Lightning*, 65–66.
29. Ibid., 70.
30. Girard, *I See Satan Fall Like Lightning*, 184.
31. Ibid., 142–143.
32. James Alison, *The Joy of Being Wrong: Original Sin Through Easter Eyes* (New York: The Crossroad Publishing Company, 1998), 139–161.
Wolfgang Palaver, *René Girard's Mimetic Theory* (East Lansing: Michigan State University Press, 2013), 255–273.
33. Paolo Diego Bubbio, "A Sacrificial Crisis Not Far Away: *Star Wars* as a Genuinely Modern Mythology," in P. Bubbio, and C. Fleming, eds., *Mimetic Theory and Film* (New York: Bloomsbury, 2019).

BIBLIOGRAPHY

AFI Life Achievement Award: A Tribute to George Lucas. Director: Louis J. Horvitz. Production Company: AFI. 2005.

Alison, James. *The Joy of Being Wrong: Original Sin through Easter Eyes*. New York: Crossroad Publishing Company, 1998.

Bailie, Gil. *Violence Unveiled: Humanity at the Crossroads*. New York: Crossroad Publishing Company, 1995.

Bubbio, Paolo Diego. "A Sacrificial Crisis Not Far Away: Star Wars as a Genuinely Modern Mythology." In *Mimetic Theory and Film*, by Paolo Diego Bubbio and Chris Fleming, 123–149. New York: Bloomsbury, 2019.

Campbell, Joseph. *The Hero with a Thousand Faces*. Novato: New World Library, 2008.

———. *The Power of Myth*. New York: Doubleday, 1991.

Fleming, Chris. *René Girard: Violence and Mimesis*. Cambridge: Polity Press, 2004.

Girard, René. "Are the Gospels Mythical?" *First Things: A Monthly Journal of Religion & Public Life*, 1996: 27–31.

———. *Battling to the End: Conversations with Benoît Chantre*. East Lansing: Michigan State University Press, 2010.

———. *Evolution and Conversion: Dialogues on the Origins of Culture*. With Pierpaolo Antonello and João Cezar de Castro Rocha. London: Continuum, 2007.

———. *I See Satan Fall Like Lightning*. Maryknoll NY: Orbis Books, 2001.

———. *The Scapegoat*. Baltimore: Johns Hopkins University Press, 1986.

———. *Things Hidden Since the Foundation of the World: Research Undertaken in Collaboration with J.-M. Oughourlian and G. Lefort*. London: Bloomsbury, 2016.

———. *Violence and the Sacred*. London: Bloomsbury, 2013.

Harari, Yuval Noah. *Sapiens: A Brief History of Humankind*. London: Vintage, 2015.

Moyers, Bill. Bill Moyers. 18 June 1999. https://billmoyers.com/content/mythology-of-star-wars-george-lucas/ (retrieved November 4, 2019).

Palaver, Wolfgang. *René Girard's Mimetic Theory*. East Lansing: Michigan State University Press, 2013.

Star Wars Episodes I–VI Box Set Blu-ray Disc. Director: Irvin Kershner, George Lucas and Richard Marquand. Production Company: Lucasfilm/20th Century Fox. 2015.

Chapter 3

Desire, the Scapegoated Other, and J.J. Abrams' *The Force Awakens*

John C. McDowell

This chapter focuses on what a productively edifying reading[1] of J.J. Abrams's *The Force Awakens* might look like.[2] It is here that the work of René Girard proves to be a useful analytical tool that encourages the movie's reader to pull back the curtain and observe the social function of this cinematic piece within the ordering of the violent social imagination. From Girard emerges the claim that this particular movie reveals much of what he frames as the social contagion of "sacred violence." In other words, Abrams's movie fails to be edifying, at least in an Augustinian sense, but instead reflects the violent order of what film scholars[3] have called post-9/11 cinema. This argument cumulatively unfolds through two main steps. Firstly, a reflection on a common use of "myth" in relation to the *Star Wars* franchise is claimed to be considerably better contextualized by engaging with Girard's treatment of myth. Girard's analysis encourages the reader of *Star Wars*-as-modern-myth to penetrate deeper and to recognize how movies serve both to reflect dominant social values and to sustain them. Secondly, these observations lead directly into reading a set of key features in Abrams's film by evaluating them through Girard's talk of the way myths socialize, even as they mask or hide the violent order, and thereby reinforce the system of violence.

MYTH AND GIRARD'S DEMYTHOLOGIZING

In 1978 Andrew Gordon composed a paper that has set the tone for much of the response to *Star Wars* by scholars ever since, suggesting that there is considerably more to it than popcorn cinematic entertainment. Working from Joseph Campbell's notion of the "monomyth," Gordon argues that myths are stories or sets of stories that explain our place in the world in order to aid self-understanding and shape our way in that world.[4] Drawing attention to a Jungian reading of mythic archetypes or primordial characters and common themes across cultures in 1977's *Star Wars*, Gordon maintains that what the director George Lucas did was translate certain mythic features from Campbell's studies into a cinematic idiom, generating "a new mythology which can satisfy the emotional needs of both children and adults."[5] This account, subsequently, has taken on a life of its own. So much so that the prominence of Campbell's PBS interviews *The Power of Myth*,[6] and the extraordinary popularity of the 1997 Smithsonian Institution's National Air and Space Museum exhibition *Star Wars* and the Magic of Myth means that "In the public's imagination, the terms 'myth' and '*Star Wars*' are very closely linked."[7] This connection has been reinforced by Lucas's own claims, although here one needs to carefully identify the range of ways in which Lucas was equally critical of Campbell's work and that the sequels to *A New Hope* distinctly complicate Campbell's simplistic notion of the hero-myth.[8] As early as 1977 (the month *before* the theatrical release of *Star Wars*) the director declared, "I wanted to do a modern fairy tale, a myth."[9] He later admitted that he "wanted to take ancient mythological motifs and update them."[10] The idea is not to create a "new myth," as such, as much as to construct a "myth" from mythic resources from the past.

To treat *Star Wars* as "myth" is controversial and deeply problematic, however. At the very least, such a blanket comparison evades the fact that myths, and indeed every text, imbibe and express a range of assumptions and values from within their own specific cultural contexts. Texts have histories, and to imagine that there are archetypes and themes common across all cultures is both an abstraction of those texts from their histories, and a projection of contemporary values onto a range of disparate materials. As Roland Barthes recognizes, "one can conceive of very ancient myths, but there are no eternal ones. . . . Mythology can only have an historical foundation."[11] Likewise, Paolo Diego Bubbio recognizes that "each version of a myth reflects the society that has produced or modified it."[12] Campbell, for instance, is far too cavalier in his use of myths so that, while he "cites hundreds of myths and extricates from them hundreds of archetypes . . . he analyzes few whole myths."[13]

The work of René Girard, however, forces the reader of movies-as-modern-myths to penetrate deeper and to recognize how they serve both to reflect dominant social values and to sustain them. Girard is certainly not innocent of exaggerating that a common feature underlies societies and their prevailing myths—the scapegoat mechanism that operates as an all-embracing metanarrative or "the only organizing principle, ... [so that] it controls everything."[14] Moreover, as Walter Wink suggests, some myths contribute to subverting violent social power relations, and I have made claims to this effect regarding Lucas's two sets of *Star Wars* trilogies.[15] Nonetheless, to read *Star Wars*, and in this chapter on J.J. Abrams's *Star Wars Episode VII: The Force Awakens* in particular, requires pressing certain questions of the material and raises some interesting possibilities.

Girard's interest has largely focused on the nature and causes of mob violence, and in this vein, he analyzes what he calls "persecution texts" and "myths." His thesis is that these mythic materials mask something that can and should be exposed. Therein, "those who create the sacred with their own violence are incapable of seeing its truth."[16] Specifically, the violence that is masked is a *necessary violence*. This is a violence that perpetuates violence rather than dissipates and resolves the difficulties that give rise to it, thereby reinforcing the violent system. The role of the cultural commentator, then, is to "demystify violence," which means tearing away the veil of self-delusion and enable (in)sight into a myth that otherwise generates "blindness."[17] Roland Barthes warns, however, that "*myth hides nothing*: its function is to distort, not to make disappear."[18] Although the warning is fair, in many ways Girard's approach can accommodate it. He argues that those who support the violence of the sacrificial system or "victim mechanism ... believe they are supporting the truth when they are really living a lie."[19] It is a system encoded, one might say, in mythic texts that deflect from practices and processes for healthy nonviolence societies. Girard helpfully refuses to read myths as primitive attempts to speak of reality in prescientific cultures, an approach that had been common among nineteenth-century scholars, and one that remains in the popular equation of "myth" with "falsity" or "untruth."[20]

Reading *The Force Awakens* through Girard's theory raises some interesting possibilities. In contrast to Lucas's prequel trilogy, Episode VII does not focus on tracing the origins of the violence, although it does come at the opening of a new stage in the violent conflict that Obi-Wan in *A New Hope* described as "the dark times" that succeeded the millennia of peace and justice, in which the Old Republic had been protected by Jedi "guardians." The film, instead, launches the viewer into the midst of conflict with the First Order's attack on the community at Tuanul in the Kelvin Ravine on Jakku. As with *A New Hope*, this is a situation in which violent contagion has escalated well beyond the ability for it to be diffused through a sacrificial ritual. It is the result of a belligerent antagonism that comes too late for political diplomacy or compromise. After all, this is *Star* WARS, and Lucas, of course, had admitted to designing a film that reflected his love for the *Flash Gordon* adventure serials. In this regard the movie functions as an echo, a kind of mimetic double, of Lucas' Episode IV.[21] "There is nothing, or next to nothing, in human behavior," Girard announces about mimetic desire, "that is not learned, and all learning is based on imitation."[22]

Without the control of violent impulses that the sacrificial order provides, the violence escalates. "Sooner or later, either humanity will renounce violence without sacrifice or it will destroy the planet."[23] This contagion has occurred because of resentment and vengefulness, the reciprocity that lashes out in pain, anger, and longing for retribution. "Violence, then, is an interminable, infinitely repetitive process. . . . Only violence can put an end to violence, and that is why violence is self-propagating. Everyone wants to strike the last blow, and reprisal can thus follow reprisal without any true conclusion ever being reached."[24] The First Order certainly displays considerable signs of resentment. It is not incidental that Kylo Ren is shown on several occasions to erupt violently in reaction to failure and loss of control. In an important scene, prior to the destruction of key New Republic planets, General Hux addresses massed military ranks. To say that the oratory is impassioned would be an understatement. As it progresses, he becomes more and more fanatical, something intensified further in Rian Johnson's *The Last Jedi*. It is full of spite and unrestrained animosity toward the New Republic, and its unworthiness to rule after having defeated Palpatine's Empire in the Galactic Civil War. This is the cause of the new stage of galactic violence for Episodes VII–IX of the saga. No compromise is possible, no peaceable accord, only the rising of the First Order to enact vengeance. The echoes of the rise of National Socialism out of, among other things, resentment at the deal forced upon Germany at Versailles, is not far from the surface.

Girard's account appears to some commentators to assume the validity of Thomas Hobbes's claim about the primal state, that human beings are involved in a perpetual struggle and therefore a "war of all against all." Terry Eagleton, for instance, complains of Girard's "bleakly Hobbesian vision."[25] The problem with Girard's suggestion is that, as John Milbank observes, "To trace violence back to imitation is equivalent to lodging sin gnostically in our finitude."[26] Likewise, Eagleton complains that Girard provides a significantly "drastic reductive" portrayal of violence in the context of mimetic desire.[27] It is simply not the case that "mimetic desire is always as destructive as he imagines."[28] Whether that is fair to Girard or not, Girard's notion of mimetic rivalry as the way in which antagonistic desire is generated and becomes violent is nonetheless a useful device for reading Abrams's movie. Crucially, it is evident in Hux's resentment of the New Republic's control of galactic governance. The First Order commander exhibits an ambitious desire to restore galactic rule-by-the-iron-fist, and thereby allow the First Order to be a worthy successor to the Galactic Empire and possess the sole monopoly on, and legal control over, violence in its militarized state.[29]

According to Wink, the combat myth of redemptive violence tends to be more common in relation to generating violence than the myth of the scapegoat. However, Hux does indeed make the New Republic itself into the scapegoat, not only for the ills of the imperial military order, but for the ills of the galaxy. It is, he announces, "a regime that acquiesces to disorder." The New Republic, he sneeringly spits, "lies to the galaxy while secretly supporting the treachery of the loathsome Resistance." This is a fundamentalism requiring complete political and ideological takeover, a fundamentalism enthusing the gathered ranks against those portrayed as politically decadent. Alan Dean Foster's novelization uses the language of "decadence" to describe the New Republic.[30] A similar characterization of the current Senate is made when Kylo Ren sneers at Rey and confronts her about "the murderers, traitors, and thieves you call friends." Here the New Republic and the Resistance are as irredeemably "other" to the First Order as it is to them. They are mirrors or mimetic doubles and rivals of each other. With such regimes there can be no compromise, no conversation, no co-operation, no negotiation, only opposition, conflict and annihilation. Even so, the desire does not appear to be one of galactic extermination, but merely the destruction of the current governing order and its replacement by the First Order. "All remaining systems," Hux vehemently predicts, "will bow to the First Order." Accordingly, violence is being socially contained, in a way, by being displaced onto a single victim—the governing order of the New Republic. The leaders and protectors of the New Republic are to be offered up as sacrificial victims.[31] Not only must the First Order strike without mercy, annihilating its enemy, but after their success there is a promise of social peace under its militarized state governance. In this regard, "social cohesion is founded on an act of destruction."[32] As Mark Heim recognizes, "The ritual cure is a homeopathic one. It uses violence to drive out violence. But a very specific dose and type are required. It is crucial that it be collective violence (in which all, at least implicitly, participate) and that it not itself set off any further cycle of vengeance."[33]

THE POLITICS OF MYTH

Girard, of course, analyzes mythic texts to understand the sociocultural conditions at play, especially as they encode a violent system and reinforce that system through culturally conditioning stories. "There are chinks and cracks. In mythology the mask is still intact; it covers the whole face so well that we have no idea it is a mask."[34] Through myths, people are socialized into a violent order that is held together only by that deflecting of its desires onto the "good" violence that scapegoats a victim. If mythologies mask an originary violence and perpetuate violent conditions, what does this then mean for *The*

Force Awakens as a cultural myth? At least six elements in the film provide clues as to its social function and its masking of social violence.

The first thing to notice is the physical otherness of Snoke and Kylo Ren, both of whom exhibit physical disfigurements. The latter bears a prominent facial scar which provides a visual reference to the Anakin of *Revenge of the Sith*; the former's wound is especially pronounced, with him bearing a deeply mutilating facial wound. To understand what this entails returning to Girard on the classes of people from whom the scapegoat is constructed for the social projection of blame, hate and hostility. There is a "whole range of victim signs," and "the more signs of a victim an individual bears, the more likely he is to attract disaster."[35] Certain qualities, then, set some apart which renders them ripe for blame under certain conditions of scarcity, fear, crisis, and disaster. "[T]he scapegoat no longer appears to be merely a passive receptacle for evil forces but is rather the mirage of an omnipotent manipulator shown by mythology to be sanctioned unanimously by society."[36] In particular, he argues, minorities, strangers or foreigners, and social outsiders tend to be on the receiving end of socially sacrificial violence. In addition, "physical and moral monstrosity are heaped together in myths that justify the persecution of the infirm."[37] They are, Girard says, transformed into the "monstrous."[38] Speaking of Girard's account of scapegoating, Richard Kearney argues that we "attempt to simplify our existence by scapegoating others as 'aliens.'" In so doing, we contrive to transmute the sacrificial alien into a monster, or into a fetish-god. But either way, we refuse to recognize the stranger as a singular other who responds, in turn, to the singular otherness in each of us. We refuse to acknowledge ourselves-as-others."[39]

The second clue is the nature of the Starkiller Base's weapon platform as a Weapon of Mass Destruction, and its utilization by a terrorist organization in a catastrophic preemptive strike against the centers of power in the New Republic. This is modeled to a significant degree, of course, on the two Death Stars as planet-destroying devices, although the destructive capability and firing range of Starkiller Base's device far outstrips the capabilities of its inferior predecessors.

The third important feature is the location of the threat that the First Order poses to the democracy of the New Republic. It is telling that the Imperials who survived the Galactic Civil War fled to, and regrouped in, the galactic margins aptly named the Unknown Regions. This is territory beyond the galaxy's Western Reaches. From there, the First Order erupts to impose itself, from outside the Republic itself. Here, of course, one needs to hesitate. The backstory given to Kylo of the Knights of Ren sees him as emerging *from within* the Republic, with a nod to a fall story for Ben Solo, an echo of Anakin's fall. It is not incidental that in one scene Kylo addresses the mangled and melted helmet of Darth Vader, a fetishized object, promising that he will finish what his grandfather had started. Yet the First Order stands on the margins, as outsiders who need to be violently conquered. They are portrayed, then, as an "alien" peril. This stands in marked contrast to the prequels, with their narrative arc that involves the fall of the Republic under the machinations of Palpatine, and the original trilogy in which Obi-Wan relates the story not only of Vader's capitulation to the dark side but the treacherous displacement of the Republic by the Empire.

In the fourth place is the almost impermeable boundary between categories of us-them and good-evil. In *The Force Awakens*, both sides blame each other, and there is no way of rationally deciding between them. Nonetheless, the opening *Flash Gordon* inspired screen crawl provides the audience some direction for the characters they should sympathize with and those they should dislike. There the reference is to "the sinister First Order" which has "arisen from the ashes of the Empire," and the contrast is drawn with the reference to "the brave Resistance" which aims at "restoring peace and justice to the galaxy." Moreover, the imagery of the red and black banners, as well as the officers' uniforms, depicts the First Order as a Nazi-like movement, in a utilization of a common cinematic trope that announces the presence of pure evil. The Force now appears not to be a singular thing which, as Yoda articulates in *Empire Strikes Back*, binds all things together in symbiotic relations of peace and co-operation, but which is misused by the Sith in a way that disrupts that balance and which comes to be referred to as the "dark side." Instead, Abrams' movie suggests that the Force has a duality of a "light" side and a "dark" side. In fact, *The Complete Star Wars Encyclopedia* earlier had claimed that "there are two sides to the Force: The light side bestows great knowledge, peace, and an inner serenity; the dark side is filled with fear, anger, and the vilest aggression."[40] The political import of these differentiations, of tightly defined inclusion and exclusion, is not lost on Kearney: "In an age crippled by crises of identity and legitimation, it would seem particularly urgent to challenge the polarization between Us and Them."[41]

Fifth, this good-evil, us-them scheme is reflected further in a process that projects not only blame upon the enemy other, but purifies the violent action of those who now see themselves as victims. As the screen crawl announces, "the sinister First Order" is opposed by a "brave Resistance" led by General Leia Organa. "The definition of victim as sinner or criminal is . . . absolute in myth, and the causal relationship between crime and collective crisis is . . . strong."[42] "Whether physical or psychological, the violence directed at the victim appears to be justified—justified by the responsibility of the scapegoat in bringing about some evil that must be avenged, something bad or harmful that must be resisted and suppressed."[43] In this way, mob and persecutors assume the validity of their violent actions, and unquestionably believe in the moral fittingness of their violent action against the scapegoat who is perceived to deserve blame. The movie's novel adaptation has Leia say that the Resistance is engaged in "A war that won't end until either it [viz., the First Order] or the Resistance is destroyed."[44] This arch-hawkishness enables deflection away from the "us" to the "them," and the "them/others" who are to be fought and defeated for "our" security. A little hyperbolically reductive, Girard declares that "all a myth is" is "an absolute faith in the victim's total power of evil that liberates the persecutors from reciprocal recriminations and, therefore, is identical with an absolute faith in the total power of good."[45] Myth, after all, Girard announces, "is the social articulating of scapegoating narrated from the viewpoint of the persecutors."[46]

Finally, a common feature of Manichaean-like sensibilities is that while good is natural and identified with "us" (whoever we are who is doing the defining), evil has no history. It erupts for no reason. This, of course, accentuates the boundary between victimization and wicked aggression. It is telling that the Supreme Leader, Snoke, has no backstory in *The Force Awakens* (Episode IX does provide a clue to his origins). He simply appears, a form of belligerent wickedness that is given no explanatory motivations. There is, however, some potential for Kylo Ren to destabilize the good-evil binary. He admits on one occasion that he feels again the "call to the light," and yet he desires to be renewed in "the power of the darkness." Lor San Tekka and Han both remind him of his heritage in an effort to tempt him to reject Snoke's hold on him (in this way, the two sides are doubles, with Kylo Ren as the object of both their desires). Yet even here *The Force Awakens* offers little more motivation than suggesting he is purely explosively emotionally reactive. He certainly does not appear to follow a path on principle, under the guidance of Snoke, towards a different "good" (such as imperial governance). Of course, one needs to ask about what went wrong in Snoke's own moral formation that resulted in him acting manipulatively and with no sympathy for the destruction of millions, possibly billions, of people (at this stage in the narrative the reveal about him in *The Rise of Skywalker* had not occurred). However, Snoke, and even Kylo Ren, are simplistically morally dehumanized as a result. Of course, more generally, this process of denying any sympathizable qualities to certain characters is extended to the depiction of the personnel of the First Order. They are denied any semblance of complex human and political motivation in a way that would contextualize and explain (which is not to justify) their actions of inhumane violence.

What does this add up to? These references all have a distinctive significance when read in the context of what Terrence McSweeney and others call "post-9/11 cinema." This is not a comment about the fact that it comes chronologically *after* 9/11 as such, but rather a statement about the movie's ethos. The cinematic response to 9/11 is one in which cinema works with a double politics of purity and of blame, the innocent victim and the intelligibly evil victimizer. McSweeney explains, consequently, that the representation of "resounding cultural trauma" reproduces "an uncritical and unreflective narrative of American victimization, a pronounced disconnection from the complexities of the geographical arena, and, in some cases, even an elaborate erasure of political and historical context. . . . These narratives share a conspicuous detachment from disconcerting questions of politics, history and causality."[47] There is nothing "innocent," then, politically or ideologically, about myths. A myth illegitimately attempts to suggest that it is to be experienced "as innocent speech" precisely because it naturalizes itself as factual and "depoliticized speech," as speech without a history or politics of use.[48]

CONCLUSION

Augustine speaks of reading together within the community of the church as a training in love, but Girard helps push this ritual further, so that dominant social engagements with cinema's "mythic" texts can be perceived as contributing to social cohesion but only at the expense of failing to love those who are reduced to the position of the scapegoat. After all, myths "are the retrospective transfiguration of sacrificial crises, the reinterpretation of these crises in the light of the cultural order that has arisen from them."[49] Girard, consequently, helps the audience detect those mechanisms in the myth that are conducive to perpetuating a violent order while covering up the social origins of its mimetic rivalry and violence against the scapegoat.

For Lucas's original trilogy, the violence belongs to a context involving, among other things, the filmmaker's critique of the politics of a country that had ended up in the Vietnam War and in the breakdown of trust in the President over the Watergate affair.[50] In his 1974 notebooks, he reflects that "The empire is like America ten years from now, after gangsters assassinated the Emperor and were elected to power in a rigged election. . . . We are at a turning point: fascism or revolution."[51] Lucas's context is one in which imperialism is being contested, with *Star Wars* and its sequels encoding references to American empire within its critiques of ancient Roman and modern British imperialism; of concern with the growth of violent fascistic government developing *from within* the system; of observation of how this government is socially hierarchical and exclusionary; and of the Alliance's violence being not self-defensive but constituting a *rebellion* against political disorder.

In many ways, the spectacle of *The Force Awakens* provides an echo, a copy even, of Lucas's *A New Hope*. The narrative progresses from a desert planet, through a threshold call involving a droid (C3PO and R2D2/BB8), and then involves the central protagonist's awakening to the reality and power of the Force (Luke on board the Falcon/Rey on Takodana), to the assault against a super-weapon of mass destruction (the Death Star/Starkiller Base, and much more. However, that recognition should not hide the fact that there is much that pulls in rather different directions between the two movies—in particular, the nature and function of violence. Abrams's contribution to the *Star Wars* saga belongs to "post 9/11 cinema," and the way it deals with violence resonates with the scapegoat mechanism. This is evident in the demonization and exclusion as a pure "other" of the enemy. Such an approach, of course, had been prevalent during the Cold War era, and it has occasionally surfaced in, among other things, *Independence Day* and *Starship Troopers*. Yet the notion of the "evil other" becomes acutely intense in a post-9/11 setting. Significantly, Abrams weakens the association of America with the cause of the disorder, in contrast to *Rogue One*'s reference to American imperial presence in the Middle East; depicts the conflict as the appearance of the threat *from outside*, from the margins beyond the New Republic's borders; reduces the First Order's motivations less to those of control and dominance than of destructive resentment and revenge; and makes it less obvious that redemption consists in anything other than the utter annihilation of the threat, thereby echoing the apocalyptic belligerence of "the myth of redemptive violence," the belief that saving peace and healing come through violence.[52] There may be resources in Lucas's *Star Wars* series that can encourage hope for a redemptive peacemaking—one that contributes to "the constantly necessary dismantling of sacral violence; and . . . critical engagement with . . . forms both of sacral violence and of conflictual mimesis."[53] Abrams's addition to the franchise, however, lends itself to a distinctive inhospitality to neighbors and a vision of healing by necessary violence or the purgative function of a holy war. The conflict is less eschatological than apocalyptic, involving not reconciliation and peaceableness as much as an all-out conflict to the bitter end.

NOTES

1. In case the reader is puzzled over how movies are spoken of as "texts" that require to be "read," help is provided by Jacques Derrida "Hospitality, Justice and Responsibility: A Dialogue with Jacques Derrida," in Richard Kearney and Mark Dooley (eds.), *Questioning Ethics: Contemporary Debates in Philosophy* (London and New York: Routledge, 1999), 65–83 (67).

2. The study pays attention both to this particular movie in its own right, and also suggests that it exhibits a particularly pronounced tension with the political sensibility of George Lucas's six episodes that have been formative for the franchise. In this way, the paper invites the opening up of further analysis of Lucas's work in comparison

with that of his successors without succumbing to a conflation of the series that would imply that they are all encoding similar sets of political values.

3. Augustine spends time early in *De Doctrina Christiana* explaining how the scriptures are to be read together, as an activity of love for the sake of building up the community of God's people [Augustine, *De Doctrina Christiana*, trans. R.P.H. Green (Oxford and New York: Oxford University Press, 1995), 1.86]. This constitutes an edifying reading for the well-being of the social body that takes place within the history of God's redemptive healing of the world.

4. Andrew Gordon, "*Star Wars*: A Myth for Our Time," *Literature and Film Quarterly* 6 (1978), 314–326. Cf. Joseph Campbell, *The Hero With a Thousand Faces* (New York: Princeton University Press, 1949), 4.

5. Gordon, 324.

6. Joseph Campbell and Bill Moyers, *The Power of Myth* (New York: Doubleday, 1988).

7. Carl Silvio and Tony M. Vinci, "Moving Away from Myth: *Star Wars* as Cultural Artifact," in Carl Silvio and Tony M. Vinci (eds.), *Culture, Identities and Technology in the* Star Wars *Films: Essays on the Two Trilogies* (Jefferson, NC: McFarland and Company Inc., 2007), 1–8 (2).

8. For a discussion of the complexity of Lucas's relation to Campbell's myth work, see John C. McDowell, "'Unlearn What You Have Learned' [Yoda]: The Critical Study of the Myth of *Star Wars*," in Terry R. Ryan and Dan W. Clayton (eds.), *Understanding Religion and Popular Culture* (London: Routledge, 2012), 104–117; and, to a lesser degree, John C. McDowell, *The Gospel According to Star Wars: Faith, Hope and the Force*, 2nd ed. (Louisville, Kentucky: Westminster John Knox Press, 2017), ch. 2. Care should be taken when drawing on Girard's reading of tragedy as myth and applying it to the configuration of Anakin Skywalker's narrative arc. For a reading of the *political* conditions of Lucas's portrayal of Anakin as a tragic figure, see *The Politics of Big Fantasy: Studies in Cultural Suspicion* (Jefferson, NC: McFarland Press, 2014), ch. 2.

9. George Lucas, in Sally Kline (ed.), *George Lucas: Interviews* (Jackson: University Press of Mississippi, 1999), 53.

10. Lucas, cited in J.W. Rinzler, *The Making of Star Wars: The Definitive Story Behind the Original Film* (Ebury Press, 2008), 5f.

11. Roland Barthes, *Mythologies*, trans. Anette Lavers (New York: Hill and Wang, 1972), 108.

12. Paolo Diego Bubbio, "A Sacrificial Crisis Not Far Away: *Star Wars* as Genuine Modern Mythology," in Paolo Diego Bubbio and Chris Fleming (eds.), *Mimetic Theory and Film* (New York and London: Bloomsbury Academic, 2019), 123–149 (126).

13. Robert A. Segal, *Joseph Campbell: An Introduction* (New York: Garland, 1987), 137f.

14. René Girard, *Job: The Victim of his People*, trans. Yvonne Freccero (London: The Athlone Press, 1987), 24.

15. Walter Wink, *Engaging the Powers: Discernment and Resistance in a World of Domination* (Minneapolis: Fortress Press, 1992), 152–155; John C. McDowell, *Identity Politics in George Lucas' Star Wars* (Jefferson, NC: McFarland, 2016).

16. Girard, *Job*, 28.

17. René Girard, *I See Satan Fall Like Lightning*, trans. James G. Williams (Maryknoll, NY: Orbis, 2001), 130, 150.

18. Barthes, 120.

19. Girard, *I See Satan*, 41.

20. For a helpful introductory guide to the approaches of the likes of E.B. Tylor, see Robert A. Segal, *Myth: A Very Short Introduction* (Oxford and New York: Oxford University Press, 2004).

21. For a tracing of a number of visual and thematic echoes, doubling, or mimicking of Episode IV in Episode VII, see McDowell, *The Gospel According to Star Wars*, ch. 8.

22. Girard, *I See Satan*, 107.

23. René Girard, *Battling to the End: Conversations with Benoît Chantre*, trans. Mary Baker (East Lansing: University of Michigan Press, 2010), xvii.

24. René Girard, *Violence and the Sacred*, trans. Patrick Gregory (Baltimore: Johns Hopkins University Press, 1977), 14, 26.

25. Eagleton, 55.

26. John Milbank, "Stories of Sacrifice," *Modern Theology* 12 (1996), 27–56 (52).

27. Terry Eagleton, *Radical Sacrifice* (New Haven and London: Yale University Press, 2018), 55.

28. Eagleton, 55.

29. Girard uses the term "monopoly on the means of revenge" to describe the judicial system's confrontation of violence [*Violence and the Sacred*, 23].

30. Alan Dean Foster, *Star Wars: The Force Awakens* (London: Century, 2016), 173.

31. It is worth indicating that Girard's account rhetorically overplays the role of violence in sacrifice, and is vulnerable to criticisms of failing to pay attention to particularity of practices. Timothy Gorringe, for example, argues that "His thesis is . . . simplistic as an account of sacrifice: . . . not *all* sacrifice can be understood as a rationalization of violence." [*God's Just Vengeance: Crime, Violence and the Rhetoric of Salvation* (Cambridge: Cambridge University Press, 1996), 45]

32. Eagleton, 54.

33. S. Mark Heim, *Saved from Sacrifice: A Theology of the Cross* (Grand Rapids, MI: William B. Eerdmans, 2006), 44.

34. René Girard, *The Scapegoat*, trans. Yvonne Freccero (Baltimore: Johns Hopkins University Press, 1986), 37.

35. Girard, *The Scapegoat*, 32, 26.

36. Girard, *The Scapegoat*, 46.

37. Girard, *The Scapegoat*, 35.

38. Girard, *The Scapegoat*, 33.

39. Richard Kearney, *Strangers, Monsters, and Gods: Interpreting Otherness* (London and New York: Routledge, 2003), 5.

40. Stephen J. Sansweet, Pablo Hidalgo, Bob Vitas and Daniel Wallace, with Chris Cassidy, Mary Franklin and Josh Kushins, *The Complete Star Wars Encyclopedia*, Volume 1 (London: Titan Books, 2008), 285.

41. Kearney, *Strangers, Monsters, and Gods*, 5.

42. Girard, *The Scapegoat*, 36.

43. Girard, "Generative Scapegoating," in Robert G. Hamerton-Kelly (ed.), *Violent Origins: Walter Burkert, René Girard, and Jonathan Z. Smith on Ritual Killing and Cultural Formation* (Stanford: Stanford University Press, 1987), 73–105 (79).

44. Dean Foster, *Star Wars: The Force Awakens*, 256.

45. Girard, *Job*, 34.

46. Girard, 'Generative Scapegoating,' 79.

47. Terrence McSweeney, *The 'War on Terror' and American Film: 9/11 Frames Per Second* (Edinburgh: Edinburgh University Press, 2014), 11f.

48. Barthes, 130, 146.

49. Girard, *Violence and the Sacred*, 64.

50. To expand on this would take too long, so the reader is directed to McDowell, *Identity Politics in George Lucas' Star Wars*, chs. 1–2.

51. Cited in Rinzler, 26.

52. Walter Wink, *The Powers That Be: Theology for a New Millennium* (New York: Doubleday, 1998), 42.

53. Rowan Williams, *Wrestling with Angels: Conversations in Modern Theology*, ed. Mike Higton (London: SCM, 2007), 183.

BIBLIOGRAPHY

Augustine. *De Doctrina Christiana*. Translated by R.P.H. Green. Oxford and New York: Oxford University Press, 1995.

Barthes, Roland. *Mythologies*. Translated by Anette Lavers. New York: Hill and Wang, 1972.

Bubbio, Paolo Diego. "A Sacrificial Crisis Not Far Away: Star Wars as Genuine Modern Mythology," in *Mimetic Theory and Film*. Edited by Paolo Diego Bubbio and Chris Fleming, 123–149. New York and London: Bloomsbury Academic, 2019.

Campbell, Joseph. *The Hero with a Thousand Faces*. New York: Princeton University Press, 1949.

Campbell, Joseph, and Bill Moyers. *The Power of Myth*. New York: Doubleday, 1988.

Dean Foster, Alan. *Star Wars: The Force Awakens*. London: Century, 2016.

Eagleton, Terry. *Radical Sacrifice*. New Haven and London: Yale University Press, 2018.

Girard, René. *Battling to the End: Conversations with Benoît Chantre*. Translated by Mary Baker. East Lansing: University of Michigan Press, 2010.

———. "Generative Scapegoating." in *Violent Origins: Walter Burkert, René Girard, and Jonathan Z. Smith on Ritual Killing and Cultural Formation*. Edited by Robert G. Hamerton-Kelly, 73–105. Stanford: Stanford University Press, 1987.

———. *Job: The Victim of his People*. Translated by Yvonne Freccero. London: The Athlone Press, 1987.

———. *I See Satan Fall Like Lightning*. Translated by James G. Williams. Maryknoll, NY: Orbis, 2001.

———. *The Scapegoat*. Translated by Yvonne Freccero. Baltimore: Johns Hopkins University Press, 1986.

———. *Violence and the Sacred*. Translated by Patrick Gregory. Baltimore: The John Hopkins University Press, 1977.

Gordon, Andrew. "Star Wars: A Myth for Our Time." *Literature and Film Quarterly* 6 (1978): 314–326.

Gorringe, Timothy. *God's Just Vengeance: Crime, Violence and the Rhetoric of Salvation*. Cambridge: Cambridge University Press, 1996.

Heim, S. Mark. *Saved from Sacrifice: A Theology of the Cross*. Grand Rapids, Mich.: William B. Eerdmans, 2006.

Kearney, Richard. *Strangers, Monsters, and Gods: Interpreting Otherness*. London and New York: Routledge, 2003.

Kline, Sally, ed. *George Lucas: Interviews*. Jackson: University Press of Mississippi, 1999.

McDowell, John C. *The Gospel According to Star Wars: Faith, Hope and the Force*, 2nd edn. Louisville, Kentucky: Westminster John Knox Press, 2017.

———. *Identity Politics in George Lucas' Star Wars*. Jefferson: McFarland, 2016.

———. *The Politics of Big Fantasy: Studies in Cultural Suspicion*. Jefferson, NC: McFarland Press, 2014.

———. "'Unlearn What You Have Learned' [Yoda]: The Critical Study of the Myth of Star Wars." In *Understanding Religion and Popular Culture*. Edited by Terry R. Ryan and Dan W. Clayton, 104–117. London: Routledge, 2012.

McSweeney, Terrence. *The "War on Terror" and American Film: 9/11 Frames per Second*. Edinburgh: Edinburgh University Press, 2014.

Milbank, John. "Stories of Sacrifice." *Modern Theology* 12 (1996): 27–56.

Rinzler, J.W. *The Making of Star Wars: The Definitive Story behind the Original Film*. Ebury Press, 2008.

Sansweet, Stephen J., Pablo Hidalgo, Bob Vitas, and Daniel Wallace, with Chris Cassidy, Mary Franklin, and Josh Kushins, eds. *The Complete Star Wars Encyclopedia*, Volume 1. London: Titan Books, 2008.

Segal, Robert A. *Joseph Campbell: An Introduction*. New York: Garland, 1987.

———. *Myth: A Very Short Introduction*. Oxford and New York: Oxford University Press, 2004.

Silvio, Carl and Vinci, Tony M., eds. *Culture, Identities and Technology in the Star Wars Films: Essays on the Two Trilogies*. Jefferson, NC: McFarland and Company Inc., 2007.

Rowan Williams, *Wrestling with Angels: Conversations in Modern Theology*, ed. Mike Higton. London: SCM, 2007.

Wink, Walter. *Engaging the Powers: Discernment and Resistance in a World of Domination*. Minneapolis: Fortress Press, 1992.

———. *The Powers That Be: Theology for a New Millennium.* New York: Doubleday, 1998.

Chapter 4

Girard's Lasso of Truth

Wonder Woman and the Overcoming of Satan

Stephanie Perdew

The 2017 motion picture *Wonder Woman* presents a new installment in the tales of superhero Diana Prince, who first premiered in DC Comics in 1941.[1] The film conforms to the plot lines of superhero fiction, in which a protagonist defeats a villain using a combination of human daring and superhuman powers. Violence is subverted by superior and supposedly morally righteous violence, all in the name of protecting the vulnerable. In many ways, Wonder Woman fulfills these expectations to the satisfaction of theatre audiences. But the 2017 film depicts a more complex battle between Wonder Woman and her antagonist, Ares, god of war. This chapter reads the relationship between Wonder Woman and Ares through the lens of René Girard.

Ares can be interpreted as a Satanic figure, following Girard's understanding of Satan as a name for the scapegoat mechanism which results from compounding mimetic crises.[2] Girard uses the terms "satan," the "devil," the "prince of this world," and "the father of lies" as signifiers for this mechanism. Thus I will refer to the Ares figure by these terms throughout this chapter.[3] In *I See Satan Fall Like Lightning*, Girard outlines the contours of how the satan appears throughout the Biblical narrative. In the opening scenes of Genesis, the satan is personified by the seducing snake who lures us into transgression and inspires us to blame each other for our predicaments. As history unfolds, the devil enthralls us all in mimetic rivalries as we imitate his invitation to transgress the prohibitions and boundaries that would protect us from conflict. Our seducer then becomes a stumbling block, the accuser and adversary who draws us deeper into mimetic rivalries and encourages us to turn on one another to resolve our crises. Finally, the satan acts as the "prince of this world" when sacrifice and expulsion of victims re-order humanity, which brings about a false but cathartic unanimity, bought at the expense of the one/s sacrificed or expelled.

In Christian patristic traditions, the devil was understood as a fallen angel in rivalrous competition with God. Irenaeus of Lyons describes the devil thus:

> The devil . . . becoming envious of man, was rendered an apostate from the divine law: for envy is a thing foreign to God. And as his apostasy was exposed by man, and man became the [means of] searching out his thoughts, he has set himself to this with greater and greater determination, in position to man, envying his life, and wishing to involve him in his own apostate power.[4]

Origen of Alexandria uses the terms "demons," "powers," and "the devil" interchangeably to refer to the forces opposed to Christ without granting these forces (powers and principalities) their own ontology: "the one diametrically opposed to him [Christ] should be called son of the evil demon, who is Satan and the devil."[5]

Girard follows these traditions as he sees that the devil's power is derivative: "the devil does not have a stable foundation; he has no *being* at all. To clothe himself in the semblance of being, he must act as a parasite on God's creatures."[6] Girard sees this parasitic activity in the scapegoat mechanism, so that the name "Satan" can be given not to a creature with an autonomous ontology, but to humans caught up in the mimetic crises resulting in the scapegoat mechanism, which are satanic. In Girard's reading of the Bible, this process or mechanism is symbolized by the figure of Satan (in Hebrew, "the accuser"), the devil, the father of lies, and the prince of this world. In *Wonder Woman*, this process or mechanism is symbolized by the character Ares.[7] Ares is a rejected son and rival god to his father Zeus, an envious antagonist to humans whom he stirs into jealousy and accusation and hopes to lure into a war of total annihilation.

Like Adam and Eve in the Garden of Eden, Wonder Woman begins her life unaware of satanic ways. Princess Diana lives in an idyllic paradise on the island of Themyscira. Unlike Eden, it is inhabited by others, the female Amazons. They know of evil, and Diana's mother Queen Hippolyta goes to great lengths to protect Diana from it. As in the primordial Jewish-Christian story, humans in Diana's world are made in the image of the divine. At the time of Diana's birth, Zeus had already created "beings born in his image, fair and good, strong and passionate."[8] But Ares, a son of Zeus, grew envious of humans and sought to corrupt them. He "poisoned men's hearts with jealousy and suspicion, he turned them against one another, and war ravaged the earth."[9] Wonder Woman's narrative is drawn peripherally from Greco-Roman mythology, not from the Gospels. But as in the Biblical narrative, her world also knows of a jealous rival force to the true god, which sets other rivalries and disorder in motion.

The figure of Ares, god of war, is a fallen prince and jealous son who has the power to sow violence and disorder, to make humans envious, suspicious, and rivalrous. Ares operates as "the prince of this world," which will be illustrated later in the movie when his character is unveiled. As "prince of this world," Ares both ignites strife between humans and keeps total apocalypse at bay. This pattern is Satanic, in that Girard calls Satan "a principle of order as much as disorder."[10] Satan is envious of God and God's creatures, and most certainly of God's son, whom he tempts in the wilderness and hopes to defeat (Mk 1: 12–13; Mt 4: 1–11; Lk 4: 1–13). Satan's evil feeds on his mimesis of the true God, but in a "manner that is jealous, grotesque, perverse, and as contrary as possible to the upright and obedient imitation of Jesus."[11] So, too, Ares is in a mimetic rivalry with his father Zeus and with the humans created by his father, enacting his jealousy by inciting them into rivalries and wars, hoping perhaps to convince his father that his beloved creatures are not so fair and good after all.

In Princess Diana's world, the powers of Ares brought about war and the enslavement of peoples, including the Amazons, who had been created to "influence men's hearts with love."[12] Eventually the Amazons rebelled, and the gods came to their defense. Diana's mother Queen Hippolyta fought bravely to liberate her people, but Ares killed the gods who defended the Amazons. Zeus was able to force Ares to retreat but used the last of his divine power to do so. This is an interesting statement about Zeus, made early in the film.[13] The viewer is put on quiet notice that Zeus is not going to enter the narrative to defeat Ares. His divine power has been emptied, and if Ares is to be defeated, it will be through some other means. The Christian viewer, particularly those who are readers of Girard, will remember that Paul also knew that salvation came through one who emptied himself of divine power (Phil 2: 1–11). The parallel is not precise, but a viewer watching through a Girardian lens may already be on alert for a potentially different kind of Hollywood ending.

Just as the devil departs Jesus after the test in the wilderness, intending to return at an opportune time (Lk 4: 13), Zeus knew that Ares would regain strength and return at an opportune time to finish his mission, which was to stir up an ultimate war in which humans would eventually destroy themselves. Although Jesus and Zeus succeeded in overcoming their foes, the war was far from over. Here, though, an interesting divergence between Jesus and Zeus occurs. After his desert battle, Jesus proceeds to gather a people as he proclaims the arrival of God's Kingdom. Zeus, facing his own waning strength, embarks upon no such extroverted program. Instead, he leaves a weapon "powerful enough to kill a god" and hides it on the island of Themyscira, entrusting it to the care of the Amazons.[14] The mission of the Amazons is to defeat Ares should he come to them; but they will not leave their island to mount an offensive.

Princess Diana, the only child on the island, grows up in isolated peace, yet all around her, women are preparing for war. She longs to join them in learning to be strong and brave. Queen Hippolyta tells her daughter the story of Zeus, Ares, and the Amazons as a bedtime tale, lovingly revealing that she longed for a child so much that she fashioned Diana out of clay, and begged Zeus to give her life. Queen Hippolyta assures Diana that Zeus left the Amazons weapons strong enough to defeat Ares. She shows Diana the tower in which these weapons are stored: a shield and a sword that Diana solemnly calls "the god-killer." The weapons are declared off-limits for Diana, and she is prohibited from learning the arts of battle.

Nevertheless, Diana continues to beg her mother to let her train. As Queen Hippolyta resists she tells her sister Antiope, "the stronger she gets the sooner he [Ares] will find her...she must never know the truth about what she is or how she came to be."[15] Eventually, Antiope convinces Hippolyta that Diana needs the training required to wield the sword and shield. In a sparring session with an older, stronger Amazon, Diana crosses her arms, generating enormous power from her wrist bracelets which deflects the power of her opponent. Diana and the viewer both realize her powers are stronger than she has been told. But her ultimate identity remains unrevealed to the viewer or to Diana herself.

Her journey of discovery begins when the American aviator Captain Steve Trevor crashes into the sea near Themyscira. The viewer learns that the German navy is in pursuit of Captain Trevor; the context is World War I. The pursuing ships at first reach a foggy mirage, catching glimpses of the island, before breaking through and bringing a battle to the Amazons. Diana fights in the battle, learning that her wrist bracelets deflect bullets, although she is unable to save her aunt, General Antiope, who dies of a gunshot wound. Steve Trevor observes the skills and strategies deployed by the Amazons, who have no firearms, yet repel the German assault.

As Diana assists Captain Trevor in recovering from his crash and the battle, the Amazons interrogate him with their lasso of truth. He reveals that he is a secret agent spying on the Germans in the war to end all wars, a war involving multiple countries with over a million soldiers and civilians dead.[16] Upon hearing this, Queen Hippolyta realizes that the powers of Ares have returned, stirring up the promised decisive battle amongst the people the Amazons are called to defend. Diana determines to leave her home and accompany Captain

Trevor back to the war in order to defeat Ares, symbolized for her and the viewer by the power of the German General Ludendorff and his specialist in chemical weapons, Dr. Sophie Moreau.

Unlike Adam and Eve, Diana is not cast out of her paradise, but leaves of her own accord, over the objections of her mother who wants nothing more than to protect her from the loss of innocence and the violence she knows is coming. Upon Diana's departure from Themyscira, Queen Hippolyta tells her daughter, "The world of men is not worthy of you," yet she gives Diana the shield and the sword (the "god-killer") and Diana sets sail for London with Captain Trevor.[17]

While in London, Diana meets Sir Patrick Morgan, a British Defence official who councils Steve Trevor that despite the revelation of Dr. Moreau's chemical formulas—recorded in a notebook that Trevor has stolen behind enemy lines—the British will press on in pursuing an armistice. Sir Patrick declares that the suffering of more civilians or soldiers due to Dr. Moreau's chemical gas is a price to be paid in bringing about a negotiated peace. Those watching through the Girardian lens will note that Sir Patrick has entered a kind of Satanic wager in which the sacrifice of victims is deemed necessary to keep peace. His proclamation is not unlike that of Caiaphas in the plot to kill Jesus: "It is better for you to have one man die . . . than to have the whole nation destroyed" (Jn 11: 50). Sir Patrick champions precisely the kind of victim mechanism which Girard describes:

> To apprehend this mechanism as the work of Satan is to understand that what Jesus asserts—"Satan expels Satan"—has a precise meaning, rationally explainable. It defines the effectiveness of the single victim mechanism. The high priest Caiaphas alludes to this mechanism when he says, "It is better that one man die and that the whole nation not perish."[18]

But perhaps Sir Patrick is not all that he seems. In a secret meeting at a pub, he grants Captain Trevor the funds needed to make one last foray into General Ludendorff's camp in order to stop Dr. Moreau. Steve, Diana, and his rag-tag trio of mercenaries trail Ludendorff to an airfield where a plane loaded with the bombs developed by Dr. Moreau will soon take flight. In the control tower, Diana gets her sought-after confrontation with General Ludendorff, whom he believes to be Ares. She draws her sword ("the god-killer") and kills him, but the war still rages.

Diana's realization sets in: "I killed him. I killed him but nothing stopped. You kill the god of war, you stop the war."[19] Diana questions the goodness of human beings and contemplates abandoning her mission. At this point the viewer who knows Girard, and who knows the Bible, knows that the father of lies is gaining a foothold with Diana, who struggles with the truth about humans.

When Steve Trevor tries to enlist her to help him stop the gas-laden plane from taking flight, she resists.

> **Diana:** No, all of this, the fighting should have stopped. Why are they doing this?
>
> **Steve:** I don't know. Maybe it's them. Maybe people aren't always good. Ares or no Ares, maybe it's who they are.
>
> **Diana:** No, no. It cannot be. It had to be him [Ares]. It cannot be them. My mother was right. She said, 'the world of men does not deserve you.' They don't deserve our help, Steve.[20]

Captain Trevor becomes, in effect, her theological teacher, illustrating the fallacy of the single victim mechanism: that a "bad guy" or enemy can be identified, eliminated, and that peace will ensue:

> **Steve:** It's not about deserve. Maybe they don't [deserve help] but it's not about that. It's about what you believe. You don't think I wish I could tell you that it was one bad guy to blame? It's not. We're all to blame.

DIANA: I'M NOT!

> **Steve:** But maybe I am. Please, help me stop it, there could be thousands more. I have to go. I have to go.[21]

Steve Trevor reveals the truth that General Ludendorff (thought to be Ares) is not to blame for human violence. As Trevor insists, "we're all to blame," or as Girard has said regarding the violence of the gospel Passion Narrative,

> Violent contagion is enough. Those responsible for the Passion are human participants themselves, incapable of resisting the violent contagion that affects them all when a mimetic snowballing comes within their range, or rather when they come within the range of this snowballing and are swept along by it. We don't have to invoke the supernatural to explicate this.[22]

Captain Trevor departs the airfield tower but Diana remains, questioning this truth.

She is joined in her questioning by Sir Patrick Morgan, who appears in the control tower. Diana and the viewer realize simultaneously that Ares can appear in many guises, and that they have been fooled. This reversal, that a British official rather than a German General personifies Ares, subverts the viewer's stereotype of who the "bad guys" and "good guys" are amidst a movie set in World War I. The Girardian lens signals that Sir Patrick's actions were Satanic all along, in that they have sown disorder and confusion. As Girard notes:

> Satan can therefore always put enough order back into the world to prevent the total destruction of what he possesses without depriving himself for too long of his favorite pastime, which is to sow disorder, violence, and misfortune among his subjects.[23]

This is what Sir Patrick has been doing amidst the war in the guise of the prince of this world. On the one hand, he advocates for an armistice. On the other, he advises Trevor to secretly attempt to defeat Ludendorff. Ludendorff is killed, the war still rages, chemical weapons are loaded onto an airplane, and Ares appears on the airfield.

There, like the father of lies, Sir Patrick seeks to lure Diana further into the satanic game, inviting her to continue to question human goodness and ally with him.

Diana: You . . . you're him.

Ares: I am, but I am not what you thought I was. [*Diana reaches for her sword, which she has lost in the battle with Ludendorff.*]

Ares: I am not your enemy, Diana. I am the only one who truly knows you and who truly knows them [humans] as you now do. They have always been, always will be weak, cruel, selfish and capable of the greatest horrors. All I ever wanted was for the gods to see how evil my Father's creation was, and they refused, so I destroyed them.

Ares is a rival for Diana's allegiance, and seeks to exploit her confusion about humans by convincing her of their evil. In doing so he reveals his jealous desire that the other gods see the Father through the lens of his lies. In naming his Father's creation "evil," Ares commits the ultimate sin as described by Jesus, the blasphemy against the Holy Spirit (Mk 3:28; Mt 12: 31, Lk 12: 10). He looks at what is good and calls it evil. And he attempts to seduce Diana into believing him.

When Diana resists his first overture and recovers her sword, Ares reveals the truth of who Diana is and how she came to be. Diana knows she is the daughter of Zeus (the father of gods). But Ares reveals that she is the god-killer, not her sword. The Christian viewer remembers Jesus teaching that those who live by the sword shall perish by the sword (Mt 26: 52). Diana is the one sent to defeat Ares, it is not her weapons that will do so. But how she will do so remains to be seen.

> **Ares:** My dear child, that is not the god-killer, you are. Only a god can kill another god. Zeus left a child with the Queen of the Amazons as a weapon.

DIANA: YOU ARE A LIAR!

Diana is right that she is conversing with the father of lies. Satan spins half-truths which are enticing and deceptive all at once. Ares is telling the truth when he says that Diana is the weapon left with the Amazons—a truth she resists hearing. He is lying when he says that humans start their wars on their own.

Through his lies, Ares believes he can lure Diana away from her divine mission to defeat him, and so tempts her by offering himself as a partner. If the humans of the world are not worthy of her, he is:

> All these years, I have struggled alone, whispering into their ear's ideas and inspirations for formulas, weapons, but I don't make them use them, they start these wars on their own. All they do is orchestrate an armistice I know they cannot keep in the hope they will destroy themselves, but it has never been enough until you. When you first arrived I was going to crush you, but I knew if only you could see what the other gods could not then you would join me and with our powers combined we would finally end all the suffering, the destruction they bring, and we could return this world to the paradise it was before them. Forever.

Ares is Satanic in precisely the way that Girard describes: "Satan wants first of all to seduce . . . [he] presents himself as a model of our desires . . . [and] counsels us to abandon ourselves to all our inclinations in defiance of morality and its prohibitions."[24] Ares reveals the way in which Satan distorts human desire such that we imitate him without even knowing we are doing so, hearing his whispers and following the desires he stirs. For her part, Diana resists:

> **Diana:** I could never be part of that.
>
> **Ares:** Oh, my dear, you have so much to learn.[25]

When Diana resists his seduction, Ares becomes her adversary, also in the way that Girard describes: "the *seducer* of the beginnings is transformed quickly into a forbidding *adversary* . . ."[26] Enraged at her resistance, Ares lashes out at Diana, tossing her down the runway with brutal force.

As Diana lies stunned from Ares' assault, Steve Trevor returns. The bombs on the airplane are on a timer and will soon detonate, so he has devised a plan to fly them away from the soldiers and civilians nearby. He tells Diana of his plan, but she cannot hear him as her ears are ringing from the force Ares inflicted. Steve departs toward the plane. Meanwhile Ares emerges in full armor and says "It is futile to imagine you can win. Give up, Diana."[27] What does a win over Satan entail? The viewer expects that Wonder Woman will engage Ares head-on. The Christian and reader of Girard suspects the defeat will not be so straightforward.

Diana sees Steve Trevor ascend in the airplane overhead, and then sees it explode. He has done what he can in his own battle against Ares: he has tried to learn and tell the truth of the chemical weapons and, ignored, he undertakes a final mission of self-sacrifice to protect the lives of the innocent even if he cannot change the terms of the entire war. Diana cries out in anguish as she witnesses his death. She breaks apart the debris of armor on the runway and seems ready to destroy Dr. Moreau.

Ares encourages her rage while continuing to perpetuate his lies as he entices Diana to turn her rage toward Dr. Moreau, the scientist deformed by her own chemical experiments. She bears all the physical marks of a likely scapegoat, as Girard describes their identification: "In addition to cultural and religious there are purely *physical* criteria. Sickness, madness, genetic deformities, accidental injuries, and even disabilities in general tend to polarize persecutors."[28] So Ares calls attention to Dr. Moreau and invites Diana's scapegoating:

> Yes, Diana, take them all. Finally, you see. Mankind did this, not me. They are ugly, filled with hatred, weak just like your Captain Trevor, gone and left you nothing, and for what? Pathetic. . . . Look at her (gesturing toward Dr. Moreau) and tell me I'm wrong. She is the perfect example of these humans and unworthy of your sympathy in every way. Destroy her, Diana. You know that she deserves it. They all do. Do it![29]

Diana resists the invitation to make a scapegoat of Dr. Moreau and turns back toward Ares with resolve.

She proclaims: "you're wrong about them. They're everything you say, but so much more."[30] Ares responds as her adversary with his full display of lightening-like power. Diana walks slowly toward him, braces her wrists, repels his advance, and continues walking deliberately. Ares screams: "they do not deserve your protection!" and Diana replies with the theology Captain Trevor taught her: "it's not about deserve. It's about what you believe. And I believe in love."[31]

At the mention of love, Ares declares in rage "I will destroy you!," rising into the air and drawing down sparking, evil tentacles. Wonder Woman becomes entangled in them. As she looks at them, slowly rotating the tentacles around her wrists, her enigmatic expression leads the viewer to momentarily wonder if she has been more deeply seduced by Ares' ways and bound by evil. But instead she realizes that the very weapons sent to ensnare her can be turned back on her enemy. As she says "goodbye, brother,"[32] she rises in a glowing white cruciform shape, crosses her wrists and sends Ares' powers back upon him. It is Ares' own power, drawn out, exposed, and turned back upon itself, that defeats him.

Girard claims that Jesus defeats the devil by exposing his lies, and turning his Satanic power back on himself: "with the satanic expulsion of Satan the mimetic cycle is really closed—the knot is really tied—for the single victim mechanism becomes explicitly defined."[33] This defeat is not just a victory by the terms of the devil's game. As Girard's says, "the powers are not put on display because they are defeated, they are defeated because they are put on display."[34] The powers of evil are "beaten by a weapon whose effectiveness they could not conceive, that contradicts all their beliefs, all their values. It is the most radical weakness that defeats the power of satanic self-expulsion."[35] The weapon of defeat is Jesus himself, and his kenotic willingness to go to the cross as the victim "whose love and suffering reveal our violence for what it is," namely, Satanic.[36]

Wonder Woman is not Jesus. If anyone plays the self-sacrificial role, it is Captain Trevor. But Diana does defeat Ares by deflecting his evil power and allowing it to destroy him. And she does so by appealing to what she has learned about self-giving love. The story of Wonder Woman is not explicitly Christian—it is still a Hollywood production. Yet readers of Girard can view the film through his lens, and Girard himself might have said that the plot of the film would have been influenced by the Gospels, whether the writers of the film knew it or not. This is because, as noted above, the Gospels announce the workings and the secret of the single victim mechanism, after which anything in the orbit of the Gospels necessarily comes under their influence.[37]

Back on the runway, the war is not over. The superhero in this film has not achieved a total, violent victory. Captain Steve Trevor has saved soldiers and civilians from Dr. Moreau's poison concoction. Dr. Moreau herself has escaped, but it is left undetermined whether she is repentant or not. The German soldiers and Trevor's crew embrace one another as they realize danger is averted. The satanic workings of Ares have been exposed. But humans retain the ability to choose between good and evil.

Diana acknowledges this at the end of the film when she attends a victory party in the streets of London, and spots a picture of Captain Trevor by his airplane. She knows that humans can still choose evil, and so knows that the victory party is temporary. She speaks:

> I used to want to save the world. To end war and bring peace to mankind. But then I glimpsed the darkness that lives within their light and learned that inside of them, there will always be both. It's a choice each must make for themselves, something no hero will ever defeat. And now I know that only love can truly save the world. So, I stay, I fight, and I give. For the world I know can be.[38]

Diana notes that she is only a superhero, and no hero will do the work that humans must do themselves, which is ever to negotiate the choice between good and evil. Yet she found and revealed Ares for the mechanisms he personified: an author of confusion amidst a war that he was both instigating and pretending to end; a rival with humans, envious and deceitful; a seducer who attempted to lure her into betraying her mission and allying with him in the destruction of humankind. When the satanic workings symbolized by Ares are defeated, Diana and others know the truth.

Girard argued that "Satan himself has thus placed the truth at the disposal of humankind; he has made it possible to overturn his own lie; he has rendered the truth of God universally understandable."[39] After this point, there can be no return to Satan's total hold on humankind:

> The princes of this world could rub their hands in satisfaction and yet it turned out that their calculations were undone. Instead of conjuring away once more the secret of the single victim mechanism, the four accounts of the Passion broadcast it to the four corners of the world, publicizing it wherever they were read and proclaimed.[40]

Knowing the truth does set us free (Jn 8:32) but knowing the truth and acting upon it are two different things. Girard also knew that that after the cross humans were not immune to satanic mechanisms, only that Jesus forever made Satan's mechanisms plain to see: "We should not conclude that to identify the truth is enough to liberate us from the lies in which we are all imprisoned."[41] What is paramount is that humans have the choice to imitate Christ and resist imitating Satan: "In order to explain this to human beings, one would have to say: God leaves it up to you to decide. In other words, he isn't responsible for the fact that human beings get caught up in satanic entanglements."[42]

On the surface, the film *Wonder Woman* presents viewers with one kind of choice: to identify with Wonder Woman over against the satanic mechanism personified by Ares. Indeed, viewers cheer her well-meaning innocence regarding the satanic ways of the world, as well as her sword-bearing, wristlet deflecting prowess in battle. To indulge this choice is what we expect after watching a superhero movie, taking delight in our good hero building up a group (including us, the viewers) over against the defeated group (Ludendorff, Ares, the Germans).

When we identify such, we are in the realm of what Girard's theological interpreter James Alison calls "functional atheism":

> Whenever the group interpretation tends to work by creating a "we" at the expense of, over against, a necessary "they," we have reason to doubt that anything is present other than the spirit of group building over against another, which is, of course, what is meant by functional atheism.[43]

Alison names this view of championing one god against another not "monotheism," as might be expected, but "functional atheism," because he declares that this belief of a god over against another god is not belief in God:

> If God really is true, then to exaggerate the strength of the wicked other so as to strengthen the faith of the believer is the worst sort of nihilistic atheism, because it really does suppose that, in practice, it is only by provoking the wicked other to act out his part in the drama that our faith will survive, which means we don't believe in God, but only in conflict.[44]

But viewers looking through the Girardian lens can see that Diana's closing reflection models a different choice to us, a choice for the love whose province belongs to the true God and not to satanic powers:

> The god who is wholly Other, genuinely "another Other," has no part in such activities; indeed, from the point of view of the functional atheists . . . the real God is a stumbling block, a scandal, an offence, something they won't be able to get over because God works in ways exactly opposed to their normal understanding of desire.[45]

Some viewers may dismiss Diana's statement that "only love can save the world." But those viewers looking through the Girardian lens will recognize the choice between God and the gods, between the God who is "another Other," and the satanic mechanism. We are responsible for resisting satanic entanglements, and the Gospels reveal everything we need to know about how to do so. As Wonder Woman experienced, Satan's menacing tentacles might entangle us and even bind us for a while, but when we learn that they are parasitic and ultimately powerless, we can summon the strength of love and turn them back upon themselves, as they collapse under their own power.

NOTES

1. Allan Heinberg, *Wonder Woman*. DVD. Directed by Patty Jenkins (Los Angeles, CA: Warner Brothers Pictures, 2017). This study is a consideration of the 2017 film and not the wider corpus of *Wonder Woman* media.

2. Girard understands the scapegoat mechanism as the means by which mimetic rivalries are focused and discharged upon a single victim, whose expulsion ensures that a community overtaken by such mimetic crisis does not totally self-destruct. Rather, the scapegoat carries the toll of the rivalry away from the group. The violence directed at the scapegoat (who is believed to be guilty even if this is not so in fact) is seen to be good, in that it restores order for a time. See Girard's own description in *The Girard Reader*, ed. James. G. Williams (New York, NY: Crossroad Publishing, 1986) 269–272.

3. See especially René Girard, *I See Satan Fall Like Lightning,* trans. James G. Williams (Maryknoll, NY: Orbis Books, 2001) and *The One by Whom Scandal Comes,* trans. M. B. DeBevoise (East Lansing, MI: Michigan State University Press, 2014).

4. *Adversus Haereses* 5. 24. 3; See the Latin as reproduced from the two extant manuscripts in Sancti Irenaei, *Libros quinque adversus Haereses*, ed. W. Wigan Harvey (Cambridge: Cambridge University Press, 1857).

5. *Contra Celsum* trans. Henry Chadwick (Cambridge: Cambridge University Press, 1953). For the Greek, J.P. Migne, ed., *Patrologiae Cursus Completus, Series graeca* (Paris, 1857–86), volume 11.

6. *I See Satan,* 42.

7. From this point I refer to Ares as a character in the film, and refer to him in the guise of Satan, the devil, the father of lies, and the prince of this world (following Girard). Referring to the character by a name is not to concede that Ares, as a representation of Satan, has "being" in the ontological sense. Indeed, Ares' "being" is derivative from and in rivalry with his father, Zeus.

8. *Wonder Woman* Chapter 1.

9. Ibid, Chapter 1.

10. Girard, *I See Satan*, 34.

11. Ibid., 45.

12. *Wonder Woman*, Chapter 1. The screenwriter does not use the inclusive "humans" or "humankind."

13. Ibid, Chapter 1.

14. Ibid, Chapter 1.

15. Ibid, Chapter 2.

16. Ibid, Chapter 3.

17. Ibid, Chapter 4.

18. Girard, *I See Satan,* 36.

19. *Wonder Woman*, Chapter 10.

20. Ibid, Chapter 10.

21. Ibid, Chapter 10.

22. Girard, *I See Satan,* 21–22.

23. Ibid, 37.

24. Ibid, 33.
25. *Wonder Woman*, Chapter 10.
26. Girard, *I See Satan*, 33, emphasis his.
27. *Wonder Woman*, Chapter 11.
28. René Girard, *The Scapegoat*, trans. Yvonne Freccero (Baltimore, MD: The Johns Hopkins University Press, 1986) 18, emphasis Girard's.
29. *Wonder Woman*, Chapter 11.
30. Ibid, Chapter 11.
31. Ibid, Chapter 11.
32. The sibling as rival/double is a theme interpreted by Girard. See *Things Hidden Since the Foundation of the World*, trans. Stephen Bann & Michael Meteer (Stanford, CA: Stanford University Press, 1987), 12–18, 221–229.
33. Girard, *I See Satan*, 46.
34. Ibid, 143.
35. Ibid, 143.
36. Ibid, 143.
37. Ibid, 149.
38. Ibid, Chapter 11.
39. Girard, *I See Satan*, 152.
40. Ibid, 149.
41. Ibid, 150.
42. Girard, *The One by Whom Scandal Comes*, 96.
43. James Alison, *Undergoing God: Dispatches from the Scene of a Break-In* (New York: Continuum International Publishing Group, 2006), 21.
44. Ibid, 22.
45. Ibid, 28.

BIBLIOGRAPHY

Alison, James. *Undergoing God: Dispatches from the Scene of a Break-In*. New York: Continuum International Publishing Group, 2006.

Girard, René. *I See Satan Fall Like Lightning*. Translated by James Williams. New York: Maryknoll, 2001.

———. *The One by Whom Scandal Comes*, trans. M. B. Debevoise. East Lansing, MI: Michigan State University Press, 2014.

———. *The Scapegoat*. Translated by Yvonne Freccero. Baltimore: Johns Hopkins University Press, 1989.

———. *Things Hidden since the Foundation of the World*. Translated by Stephen Bann and Michael Metteer. Stanford: Stanford University Press, 2014.

———. *Violence and the Sacred*. Translated by Patrick Gregory. Baltimore: Johns Hopkins University Press, 1979.

Heinberg, Allen. *Wonder Woman*. DVD. Directed by Patty Jenkins. Los Angeles, CA: Warner Brothers Pictures, 2017.

Chapter 5

Those Who Have Eyes to See

The Divine Origins of the Modern Plot Twist

Jordan Almanzar

Toward the end of his dialogue with Gianni Vattimo, René Girard concluded, almost in passing, that the destruction of the scapegoat mechanism required a group of dissenters who were willing to report what they had truly seen—namely, that the victim, Jesus, was innocent. "The main clue," Girard says, "is the presence in the crucifixion accounts of something totally absent from mythology, a group of unbelievers in scapegoating."[1] The reality of this group must be taken seriously, since they are the first visible body in history to proclaim the innocence of the victim. Further, Girard states, "Next to the loyal scapegoaters, who remain the largest group by far, we have a dissident minority. . . . This minority is indispensable, obviously, to the unconcealment of scapegoating."[2] In other words, Girard necessarily argued that a community primed with eyes to see is paramount in undoing the concealing component—the mythology—of the scapegoat mechanism.

It is clear that the revealing of the scapegoat mechanism represents a permanent shift in our understanding of the world's story and that this revelation occurred most fully during the Paschal Mystery—namely, the Passion, Burial and Resurrection of Jesus. "The Crucifixion," Girard says, "is what highlights the victimary mechanism and [thereby] explains history."[3] The death of Jesus seems to be the absolute peak of a continental divide which forces a distinction between kinds of people—those who have eyes to see and those who do not. In other words, there was now a group of people who were capable of apprehending the revelation, who were living in the light of truth right alongside those who were yet living in the world of mythology. Just as a plot twist does not actually change a story but only reveals what is true while destroying what was merely perceived, the true flow of history did not actually shift but was apprehended. In this way we can say that plot twists are revelations of truth, and the shift happens only to the observer who has grasped the truth—and this we call a revelation. A revelation, then, is the act of grasping a truth that had been hidden and is now dramatically, suddenly disclosed—and makes a claim, demands a response and causes indifference to be impossible.

In this chapter, I am building on Girard's insight that a community of unbelievers in scapegoating, the Church, was and is absolutely necessary for the revelation to be manifest. The primitive Church is likened to a movie audience who experiences a plot twist. Lest the reader be scandalized by my comparison of the supreme, divine narrative shift that took place at the Cross to the plot twists that occur in the films *Fight Club*, *The Village*, and *The Others*, I ask that a singular line of comparison be held in view. For it is not the details of any particular film that can be likened to the Crucifixion, but rather the shift in understanding that takes place once truth's revelation has been apprehended. Girard hit upon this consequence of his theory most clearly in the quote above, and it seems convenient to develop it further under the guise of what most of us have experienced in film or literature—namely, a plot twist. Those who are familiar with Girard's discrepancy between mythology and revelation will recognize the distinction at once—most generally, that a story that seemed to be unfolding before a plot twist represents mythology while a post–plot twist narrative, guided by the white light of some truth disclosure, represents revelation.

A further disclosure must be made at the outset. When I reference the "Cross" or "Crucifixion" I am merely indicating that specific moment inside the broader Paschal event. This attention to the Crucifixion, while holding the entire event in view, stems from my interpretation of Girard and his emphasis on the significance of the Cross.[4] Girard does not feel compelled to cite the Resurrection each time he writes about the Crucifixion. And yet, it is clear that he rightly sees the two occurrences as inseparable components of a larger event.[5] Just as James Alison, when writing about the Resurrection, indicates that, "[T]he risen Lord is simultaneously the dead-and-risen Lord . . . who lives forever slain,"[6] the same but reversed implication is placed here—namely that the Crucified Christ is the "Lamb that lives forever."[7]

NOBODY IN THE AUDIENCE HAS ANY IDEA

The necessity of a community in the act of revelation, for purposes of analysis, can be likened to an audience. The revelation at the Cross, embodied by the centurion's words, "Indeed this was the Son of God" (Mt 27:54), is not unlike a moviegoer who has apprehended a plot twist. The story he thought he had been watching was torn away in an instant and permanently replaced by a new narrative—and once apprehended, he can never return to the original, concealing story. For those who saw the horrific event of the Crucifixion to its bitter end, those whose community would later proclaim the Gospel of the Risen Christ, the narrative shift was indescribably powerful. Each of the synoptic Gospels report the words of the centurion, with two of them, Matthew and Mark, more or less agreeing on the quote above, that Jesus is the Son of God.[8] Scholars are often baffled by the reasoning behind the centurion's statement, which seems so out of place coming as it does just after Jesus died. What did he see, what was revealed to him yet left undisclosed to so many others?

Turning to Luke's account we discover exactly what, from the standpoint of mimetic theory, we might expect—namely, that Jesus's innocence was revealed to the centurion. According to Luke, the centurion states: "Indeed this was a just man" (Lk 23:47). The centurion utters the truth, Jesus was just, which is the same as saying that he was innocent. So powerful was that apprehension—which was for the first time also proclaimed—that the other Gospel writers take it to mean the same thing as Jesus was the Son of God.[9] A new kind of community was created, one who proclaimed the truth of what they apprehended, one who no longer took recourse to mythology for a divine overcoming of evil. From the outset, the Church held the "forever living having been slain" Christ (*vivit semper occisus*) as its preeminent symbol. The inversion of mythology depended upon a community who would champion the innocence of the victim, Christ, and subsequently the first became last and the least became greatest.[10]

This point of analysis leads directly to the notion that plot twists in film and literature are likewise engaged in revealing a truth otherwise unknown, which is precisely why they are satisfying to us—disclosing, as they do, the story's meaning. In contrast to concealing truth, as in mythology, plot twists, as vehicles of truth revelation, came into focus with the death and Resurrection of Jesus. From the perspective of mimetic theory, there is a distinguishable link between the plot twists that occur in such films as *Fight Club*, *The Village*, and *The Others*, and the Crucifixion of Jesus. Most obviously, the item that connects these movies is that each contains an effective plot twist, that is to say, a revelation of some truth that furnishes the meaning of the film. Reality is disclosed in a plot twist, and, "reality," according to Girard, "is not rational, but religious."[11] The Cross pierces the mythic layer of culture and releases the Good News, just as a thematic plot twist pierces the mythic layer of a perceived narrative and reveals a true one.

To apprehend the narrative shift is to be a member of an audience, an audience with eyes to see. The original primed audience who saw the Crucifixion is echoed and reenacted by moviegoers and book readers who themselves enjoy the experience of being made privy to a narrative shift, or rather, a truth revelation in the form of a plot twist. They are members of a group that was duped before but has now been enlightened. For a plot twist to be recognized, there must be an audience who can make the transition from false belief to true apprehension. To various degrees and in hindsight (for example, when rewatching a film) we can clearly see that the truth was there all along.

It should be noted that some more intuitive members of an audience may possibly anticipate a plot twist before it occurs. They are like Simeon or the Magi from the Gospels, who, aided by grace, recognized the true story and merely waited for full disclosure. These are those who trusted the clues which were provided before the full disclosure had transpired, concluding now and being proven right later. But they are the exception to the rule. In modern plot twists, due to the skill of storytellers, there is scarcely enough information provided before the twist to anticipate it ahead of time.

Regardless, as hindsight shows us, it is theoretically possible to infer the plot twist before it happens. *Fight Club*, for example, is chockfull with foreshadowing clearly indicating that the two main characters, played by Brad Pitt and Edward Norton, are one and the same person.[12] In fact, in nearly every scene there is some indication that Brad Pitt's character, Tyler Durden, is a figment of Norton's character's (the unnamed narrator) imagination. When they first meet, they notice they have the exact same briefcase. This detail only becomes important after the plot twist, as it then, subtle as it is, fits perfectly with the new narrative—they are the same man. And there are numerous additional hints, such as Tyler flashing on the screen in many scenes when he is thought to be absent, or the two only paying one bus fare, or the phone call from Tyler arriving to a payphone that says in tiny letters "No Incoming Calls." From the very beginning of the film, in fact, we should be able to tell that nothing is as it seems when the narrator, played by Norton, says, "When you're suffering from insomnia, nothing's really real." And yet, nearly everyone who sees the movie for the first time does not notice the clues that seem so obvious and numerous when rewatching.

It is remarkable that even while the film teems with clues indicating that the story being shown is not the real one, Tyler Durden is himself engaged in blowing up narratives and then concealing them. Consider these lines: "In old theaters, two projectors are used, so someone has to change projectors at the exact second when one reel ends, and another reel begins. . . . It's called a 'changeover.' The movie goes on, and nobody in the audience has any idea." This indicates that the writer and director understood the power they wielded when creating and producing this plot-twisting story.[13] Beneath the movie's "text" there is a subtext that can only be apprehended by those made privy to it. The creators of *Fight Club* recognized that changeovers perpetuate the myth, while plot twists destroy a perceived narrative and replace it with a new one. To link to Girard's theory, a changeover is equated with mythology, a plot twist with revelation.

In M. Night Shyamalan's *The Village*,[14] we encounter a formidable plot twist which is most interesting because it exclusively enlightens the audience and not the characters in the film. *The Village* is set in a 19th century Pennsylvania town called Covington. Near the end of the movie, Ivy, the chief elder's blind daughter, sets out through the forbidden woods to fetch medicine and supplies for one of the villagers who has been stabbed and will die without treatment. When she reaches the edge of the woods, she discovers an ivy-covered fence, which she then struggles to climb and ultimately is successful. Just then, the scene cuts to Ivy's father opening a black box containing a worn photograph of his much-younger self along with the rest of the village leaders garbed in 1970s clothing—this alone reveals the hoax. At once the audience is enlightened to the fact that the villagers are not living in the 19th century at all, but rather, the 21st century! But to make the revelation unmistakable, the movie cuts back to Ivy when a park ranger, carrying a CB radio and driving a jeep, discovers her. Although she is blind and cannot see the modern world around her, the audience can. The audience is stripped away from a 19th century village and thrust into their own time. The seamless changeover is interrupted, and a rift appears as the plot twists to reveal a long-concealed truth. Ivy, being blind, has no eyes to see the revelation and continues in the myth. Along with the majority of the village, she remains in the pre-plot twist narrative while the leaders, or founders, of the village, perpetuate the myth by concealing the revelation from the others—but the audience knows.

THAT IS WHAT WE HAVE PROTECTED HERE, INNOCENCE!

It is tempting to compare the revelation provided by a plot twist to what the Greeks called *anagnorisis*, what Aristotle, in his *Poetics*, defines as, "a change from ignorance to knowledge, producing love or hate between the persons destined by the poet for good or bad fortune."[15] This "change from ignorance to knowledge" is where the perceived connection lies, but the contrast is due to the fact that anagnorisis perpetuates the guilt of the victim. In other words, it continues the myth. Aristotle uses the *Oedipus* myth to demonstrate anagnorisis. "Reversal of the situation," he says, "is a change by which the action veers round to its opposite . . . in the Oedipus, the messenger comes to cheer Oedipus and free him from his alarms about his mother, but by revealing who he is, he produces the opposite effect."[16] Aristotle shows no recognition, as Girard has demonstrated in numerous publications, that Oedipus was a stereotypical scapegoat. In Girard's masterful analysis, the *Oedipus* myth is clearly shown to be a concealed persecution text.[17] Anagnorisis, in all its pre-Christian, mythological manifestations, perpetuates the guilt of the victim by supplying false knowledge. In contrast to a plot twist, it conceals by diversion rather than revealing by truth. While claiming to disclose knowledge, anagnorisis is the channel of deception meant to maintain the myth.

A similar situation is displayed at the end of *The Village* when the only person, besides Ivy, who might have discovered the truth is killed and upon discovery of this man's death, Ivy's father says to his grieving mother, "Your son has made our stories real. Noah has given us a chance to continue this place." Although the audience is no longer deceived, there is an opportunity for a successful changeover for the community of villagers. That is to say, the leaders decide to perpetuate the myth by deception.[18] The myth and the myth-makers are revealed to the audience, but not to the main characters of the movie. The movie's light opens the audience's eyes, but most of the characters in the film remain blind to the truth surrounding them.

In the world of mythology, in which the villagers in *The Village* live, what is expected is always maintained—the myth is true and there is no reason to doubt. It is interesting to note that, along with the revelation provided to the audience in *The Village*, the only other person who experiences the plot-twist revelation is the park ranger, who lives not in the mythological world of the village, but in contemporary society. No one from the village (the world of myth) apprehended a plot twist. By keeping their people in the dark, the leaders of the town maintain what the world of mythology had always done. Their actions reflect the understanding captured in this mysterious mnemonic:

quae non sunt simulo; quae sunt, ea dissimulantur. [I pretend the things that are not; the things that are, they are hidden.][19]

Anagnorisis is the device that assures there is nothing new to see. As mimetic theory shows, the "revelation" of anagnorisis is no revelation at all, because it merely reaffirms and establishes what was expected. Truly revelatory plot twists, on the other hand, shatter all mythological perceptions in an instant and forever. The unexpected truth they reveal makes a plot twist a plot twist. In this alone can all modern plot twists be linked to the singular source at the Cross—in that they each reveal a truth that breaks through deceptions to which we have become accustomed.

SOONER OR LATER EVERYTHING WILL BE DIFFERENT

As in life, so in fiction; as in history, so in cinema. Most of life—and long stretches of books or movies—is composed of singular moments which flash on the screen and then seem to be carried away into some purpose, the meaning of which is either lost or only vaguely understood. In isolation, the majority of moments seem to neither contribute to a greater story nor take away from it. They appear to exist for themselves, like words on a Scrabble board, appropriated, disjointed and thereby divested of playing a role in some meaningful narrative. However, there are certain distinctive moments that rise above others because they disclose some truth which furnishes meaning to the rest. They unite all that came before and after into a meaningful, traceable narrative. These distinctive moments—in which plot twists occur—can be called *kairotic* because they disclose the nonchronological center of an unfolding event.[20] Kairotic moments serve as the engine of a plot twist, locating the exact instant that everything coming before and after is shot through with new significance. Prior to the revelation of the kairotic center, the event is not fully disclosed. Afterwards, it cannot be honestly denied.

These are the moments of foundational significance, when the truth of an unfolding event or story, with all its parts, is revealed. In mimetic theory, the kairotic center of all of history is located at the Death, Burial and Resurrection. An illustrative example from the film *The Others* is when Grace, played by Nicole Kidman, realizes that she, her children and the servants living in her house are all dead, while those who they had thought were haunting their house are actually living persons.[21] The kairotic center of *The Others* is the moment Grace realizes that it is she—along with her children and servants—who is the ghost. And this revelation is shared fully and simultaneously with the audience, the watchers to whom the entire event is revealed. Once the truth has been shown, reversion to the previous narrative is impossible.

The Others is a powerful film because the kairotic moment happens so unexpectedly, yet it is immediately perceivable and convincing. The entire plot in which the audience has been engaged is destroyed and replaced by a new one—one that compels the audience to rewatch the film now equipped with the unconcealed information. Rewatching a movie such as *The Others*, after the kairotic center, is nearly equivalent to watching a new movie. For the old one, the original prekairotic story, once destroyed, can never be believed again. The entire movie is now viewed in light of the kairotic center, a moment now waited for and anticipated from the beginning.

In the case of Jesus's Crucifixion, the kairotic moment was apprehended only by a small minority of witnesses, yet it was foundational in binding together and establishing this group into the future.[22] A group member later reported, "That which was from the beginning, which we have heard, which we have seen with our eyes . . . that which we have seen and heard, we declare unto you." (1 John 1:1, 3). The writer is speaking about Jesus Christ, but why would he need to declare to others what was from the beginning? Would they not also know? His words ring like someone who has apprehended the original plot of the world's story, one who has seen the plot twist, and he is writing to those who may be living in the prekairotic period, the world before the divine plot twist. He is a member of the audience who encountered the always-Crucified-always-living Lord and who recognized this Lord's true significance.[23]

The audience, composed of people with eyes to see, is the Church. It would take centuries for them to no longer be considered a dissenting minority, but it was absolutely characterized in its earliest form as nothing more than such. Before the Gospels were composed, there were people in this world who had heard and seen what was from the beginning, the Word made flesh dwelling among us, the innocent scapegoat who bore the iniquities of all. The test, let it be remembered, of true membership in this group of dissenters was faithfulness to the truth of the divine plot twist, to the revelation of the innocent scapegoat, even unto death. The new religion was not a choice among many established beliefs but the embodiment of an entirely new narrative. What was seen could never be unseen. Those who failed the test, it appeared, had either never apprehended the plot twist or were willing to pretend the things which are not. They would remain in the prekairotic story.

To the vast majority of those who were in attendance at the Crucifixion of Jesus, nothing new had happened.[24] Someone died to preserve peace; it was the age-old story.[25] The changeover happened, and nobody, aside from the few dissenters, knew anything. It is amazing to consider that on the day Jesus died, the world went on as though nothing new had taken place. They remained in their myth. Most of the world continued in the false peace provided by mythology. To be sure, on the day of the Crucifixion, Romans made their languid trips to the baths, bison grazed unknowingly in verdant grasslands on faraway continents, people somewhere celebrated a wedding or the birth of a child, birds nested in the sequoias just as they had done since time eternal. The death of Jesus, as a purely human event, was largely insignificant. And even at Calvary, most witnesses went home that day content in the peace they had always enjoyed. But those with eyes to see, eyes opened by the Grace of God, saw in a flash that there was another story. Revelation destroyed their myth.[26]

Regardless of the events that took place in and around Jerusalem that day—the sky being darkened for three hours, the tearing of the curtain in the temple, the earthquake—there is nothing in extrabiblical records telling us of such events on any specific day. The secular world is silent on Jesus for centuries after his earthly ministry. About the man Jesus and his death, however, there is only darkness, as portrayed by the Gospel writers at the Cross. The movie went on, and almost no one in the audience had any idea.

And yet to those who had eyes to see the true event, the entire thing can only be characterized by the miraculous and catastrophic. "This is the history," Girard says, "not of the events themselves, but of their *representation*."[27] The plot twist was so powerful to the dissenting minority that they actually remembered details which, to the rest of the world, were shrouded in darkness, like blank spots on some map of history. Those who did not see what had happened, who did not apprehend Jesus' innocence were like moviegoers who do not apprehend a plot twist. To them, the story never changes. It is as though someone had watched *Fight Club* and missed the revelation that the two characters were one. Perhaps the movie would still be entertaining on some level, but the meaning would be lost entirely.

MY EYES ARE OPEN

A plot twist is specifically designed for an audience to know of its existence. Therefore, those who write a plot twist into their story must make the narrative shift obvious enough that the observers cannot miss it. As mentioned before, this is most effectively done in *The Village* with the director utilizing two powerful scenes to demonstrate the shift—the one showing a photo of the 1970s, the other involving the ranger with his modern gear. The unpredictable twist at the end of *The Others* stands out in its abruptness and clarity. Even the title comes immediately into focus for an audience who concretely grasps that the "others" are humans and it is the star cast that are ghosts. The plot twist is grasped with almost no effort, and, with the twist, it is as though the movie inside the movie is released. The true narrative emerges, and everything is seen anew. And we moderns who have experienced plot twists in film or literature are able to understand something extraordinarily unique about the Cross and the earth-shattering outcome conveyed by its revelation as a historical moment.

Could it be that true plot twists—as vehicles of truth as opposed to the anagnorisis device which controlled classical mythology—were not possible before the Cross, that it is only in a post-Easter society that people can expect the unexpected? According to Girard, "One can deconstruct any form of mythical or ideological 'truth,' but not the Cross, the actual death of the Son of God. That is the center around which our culture rotates and from which it has evolved. Why should the world have changed if that event did not convey a radical and fundamental anthropological truth to the human being?"[28] This radical and fundamental change creates a new situation in which there are now reasons for searching, whether in movies, books or life, for some deeper meaning, some twist of the plot. It must be remembered that all modern plot twists have their origins in the Christological event. Revelation, in all its forms, culminated at the Cross in the death of the innocent victim, the canon for all subsequent twists and revelations.

But here it should be emphasized that the significance of Jesus, his truth bearing death and resurrection, was dependent upon the dissenting minority who had been primed with eyes to see. It was they who walked away from the scene of his death having apprehended something truly other than the rest of the attendees. Had this minority not reported truly what they had seen, the event of Jesus may have been mythologized to the point of insignificance. They felt earthquakes and saw darkness covering the land, events which the centurion standing by must have felt either fully or in part. For the first time in history, one truly innocent, the paragon of all victims, had been put to death, and this event was remembered by some in all its significance.

In more ways than one, Jesus committed himself to humanity. All that he had done was entrusted to a group of people who had, small as their number was, seen the same thing. No person in isolation has historical significance. It takes a community to realize, remember and make the significance known. Something similar happens when moviegoers experience a plot twist, discussing it after the fact, and thereby affirming that each has seen what the others have. In the case of Jesus, it was a group largely made up of people that knew him during his life. These were those prepared with eyes to see and ears to hear. An audience of a movie plot twist can share, in a small but very real way, the experience of having eyes to see.

CONCLUSION

I hope to have conveyed that applying film to key features of Girard's theory opens up new vistas not only for viewing the world around us but also for understanding the significance of his key insights. Since plot twists highlight a distinction Girard made between two worlds—mythology and post-Christ—they likewise enable us to more readily comprehend what the Cross means to Girard. We enjoy plot twists because they bring us out of a mythology and give us "eyes to see" a story. With that common experience as a point of departure, the truth revelation contained in plot twists can be linked to the divine plot twist and thereafter be utilized as a vehicle for zooming in closely to the moment when the old world died and the new one began.

NOTES

1. Gianni Vattimo and René Girard, *Christianity, Truth, and Weakening Faith* (New York: Columbia University Press, 2010), 103.

2. Ibid, 103–104.

3. René Girard, *Battling to the End* (East Lansing, MI: Michigan State University Press, 2010), 196.

4. According to Girard, "The Cross is not only knowledge of God, but first and foremost an understanding of mankind," *The One by Whom Scandal Comes* (East Lansing, MI: Michigan State University Press, 2014), 95. Another Girardian, while arguing that Christian theology is "transformative anthropology," says, "[T]he essential transformation of Christian theology can and will only occur when we begin our anthropology and our theology from the point of reference provided by the Cross of Jesus (. . .) from the point of view of the victim, or what Bonhoeffer called 'the view from below,'" Michael E. Hardin, "Mimetic Theory and Christian Theology," in *For René Girard: Essays in Friendship and in Truth*, edited by Sandor Goodhart, et al., 265–272 (East Lansing, MI: Michigan State University Press, 2009), 269.

5. See Girard, *Christianity, Truth, and Weakening Faith*, 104–105.

6. James Alison, *Knowing Jesus* (Springfield, IL: Templegate Publishers, 1994), 20.

7. Ibid, 19–25.

8. Mark reads, "Indeed this man was the Son of God." Mk 15:39.

9. Perhaps the centurion said both statements and much more besides, but we are left only with the two statements that had most impressed the Gospel writers—each in turn striving to demonstrate that something powerfully new had happened.

10. Nietzsche, too, saw Jesus' innocence; however, he rejects rather than embraces it. See especially Friedrich Nietzsche, *The Will to Power* (New York: Vintage Books, 1968), 542–543.

11. René Girard, *Battling to the End*, 112.

12. *Fight Club*, Directed by David Fincher (1999; Los Angeles, CA: 20th Century Fox Home Entertainment), DVD.

13. James Alison also draws an illustration from the world of cinema when he says, "It is as though we are watching a film; the film doesn't change, but the projectionist subtly puts a filter into the projector, so that exactly the same film comes out, but is changed into sepia, or pink, or whatever," Alison, 40.

14. *The Village*, Directed by M. Night Shyamalan (2004; PA, DE, NJ: Touchstone Home Entertainment), DVD.

15. Aristotle translated by S. H. Butcher, *Aristotle's Theory of Poetry and Fine Art* (Mineola, NY: Dover Publications, 1951), 41 (1452a).

16. Ibid.

17. See especially, René Girard, *The Scapegoat* (Baltimore, MD: Johns Hopkins University Press, 1986), 27.

18. Although the villagers did not kill the man, all the classic signs are there that he was a scapegoatable person. Not only was he apparently developmentally challenge, he was the one member of the group, aside from blind Ivy, who came close to discovering the secret.

19. This mnemonic of obscure origins is cited by many 20th century Latin grammars from both Germany and the English-speaking world.

20. Kairotic is taken from the Greek term *kairos* which signifies *occasion* or *appropriate time* as opposed to *chronos* which indicates *chrological time*. Paul Tillich used the term "kairotic moments," but his usage is not the same concept discussed here. See Paul Tillich, *The Interpretation of History* (New York: Charles Scribner's Sons, 1936).

21. *The Others*, Directed by Alejandro Amenábar (2001; Spain, England: Cruise/Wagner Productions), DVD.

22. See James Alison on "The Intelligence of the Victim," Alison, 33–58. Alison underscores the fact that Jesus' own understanding of himself and his mission was only later imparted to the disciples. In other words, there was no kairotic center for Jesus, since he had had intelligence of what was going on. His intelligence was grasped by the disciples after the Resurrection.

23. Ibid.

24. See Girard's argument that, in order for the Gospel revelation to occur, the violent contagion against Jesus had to be both unanimous and not unanimous, *I See Satan Fall Like Lightening* (Maryknoll, NY: Orbis Books, 2001), 188.

25. See Caiaphas' words, "[I]t is expedient for you that one man should die for the people, and that the whole nation perish not," John 11:50.

26. According to Girard, "What's unique about the Passion is not the way in which Christ dies (. . .) it's that, instead of ending with a sacralization of the scapegoat, it ends with a *desacralization* of the whole system." *When These Things Begin: Conversations with Michel Treguer* (East Lansing, MI: Michigan State University Press, 2014), 32.

27. René Girard, *I See Satan*, 141.

28. René Girard, *Evolution and Conversion* (New York, NY: Continuum Publishing, 2010), 256.

BIBLIOGRAPHY

Aristotle translated by S. H. Butcher. *Aristotle's Theory of Poetry and Fine Art*. Mineola, NY: Dover Publications, 1951.

Fight Club, Directed by David Fincher. 1999; Los Angeles, CA: 20th Century Fox Home Entertainment, DVD.

Girard, René. *Battling to the End*. East Lansing, MI: Michigan State University Press, 2010.

———. *Evolution and Conversion*. New York, NY: Continuum Publishing, 2010.

———. *I See Satan Fall Like Lightning*. Maryknoll, NY: Orbis Books, 2001.

———. *The Scapegoat*. Baltimore, MD: Johns Hopkins University Press, 1986.

Holy Bible. Douay-Rheims, 1899 American Edition Version.
Nietzsche, Friedrich. *The Will to Power*. New York: Vintage Books, 1968.
The Others. Directed by Alejandro Amenábar. 2001; Spain, England: Cruise/Wagner Productions, DVD.
Tillich, Paul. *The Interpretation of History*. New York: Charles Scribner's Sons, 1936.
Vattimo, Gianni and René Girard. *Christianity, Truth, and Weakening Faith*. New York: Columbia University Press, 2010.
The Village. Directed by M. Night Shyamalan. 2004; PA, DE, NJ: Touchstone Home Entertainment, DVD.

Chapter 6

Gazing into a Mirror

Watching Hoarders *with Girard*

Ryan G. Duns

Since its 2009 debut, the cable series *Hoarders* has given viewers a vivid, albeit ethically troubling, glimpse into what the DSM-5 recognizes as Hoarding Disorder. Individual episodes follow an attempt to intervene and "clean up" the home of someone living with this illness. Each episode's plot tends to follow a tripartite pattern. First, viewers see the hoard's scope. Some houses teem with vermin, others are nearly impassible, while still others reveal deplorable sanitary conditions. Viewers learn, too, of the crisis necessitating the intervention: eviction, health risk, imminent loss of children. Next, viewers follow a two-fold decluttering process where cleaners remove the physical hoard and a therapist explores the subject's psychic and emotional baggage. Some installments end by resolving the crisis and updating viewers on the subject's progress; other episodes conclude less optimistically with the subject slipping back into old hoarding ways.

    This chapter uses Girard's mimetic theory as a lens through which to view, critique, and glean a theological insight from *Hoarders*. I begin by discussing hoarding disorder and connecting it to Girard's understanding of mimetic desire and what he calls "ontological sickness." I then show the way mimetic theory can transform how viewers watch *Hoarders* by recasting the show as a mirror that reveals, to attentive viewers, their own distorted patterns of desire. The show, so approached, diagnoses viewers' own ontological sickness. More critically, mimetic theory exposes the sinister truth that *Hoarders* contributes to and profits from the exploitation of mental illness—and, in the process, implicates the viewer. Under entertainment's guise, it transforms viewers into victimizers and perpetuates the stigmatization of those afflicted with hoarding disorder. After this critique, I conclude by teasing out the show's theological significance. Seen from the right angle, the astute viewer may recognize that each episode unfolds along to a secularized version of mysticism's purgative, illuminative, and unitive ways. With Girard's assistance, one may begin to discover within *Hoarders* an invitation to reflect more intensively on the health of one's own desire and to consider just what, or perhaps *who*, it is for which the heart most deeply longs.

HOARDING DISORDER: ILL GIVING AND ILL KEEPING

In their introduction to *The Oxford Handbook of Hoarding and Acquiring*, Frost and Steketee note a near-absence of clinical research into hoarding, or instance of hoarding disorder, prior to 1993.[1] In recent years, such research has expanded, no doubt fueled by shows like *Hoarders*. Although among the first conduct clinical research into it, Frost and Steketee were hardly the first to notice hoarding. Fred Penzel finds evidence of it dating back 10,000 years.[2] Greek and Norse mythology, the Bible, Renaissance and Victorian literature all contain allusions to, if not warnings against, unbridled acquisition. In Canto VII of the *Inferno*, Dante places those who hoard and those who waste in hell's fourth level. In life, these hoarders and wasters neither exercised moderation in amassing nor spending money. In death they roll weights in a circle, only to collide with one another without ever completing their circuit. Opposites in life, they spend eternity as each other's obstacles:

> So they struck one another as they met;
> And then turned round, and, rolling back again
> Some shouted "Why hold on?" some "Why let go?"
> So they flowed back around the dark circle,
> From each side of us, to meet on the other side,
> Where once again they shouted their shameful chant.[3]

Long before the DSM-5, Virgil aptly diagnosed the condition of those condemned to this fate: "Ill giving and ill taking have taken from them the lovely world, and put them in this scrum."[4] It is the overdrive of acquisitive desire, an irresistible urge amass more goods without parting with any, that so burdens those who struggle with this illness. This is aptly capture by the title of book written by Tolin, Frost, and Steketee: *Buried in Treasure*.

Virgil's "ill keeping" presaged hoarding disorder's clinical description as "(1) the acquisition of and failure to discard a large number of possessions that appear to be useless or of limited value; (2) living spaces sufficiently cluttered so as to preclude activities for which those spaces were designed; and (3) significant distress or impairment in functioning caused by the hoarding."[5] Recently, the DSM-5 nuanced this definition, now recognizing that not all of the hoarded objects can be deemed "useless." Although the disorder can, in some cases, lead those it afflicts to hoard garbage or waste, this need not be the case. Some hoard animals, new clothes, dollar store deals, or anything else that strikes one's fancy. One trait common among many living with hoarding disorder has been identified by researchers as a lack of impulse control and an inability to check one's buying and acquiring habits. Spatial constraints prevent us from digging deeper into the condition's clinical diagnosis and treatment. Our goal is limited, namely, to considering how the patterns of desire seen on *Hoarders*, when viewed through mimetic theory's lens, sheds light on our patterns of desire. Our focus will be, accordingly, limited to the way *Hoarders* depicts the disorder's immoderate drive to acquire objects and the way those afflicted with this condition are inordinately attached to these objects.

Although many who struggle with hoarding have a purpose behind saving and amassing what they save, the disorder prevents them from parting with anything. Some clinicians attribute this to *anosognosia*, a blindness or "lack of awareness of a disorder or problem."[6] *Anosognosia* renders those it afflicts "hoard blind" so that they cannot see the clutter around them. Even for those who see the threat the hoard poses, their impulse to acquire cannot be overcome. Watching their struggles to break free of the hoard's hold recalls the apostle Paul: "I do not do what I want, but I do what I hate" (Romans 7:15). Many are caught in a double-bind, a dialectic commanding "Do Not Hoard" and "Hoard," a command that paralyzes them and effectively consigns them to a version of Dante's hell.

Girard never wrote about hoarding, but familiarity with mimetic theory makes apparent various analogies between the way we desire and the patterns of desire associated with hoarding disorder. For Girard, all desire is imitative and "there is nothing, or next to nothing, in human behavior that is not learned, and all learning is based on imitation."[7] Advertisers get this and, as I discussed in the Introduction, so does the fashion industry. Commercials feature models and athletes to draw attention to a new line of cosmetics or shoes. Endorsements endow objects with an aura of desirability: I want *that* object because famous people desire it. Desire, he contends, is triangular: *My desire (subject) is oriented to an object by the desire of another (model)*. Yet there is more to desire than copying. "To say that our desires are imitative or mimetic," Girard writes, "is to root them neither in their objects nor in ourselves but in a third party, the *model* or *mediator*, whose desire we imitate in the hope of resembling him or her, in the hope that our two beings will be fused."[8] This is crucial, because "acquisitive mimesis" intends more than attaining *this* or *that* object. Imitative desire, he argues, "is always a desire to be Another."[9] The drive to acquire is not an impulse to have *something* but is a desire to possesses another's being. This desire for being is metaphysical desire.

Viewed through Girard's lens, each *Hoarders* episode provides an example of persons suffering from a disoriented form of acquisitive desire. This is apparent when we see how objects with little value (junk mail) or negative value (feces) are clung to so fiercely. If we accept Girard's depiction of desire's triangularity, we might notice how often the model-corner of the triangle has been violently or tragically torn away, creating a vacuum the hoarding disorder aims to fill. It's as though metaphysical desire, when bereft of a model, possesses no direction and grasps at anything and clings to everything to secure one's being. Without a model to endow things with value, *everything* possesses value, so everything must be acquired. This desire expands, yet the hoard fails to satisfy one's desire. To the contrary, the hoard is inimical to flourishing and sabotages homes, lives, and relationships. For those afflicted, ill keeping and ill giving eventuate in ill living.

Statistically, hoarding occurs in 2–5% of adults in the USA and Europe.[10] Yet its insatiable appetite is not limited to those diagnosed with this disorder. In a consumer culture, one reassures oneself about one's acquisitive habits by saying, "If I just get *this* (house, position), *then* I will be satisfied." Buy the house, get the promotion, and the sought-for happiness evanesces; yet no matter how much one acquires, one cannot escape a gnawing desire for *more*. Psychologists call "hedonic adaptation" our rapid acclimatization to positive situations. What one swears will "be enough" never is. In fact, consuming the finite and temporal only piques our hunger for the infinite and eternal. The metaphysical desire *to be* refuses satisfaction, a condition Augustine knew well: "you have made us for yourself, and our heart is restless until it comes to rest in you."[11]

Augustine and Girard appreciate that desire is not something we *have*. We incarnate it; it is life's driving force. And, when we watch *Hoarders* with an eye to desire, each episode becomes an opportunity to undertake an "autopsy" of the way this driving force can be derailed. Let us take, then, a critical look at *Hoarders* to consider what we might learn about desire from the show.

ONTOLOGICAL SICKNESS

When Girard introduced "ontological sickness," it was synonymous with metaphysical desire and had a negative connotation.[12] "Don Quixote spreads the ontological sickness to those around him. The contagion, which is obvious in the case of Sancho, affects everyone in contact with the hero."[13] He later revised this assessment of desire and saw desire as good, even if susceptible to negative influence.[14] One of the appeals of *Hoarders* is the way it probes desire's dark side, often sensationally depicting its pathologies. It is a trait of hoarding disorder that there seems to be no cessation of the desire to acquire. Those who struggle with this disorder are persecuted by a lack they cannot fill, a hunger they cannot satisfy. Girard offers an insight into why this longing can never be totally sated:

> The reason is that [the subject] desires *being*, something he himself lacks and which some other person seems to possess. The subject looks to that other person to inform him of what he should desire in order to acquire that being. If the model, who is apparently already endowed with superior being, desires some object, that object must surely be capable of conferring an even greater plentitude of being.[15]

Our desire, Girard understood, is always borrowed from others. It is directed and influenced by the presence of a model. For whatever reason, it appears that those with hoarding disorder possess a desire that is wholly undirected. Each episode does try to account for the causes behind the subject's disoriented desire. Often enough, it's a past trauma or some form of mental illness that impedes desire's function. Without a viable model, hoarding disorder manifests itself as something a blindness, an *anosognosia*, that directs one's desire away from others and toward acquiring things. The desire *to be* another is limited to the desire *to have*. In many cases, the hoard fills a void that would otherwise be filled by a person.

Girard helps us to recognize the deforming shift to which desire is susceptible. Albeit in a dramatic way in cases of hoarding disorder, many in modern society have forgotten what Vittorio Gallese calls our "we-centricity."[16] As Brian Robinette puts it, we need to recall that individuality is "emergent from a vast realm of alterity and inhabited by innumerable others (familial, peer, social, cultural, etc.) whose desires and comportments we tacitly mirror, appropriate, negotiate, and creatively refashion in the tentative project of becoming."[17] Those familiar with Girard will hear his critique of the "romantic lie" of absolute autonomy and a call to embrace the "novelistic truth" of mediated desire. For Girard, no self exists *apart* from, but only as *a part* of, a relationship with others. This is why, I think, so many find *Hoarders* so alluring: it's a show about desire run amok where one possesses everything one wants (the hoard) yet remains tragically unfulfilled.

Holding this Girardian lens up to the television brings out these elements of *Hoarders* that many viewers would not perceive. Recall desire's triangular pattern:

> People influence one another and, when they're together, they have a tendency to desire the same things, primarily not because those things are rare but because, contrary to what most philosophers think, imitation also bears on desire. Humans essentially try to base their being, their profound nature and essence, on the desire of their peers.[18]

Models communicate *what* we want and *who* we desire to become. But, in most episodes of *Hoarders*, there is an absence of a model. Typically, some trauma—death, divorce, abuse, loss—has isolated the one with hoarding disorder from a broader network. To the mimetic theorist, the loss of one's model permits desire to go haywire and expand uncontrollably. Without a model to direct it, the desire *to be* grasps at anything and everything to fill its void. If desire is directed by a model who endows objects with value, in the absence of a viable model one can grow "value blind" and come to regard everything as desirable. One tries to fill the space left by trauma with the hoard, yet nothing fills the void. A cruel consolation, as hedonic adaptation prevents the attainment of permanent satisfaction. As viewers learn, and those touched personally by the condition know well, the desire to augment the hoard never abates. Those who suffer with this condition are possessed by their possessions and, as we see each week, it is devastatingly difficult to free those held captive by these chains.

Now, my claim is not that Girard can be read as providing any sort of clinical diagnosis. But Girard may, however, give *Hoarders'* viewers reason to pause. Refracted through the lens of mimetic theory, the affliction depicted on the screen may shed light on aspects of the viewers' lives and patterns of desire. To bring this out, I want to discuss two episodes. But before reflecting on the cases of Terry (Season 6, Episode 8) and Shanna (Season 6, Episode 4), allow me a critical observation. One of the disturbing features of *Hoarders* is its marketing. The show has no problem labeling people who struggle with a serious mental illness with demeaning nicknames. The show callously heaps insults onto its subject, dubbing Terry the "Liquid Cat Lady" and Shanna "The Poop Lady." Not only are these women's lives exploited and sensationalized, they are dehumanized and made ever more "other" to the viewer. The astute Girardian's radar pings, for here we find an otherwise neglected instance of scapegoating at play. The subjects are further marked as outsiders as their very real struggles are reduced to a catchy slogan intended to entice viewers to watch. Sure, the show is hardly a mob stoning or public execution. Yet the show deliberately polarizes the viewing audience over and against the subject; it canalizes feelings of disgust and directs them toward this other. The scapegoating cycle turns and its bloodless yet real effect can be seen: the many (viewers) become one (audience) at the expense of one (mentally ill subject). I will return shortly to probe further the ethical issues this raises.

Terry is a middle-aged woman who hoards animals. She shares her house, covered in feces and reeking of ammonia, with nearly fifty pets. Her notoriety stems not from her hoarding of live animals but from the hoard of dead cats in her refrigerator. Over the years, she collected nearly one-hundred cats and, planning to cremate them, kept their remains in her garage. During the cleanup, the crew discover that many cats had liquefied and, when they moved the refrigerator, cat-soup poured out. Ratings gold: an "ick factor" sure to titillate intrigued viewers. Yet, to the producers' credit, the episode does take a poignant turn when Terry describes how her father's death precipitated her hoarding. She blames herself for being incapable of helping her dad, and she realizes that she has transferred her desire to help him to her commitment to her cats. Inadvertently, she subverts her desire because their needs exceed her capacity to provide care. Her illness presents as a desire *to be* a caregiver but, unfocused, it fractures her health, her home, and hastens the death of her cats.

Shanna is described as owning the worst hoard in the show's history. Shanna lived with her mother until the latter's death. At some point, worried about overflowing the septic system, the women began to relieve themselves in buckets and to store the waste in jugs. Matt Paxton, a professional cleaner, estimates nearly nine tons of human waste were stored in the house. When confronted over the house's stench, Shanna seems perplexed. She blames the "musty" odor on mold and appears genuinely surprised to find out that the stench comes from feces. Later, in a heated exchange with the psychologist, Shanna insists on eating food removed from the house. The psychologist demurs, citing fecal contamination. Shanna's devastating reply, much teased by producers: "I've been eating poop for twelve years" and alludes to "getting high" from it.

No question: big "ick factor." On social media, a lot of chatter erupted with some claiming this to be the "grossest episode ever." A ratings winner, perhaps, but a loss for producers who profited at her plight. It is true that the show does have a few heart-tugging moments when we learn about Shanna's affective history, but does a touch of sympathy make up for turning her into "The Poop Lady"? More generally, do producers, furthermore, expend any effort to explore *how* the person who lives with hoarding disorder experiences the intrusion into their space and the violation of their lifestyle? Even if it makes logical sense to viewers that many who live such dire situations need and deserve help, viewers cannot forget that these are human beings for whom this logic has little purchase. Viewers may regard the clean-up crew and team of psychologists as virtuous, but to those who own the hoard the clean-up can be experienced only as violence. The producers, driven to maximize the "ick" factor, fail miserably to cultivate any empathy for those depicted.

Girard's theory here produces great light. Watching *Hoarders* in his company enables viewers to recognize the shadow of hoarding in their lives. Viewers can notice the pattern of desire, observe how it can go off the rails, and then ask themselves how they have experienced this. To be sure, many today do not regard *our* behavior as hoarding, for we have found culturally sanctioned ways to acquire what we have agreed has value: riches, honors, goods. We brag of "binging" on shoes, "splurging" on shopping, and amassing power. In the heel of the hunt, however, can any of us say "enough is enough" any faster than those with hoarding disorder? It may be neater and cleaner, but many today are afflicted with a form of bourgeois *anosognosia* blinding them to their own self-destructive patterns of desire. This misrecognition licenses them to take sordid delight in the suffering of another while shielding them from acknowledging the many ways they themselves live within a hoard.

As Girard passes the popcorn, one is struck with an insight. Perhaps what is alluring about *Hoarders* is not that it showcases a reality that is radically anomalous but, rather, one that is uncannily familiar to many of us. Perhaps the reason viewers are shocked and titillated is less because of the *differences* they observe on the small screen than because, deep down, they see in each episode the intimations of a *sameness* that hits very close to home. At the hands of its priests—the producers and marketers—each episode enacts a profane liturgy structured to create *just enough* sympathy for viewers to keep watching but not enough for them to see how they are being manipulated or implicated within these rites. For these "rites" work by concealing likeness and exacerbating a trait—here, a severe mental illness—in such a way as to exaggerate alterity. The result, in many cases, is an episode that transforms the "star" into a sort of monster. I can imagine Girard cocking an eyebrow and whispering, "So, are you tuning in because you want to see something monstrous and other or, maybe, because deep down it gives you a glimpse of a sameness that you would rather keep concealed? You think you're so advanced, but have you really outgrown P. T. Barnum's Freak Shows? Who, do you suppose, is the *real* monster?"

Girard's query should strike an empathic chord and enkindle a new knowing. For one need not be *Buried Alive* within a hoard to say, "Ah, I know something of this drive to acquire, this incessant hunger for more. The reality depicted on the screen may not be mine, but I can see elements of this person's life within my own." One might question, "Are the things I amass—cars, prestige, electronics, money, books—so different than the things they experience as providing comfort and security? Are we so different from those we watch on *Hoarders*?" As one ponders the humanity concealed by the producers' rites, the impulse to exploit cedes as empathy stirs. It's a dark grace, to be sure, and one that comes at the expense of vulnerable women and men who have been subjected to terrible public humiliation. But by opening the viewer's eyes to the evil perpetrated by this form of entertainment, a cry may begin to resound. For as the gaze pierces the show's mythic veil and sees the person beneath the illness, the viewer can begin to stand in solidarity with those depicted. For those with eyes to see it, recognition of the *Hoarders* inhumanity can give rise to a response to struggle in an effort to restore the humanity of those whom we have hitherto taken for granted.

The reader may experience a bit of a cognitive ricochet as our investigation into the "ontological sickness" depicted in *Hoarders* now casts a light, almost certainly an unwanted illumination, onto the sickness of the show's viewers. Instead of being informed or entertained by the series, those with mimetically attuned senses can experiences themselves as implicated in an exploitative industry. I can envision no greater conversion than that of the artfully produced "ick factor" being turned back on the producers, a conversion that would lead more viewers to decry the way the mentally ill and marginalized have been exploited for profit and viewing pleasure.

Nevertheless, despite my misgivings about the series, I do want to tease out what I see as a theologically relevant element from the show. I detect within the show a secularized itinerary of the purgative, illuminative, and unitive "ways" familiar to students of Christian mysticism. With Girard, I now consider how the show might be regarded as a graphic depiction of a pathway believers are called to follow, namely, a purgation of one's disordered attachments and a movement toward the One for whom our desire *to be* truly longs.

FROM HOARDING TO HEALING: DESIRE AND THE THREEFOLD WAY

Christian mystics regularly describe the spiritual life as a pilgrimage or journey undertaken in stages, and the tripartite movement of each *Hoarders* episode parallels the "ways" made famous by Pseudo-Dionysius.[19] In *The Celestial Hierarchy*, he describes these as purgative, illuminative, and unitive. Roughly speaking, the purgative way purifies the soul and loosens sinful attachments, the illuminative way enlightens and directs one toward God, and the unitive stage enters into communion with God. Rather than discrete chronological stages, elements of each is present in the other: the purgative stage only begins, for instance, when one's reality is divinely illuminated by grace and one begins to move toward wholeness guided by the summons drawing one from captivity into freedom.

Authors like Bonaventure, Teresa of Avila, and John of the Cross adopted this threefold schema and filled out its contours based on their experiences. Each saw spiritual growth as a progressive deepening of relationship with

God and a journey toward spiritual perfection. Like those treated for hoarding, mystics begin their journeys not at their initiative but at the prompting of another. In *Hoarders*, interventions seek to cure hoard-blindness; for mystics, the experience of grace empowers one to leave behind one's attachments to attain union with God. James Alison describes how grace transforms the way one relates to the Holy One:

> If the "social other" tends to teach us a pattern of desire such that what is normal is reciprocity, which of course includes retaliation, then Jesus presents God as what I call "the Other other," one who is entirely outside any being moved, pushed, offended or any retaliation of any sort at all. On the contrary, God is able to be *towards* each one of us without ever being *over against* any one of us. God is in no sort of rivalry at all with any one of us; he is not part of the same order of being as us, which is how God can create and move us without displacing us.[20]

Divine grace does not annul human desire but heals and reorients it. It irrupts the darkness, exposes distorted patterns of relationality, and illuminates a way leading to peace and healing. Grace redeems its recipient from destructive double-binds by grafting those who say "yes" into a re-creative process that purges one of ontological sickness and tutors one to desire according to the Holy Other whose desire is not acquisitive and dominative but, rather, self-giving and donative.

Consider this itinerary as found in one episode of *Hoarders*. Glen, dubbed by producers "The Rat Man" (Season 3, Episode 20), used to breed rats as pets. Three escaped and mated. Many times. The episode opens with a shocking scene: a living hoard of 2,500 rodents. Unlike Terry's cats, his rats are in relatively good health. There are just too many of them. Yet Glen, as seen in other episodes, demonstrates symptoms of *anosognosia*: he registers that there are many rats, but he remains blind to the effect the hoard has on him and his home. He simply cannot see the depths of the problem. Whereas viewers probably cannot imagine living in a house overrun by rodents, Glen can't take in the scope of the problem.

Purgation begins when Dr. Zasio helps him to perceive the hoard. Rather than imposing her vision upon him, she reorients his gaze to see it anew, revealing its scope while creating space for self-examination. Glen shares how his hoarding began after his wife's death, with the rats serving as surrogates for her and her love. For him, this disclosure permits a chink of light to pierce the hoard's darkness and provides him the courage to accept help in the hope of finding healing in his life. To call this a breakthrough would be an understatement, for the infestation necessitates knocking out the walls to flush out and capture the rats. With Zasio's help, Glen undertakes an inner purge. He names his grief and begins to process it with her assistance. While it requires some prompting, he see the consequences of "ill giving and ill keeping" and allows his furry friends to be put up for adoption. Until his 2015 death, he succeeded, assisted by a therapist, in remaining hoard-free.

Glen's case, like Terry's and Shanna's, is extreme. That's the hook the show uses to entice viewers to watch week after week. Even though the purge can have benefits, we would do well to cast a self-critical eye on the process. What does a viewer's attraction to peer voyeuristically into another's life, to gawk at another's suffering, reveal? How do we, as a society, countenance a show purporting to be about human interest when, in fact, it implicates viewers in the inhuman exploitation of the mentally ill? Matt Seitz is too charitable when he observes that *Hoarders* "depicts extreme behavior, but only as a means of finding a colorful analogue for a psychological process that 'normal' people go through every day: the struggle to identify obsessive and/ or self-destructive behavior and then do something about it."[21] Seldom does the show encourage such self-reflection; one needs "eyes to see" and reflect on the analogue Seitz describes. Mimetic theory provides the lens to expose the "myth" of hoarding that sensationally blinds viewers to the plight of its victims. If television can be a mediator of gracious light, a more reflective and theologically informed viewing of *Hoarders* can illuminate the darkness in which so many are trapped.

This, today, is needful. In an age of one-click shopping, *Hoarders* should provoke viewers to scrutinize the nature and patterns of their desire. Do we buy because it is a deal or because we are trying to conceal or deaden a sense of internal emptiness? Are our lives engulfed by mountains of spiritual debris—resentment, anger, unprocessed grief, disappointment—that alienate us from others? Does grasping at and tenaciously clinging to at all the things we think we want subvert our efforts to attain what we truly desire? If *Hoarders* acts as a cracked mirror, can we discern in its distorted reflection glimpses of our own socially-sanctioned hoarding of wealth, power, prestige, and possessions? Summoning the courage to gaze into this cracked mirror can lead one to discover and claim a truth Augustine well knew: no finite thing can, or ever will, satisfy desire's hunger. Desire is not for *this* or *that* but for the source of everything. One may roam creation's map and delight in every sensation and acquisition, yet the gnawing hunger is sure to return. At our core we are, Girard recognizes with the Bishop of Hippo, made for more; desire intends nothing less than the author and creator of being itself: God.

The cracked mirror that reflects our own distorted and self-destructive patterns can be salutary and therapeutic. By the light of our "smart televisions," one can peer into the darkness of one's life and confront the compulsion to hoard. And, by this high definition light, one may find a way to walk away from this hoard and to begin to walk in greater spiritual freedom. In the chaos of the rubbled-over heart, one may yet hear the call of the One who enters the messy reality of history and offers to heal it. For Christians, this is heard as the liberating Good News of Jesus who fulfills Isaiah's prophecy: "He has sent me to proclaim release to the captives and recovery of sight to the blind, to let the oppressed go free" (Luke 4:18). One is freed *from* the hoard and liberated *for* a spiritual journey leading toward communion with the One, revealed by Jesus Christ, who offers to sate our infinite desire to be. For those spiritually buried alive, this is the inbreaking of the savior who leads one along a spiritual pilgrimage whose itinerary is captured in the epitaph on Cardinal Newman's tomb: *Ex umbris et imaginibus in veritatem*, "out of shadow and fantasy into truth." It is a pilgrimage out of self-enclosed fantasy toward the truth that, without a relationship with the Holy Other for whom the heart pines, desire will never be satisfied.

When watched with Girard, *Hoarders* ceases to be an object of entertainment and becomes an occasion for critical discernment. Girard instructs us to notice the way desire works, to appreciate its susceptibility to distortion, and to grow attuned the ways it can be redirected and healed. By drawing attention to our interdividuality, he challenges us to consider the ways our desires have been shaped by, and in turn shaped, the desires of others. When watched through mimetic theory's lens, we find these dynamics present within *Hoarders*, yet do so in a way that notices what the producers assiduously attempt to conceal. One notices the presence of the victim and the way an industry profits by making us complicit in the mob who watches and delights in the travails of the exploited other. Where producers and executives bank on an "ick factor" to elicit thrills and *Schadenfreude*, the mimetic theory casts a penetrating light into the show's mythic darkness and reveals its victim-making mechanism. Instead of rendering us passive spectators, Girard spurs one into a solidarity that stands with and struggles on the side of those who are in need. The Gospel's revelation of the innocent victim refuses to allow those touched by its light to ignore the plight of today's victims. Girard's theory, in this way, enables us to see the crack in an exploitative industry and galvanizes efforts to respond to the needs of the victimized.

In addition to exposing the ethically troubling practices of the entertainment industry, the mimetic theory permits one to recognize that *Hoarders* is not "his story" or "her story" but is, in a way, very much "our story." With Girard's assistance, the self-reflective viewer may detect similarities between what is watched on television and lived out in daily life. The self-critical gaze may then make an inventory of one's own spiritual hoard and note the effects it has on oneself and others. But where the show depicts the purgative process taking place over the course of a few days, spiritual purgation, illumination, and unification is an unending process. If there is a dark grace to be found in *Hoarders*, it is the way the show can reveal our own hoarding tendencies and, by the television's hoary glow, begin to guide our pilgrimage from darkness into light. Our progressive liberation *from* the hoard and desire's gradual healing becomes, in turn, a liberation *for* solidarity with others lived out as a response to the Innocent Victim's call: "Go and do likewise" (Luke 10:38).

I conclude with part of a prayer from Anselm of Canterbury's *Proslogion*. On the surface, it appears as a lament arising from frustrated desire, a desire hungering for the infinite yet confronting the reality that, in the terrestrial realm, its hunger will go unsatisfied. An insuperable gulf threatens to frustrate forever desire's deepest longing and leads Anselm to cry out:

> Alas, I am indeed wretched,
> one of those wretched sons of Eve,
> separated from God!
> What have I begun, and what accomplished?
> Where was I going and where have I got to?
> To what did I reach out, for what do I long?[22]

No less than Augustine and Girard, Anselm knew the heart's restlessness and its longing for the infinite, for God. Separated from the source of being itself, Anselm felt the sting and stir of desire. In daily life, *this* thing and *that* jockey for attention, each promising seductively to fulfill the deepest desire of the heart. Frustrated over and again by these false promises, he admits that nothing finite can make him whole. No breakdown, this is a breakthrough. For it is this lesson, graphically and grotesquely depicted on *Hoarders* yet lived out by most of us: no finite thing can sate the desire for being. The mystics knew firsthand this breakthrough, and their many testimonies recount their deliverances from darkness into light as they journeyed as pilgrims toward communion.

Guided by Girard and impelled by grace, spiritual pilgrims continue to embark on the threefold path that heals desire and promises to satisfy it as they journey toward communion with the one for whom we most intensely long. If we listen to Anselm's prayer with Girard, it may be heard not as a lament but as a canticle of desire. Ranging across creation's map one discovers that no created entity, no finite thing that can be grasped and hoarded, will ever be enough. But this breakdown, this failure, is desire's great triumph. In desire's void, one discovers the intimations of a fullness that cannot be hoarded or controlled. By its light, one recognizes the hoards that hold us back and it encourages one to begin the purgative process that leads toward freedom. And by this light, one ventures forth on a pilgrimage in communion with fellow travelers who have similarly been freed from their hoards and freed for a journey animated by desire toward the Holy One in whom the restless heart may find that for which it longs.

NOTES

1. Randy Frost and Gail Steketee, "Introduction and Overview," in *The Oxford Handbook of Hoarding and Acquiring*, eds. Randy Frost and Gail Steketee (New York: Oxford, 2014), 3.
2. Fred Penzel, "Hoarding in History," *The Oxford Handbook of Hoarding and Acquiring*, 6–16.
3. Dante Alighieri, *The Divine Comedy*, trans. C.H. Sisson (New York: Oxford University Press, 2008), 73.
4. Ibid., 74. Emphasis added.
5. Frost and Steketee, "Phenomenology of Hoarding," in *The Oxford Handbook of Hoarding and Acquiring*, 20.
6. Blaise Worden, James DiLoreto, and David Tolin, "Insight and Motivation," in *The Oxford Handbook of Hoarding and Acquiring*, 249.
7. René Girard, *Things Hidden Since the Foundation of the World*, trans. Stephen Bann & Michael Metteer (Stanford: Stanford University Press, 1978), 7.
8. René Girard, *Resurrection from the Underground*, trans. James Williams (East Lansing: MSU Press, 1996), 76.
9. René Girard, *Deceit, Desire, & the Novel*, trans. Yvonne Freccero (Baltimore: Johns Hopkins, 1965), 83.
10. Kiara Timpano, Ashley Smith, Julia Yang, and Demet Cek, "Information Processing," in *The Oxford Handbook of Hoarding and Acquiring*, 100.
11. Augustine, *Confessions*, trans. Thomas Williams (Indianapolis: Hackett, 2019), 1.
12. Girard, *Deceit, Desire, & the Novel*, 97.
13. Ibid.
14. Scott Cowdell, *René Girard and the Nonviolent God* (Notre Dame: Notre Dame Press, 2018), 95.
15. René Girard, *Violence and the Sacred*, trans. Patrick Gregory (Baltimore: Johns Hopkins University Press, 1979), 146.
16. Vittorio Gellese, "The Two Sides of Mimesis: Mimetic Theory, Embodied Simulation, and Social Identification," in *Mimesis and Science*, ed. Scott. Garrels (East Lansing: MSU Press, 2011), 87–108.
17. Brian Robinette, "Contemplative Practice and the Therapy of Mimetic Desire," *Contagion: Journal of Violence, Mimesis, and Culture* 24 (2017): 73–100 at 82.
18. Girard, *When These Things*, 11.
19. Pseudo-Dionysius, *The Complete Works*, trans. Colm Luibheid (New York: Paulist Press, 1987), 145–191.
20. James Alison, *Broken Hearts and New Creations: Intimations of a Great Reversal* (New York: Continuum, 2010), 166.
21. Matt Zoller Seitz, "'Hoarders' Unforgettable Rat Episode," *Salon*, 25 September 2011, www.salon.com/2011/01/11/hoarders_2/. Accessed 3 July 2019.
22. Anselm of Canterbury, *Proslogion*, trans. Benedicta Ward (Harmondsworth: Penguin, 1973), 242.

BIBLIOGRAPHY

Alighieri, Dante. *The Divine Comedy*. Translated by C.H. Sisson. New York: Oxford University Press, 2008.

Alison, James. *Broken Hearts and New Creations: Intimations of a Great Reversal*. New York: Continuum, 2010.

Anselm of Canterbury. *The Major Works*. Edited by Brian Davies and G. R. Evans. New York: Oxford University Press, 2008.

Augustine. *Confessions*. Translated by Thomas Williams. Indianapolis: Hackett, 2019.

Cowdell, Scott. *René Girard and the Nonviolent God*. Notre Dame: Notre Dame Press, 2018.

Frost, Randy, and Gail Steketee, "Introduction and Overview" in *The Oxford Handbook of Hoarding and Acquiring*, edited by Randy Frost and Gail Steketee, 3–5. New York: Oxford University Press, 2014

Gellese, Vittorio. "The Two Sides of Mimesis: Mimetic Theory, Embodied Simulation, and Social Identification." In *Mimesis and Science*, edited by Scott Garrels, 87–108. East Lansing: Michigan State University Press, 2011.

Girard, René. *Deceit, Desire, and the Novel: Self and Other in Literary Structure*. Translated by Yvonne Freccero. Baltimore: Johns Hopkins University Press, 1976.

———. *Resurrection from the Underground*. Translated by James Williams. East Lansing: Michigan State University Press, 1996.

———. *Things Hidden since the Foundation of the World*. Translated by Stephen Bann and Michael Metteer. Stanford: Stanford University Press, 1987.

———. *When These Things Begin: Conversations with Michael Treguer*. Translated by Trevor Cribben Merrill. East Lansing: Michigan State University Press, 2014.

———. *Violence and the Sacred*. Translated by Patrick Gregory. Baltimore: Johns Hopkins University Press.

Luibheid, Colm, trans. *Pseudo-Dionysius: The Complete Works*. Mahwah, NJ: Paulist Press, 1987.

Penzel, Fred. "Hoarding in History." In Frost and Steketee, 6–16.

Robinette, Brian. "Contemplative Practice and the Therapy of Mimetic Desire." *Contagion: Journal of Violence, Mimesis, and Culture*, 24 (2017): 73–100.

Seitz, Matt Zoller. "'*Hoarders*' Unforgettable Rat Episode." *Salon*, September 25, 2011. Accessed February 18, 2020. https://www.salon.com/2011/01/11/hoarders_2/

Timpano, Kiara, Ashley Smith, Julia Yang, and Dernet Cek. "Information Processing." In Frost and Steketee, 100–119.

Worden, Blaise, James DiLoreto, and David Tolin. "Insight and Motivation." In Frost and Steketee, 247–259.

Chapter 7

From the Hermeneutic of Violence to Redemption

The 100 and Mimetic Theory

Paolo Diego Bubbio

The year is 2149. Ninety-seven years earlier, a nuclear holocaust wiped out almost all life on Earth. 2,400 people live on a space station, named "The Ark." This is the backstory of the TV series *The 100*.[1] In this chapter, I argue that watching *The 100* through the lens of Girard's mimetic theory allows us to appreciate the path the protagonists need to follow to overcome mimetic violence and the temptations of sacrificial peace, and eventually undertake a process of conversion. At the same time, the application of mimetic theory to *The 100* allows us to see how, in Girard's thought, the theological category of conversion dovetails with conceptions of the good life.

The Ark's systems are failing. It is imperative to determine whether humans can live on Earth again. 100 juvenile "expendable" prisoners are sent to Earth. They are not the only humans on Earth, however. The "Grounders" have also survived the nuclear holocaust, regressing to a barbaric stage, and live in clans locked in a power struggle. Their society is based on a warrior ethic. Their main socioethical principle is "Blood must have blood," applied through a rigid system of compensatory measures.

As argued by Girard, all the methods to control violence, from the "primitive" compensatory measures to judicial systems, are grounded in the sacred.[2] The victim, held responsible for the violence, is killed. The expulsion of the scapegoat restores peace to the community, and sometimes the scapegoat, after its death, is worshiped as the community's founder. The society of the Grounders is exemplary of this dynamic. The mythical figure that the Grounders call *Bekka Pramheda* ("Becca First Commander") was actually the scientist Becca Franco, who created the Artificial Intelligence (A.L.I.E.) that launched a nuclear apocalypse meant to solve the problem of human overpopulation. To atone for her creation of an inhumane A.I., Becca created A.L.I.E. 2.0, a computer chip (later known to the Grounders as "the Flame") that holds the consciousness and memories of previous hosts. Becca was burned alive by a group of survivors, and subsequently became a divine figure for their descendants: the Grounders.

The Sky People (as the 100 from the Ark are called now that the people from the Ark have joined them) and the Grounders are not alone. A third group live in Mount Weather: these "Mountain Men" are the descendants of survivors who locked themselves in a bunker before the apocalypse. When medical tests show that a transplant of bone marrow from the Sky People would have antiradiation effects and would allow the Mountain Men to live on the surface again, their leaders decide to use the Sky People as forced donors, even if that means killing them. The Mountain Men do not entertain a nonviolent solution, such as the willing cooperation of the Sky People to discover treatments that do not require the sacrifice of the donors. They are trapped in the sacrificial way of thinking.

Violence is mimetic: the proximity with a violent antagonist, in this case the Mountain Men, is enough for one to become violent. The violent way of thinking works as a contagion. Even Clarke, the protagonist, is infected by violence. As 47 Sky People are waiting for the bone marrow extraction that will kill them, Clarke gives Cage Wallace, the Mountain Men's leader, an ultimatum: she will poison the bunker with radiation using the air filtration system unless he frees the prisoners. The radiation would kill hundreds of people in the bunker, including innocent civilians and children. When Cage refuses, Clarke sees no other option and irradiates the bunker, killing the entire population of Mount Weather. Shattered with guilt, Clarke leaves. For a while, she lives like a hermit, feared and revered among the Grounders by the name of "Wanheda," "Commander of death."

Clarke returns when a group of her own people, under the rule of the aggressive Chancellor Pike, massacres the army of the Grounders without provocation. Clarke manages to convince Lexa, the Commander ("Heda") of the Grounders, to give up on her revenge:

> **Clarke:** Your army was here to help us and my people slaughtered them. You have every right to respond. Every right to wipe us out. Or, you can change the way you do things.
>
> **Indra [Lexa's aid]:** Why should she change? Blood must have blood.

Clarke: Really? Because from where I stand, the only way that ends is with everyone dead. So what kind of leader you want to be? The kind who kills every chance she gets because that's your way? Or the kind who shows the world a better way?

Lexa: You consider letting massacre go unavenged a better way?

Clarke: If it ends a cycle of violence, yes. If it brings about peace, yes. Someone has to take the first step. Let it be you. You say you want peace, that everything you've done was to achieve that, yet here we stand on the brink of another war. A war you can stop.

Indra: Commander, you can't seriously be considering this.

Lexa: I'm not considering it. I'm doing it.

Indra: Heda, please.

Lexa: Indra, our people act as if war is easier than peace. If that's so, should we not try and achieve the more difficult goal?

. . .

Lexa: (turning back to Clarke) Then let it be known. Blood must not have blood. (3.05, "Hakeldama")

The massacre at Mount Weather has triggered a moral crisis in Clarke, who now tries to "end the cycle of violence." Lexa seems positively infected by Clarke's desire for peace. Lexa's choice of words is noteworthy: she is not "considering" it—in light of "considerations," it would be *easy* to find justifications to stick to the traditional way of thinking. She is simply "doing" it, with the awareness that violence is the easier path, and that it is more difficult to refrain from violence than surrender to it.

It is also difficult to resist to the temptations of sacrificial peace—temptations that Clarke has to face to complete her journey of conversion.

"VIOLENCE IS A CONTAGION": THE TEMPTATIONS OF SACRIFICIAL PEACE

In season 3, A.L.I.E., the Artificial Intelligence that launched the nuclear apocalypse, tries to lure people into the "City of Light," a virtual simulation of the world. Joining the City of Light erases any physical or emotional pain, but also the memories of the event originally causing that pain. In the City of Light there is "no pain, hate, or envy."[3] However, this comes at the expense of human free will; and yet, A.L.I.E. thinks that she is providing a better life to human beings. More and more people fall under the mind-controlling influence of A.L.I.E. They all behave and think in the same way, and have the same common goal. The overriding directive: lure everybody else into the City of Light, using any means necessary, including torture and violence.

This is how mimetic violence spreads. The subject's object of desire and their model's object of desire overlap. This mutual convergence on a desired object makes people resemble each other more and more and becomes a pretext for violent rivalry (conflictual mimesis). Each adversary "does everything he or she can to be different from the other," but "the opposite, symmetrical thirst to differentiate themselves makes them even more similar."[4] This perceived loss of differentiation escalates up to the point when violence erupts against those who are, or appear, different. They are held responsible for the community's unrest and their removal (their scapegoating) restores peace, at least temporarily. An analogy can be drawn here between A.L.I.E. and the Inquisitor, the character from the *Legend of the Grand Inquisitor* as narrated in Dostoevsky's *The Brothers Karamazov*. According to the *Legend*, Christ returns on Earth; the Inquisitor has him arrested and "shows him, in a long discourse, the folly of his "idea.""[5] The Inquisitor's point is that the freedom that Christ gave humanity is the source of most suffering: 'Have You forgotten that peace, and even death, is more attractive to man than the freedom of choice that derives from the knowledge of good and evil?'[6] Like the Inquisitor, A.L.I.E.wants to get rid of the source of all pain and suffering—free will. In order to attain this goal, violence becomes necessary. Clarke is called again to decide on behalf of her people. She decides that the loss of free will is too a high a price to pay, and destroys A.L.I.E. by using the Flame to enter the City of Light and activate A.L.I.E.'s kill switch.

Before she is terminated, A.L.I.E. warns Clarke that hundreds of nuclear reactors are melting down and soon the planet will become uninhabitable. An old bunker is discovered that can protect 1,200 people. Octavia Blake (one of the original 100) reigns over the bunker with the name of *Blodreina*, or Red Queen. She sentences anyone breaking the rules to trials by combat and, since the community does not have enough protein, harvests it from the bodies of those who die during the matches. Six years later, back on the surface, Octavia's violent ruling and poor leadership determine a series of events that eventually make the Earth uninhabitable and force the survivors to leave Earth on a starship.

After 125 years on cryosleep, the survivors wake up in the proximity of a habitable moon. After landing, they find a human colony, called Sanctum, ruled by families known as the Primes, who are worshiped as gods. The people of Sanctum are the descendants of an expedition who landed on that moon 236 years earlier. The Primes have been using "mind drives" (modified versions of A.L.I.E. 2.0) to transfer their consciousnesses to new host bodies, thus living forever. They make their people believe that by receiving the drive, the host will become "one with the Primes" so that they sacrifice themselves willingly. The truth is that the original consciousness and personality of the host are erased when they receive the mind drive. The society of Sanctum seems peaceful, and Russell, the leader of the Primes, is determined to guarantee such peace. In his words, "Violence is a contagion."[7] This peace, however, is the peace of the persecutors, secured at the expense of the victims and grounded on a lie. It is ironic, but also appropriate, that Russell, originally an astronomer, chose his career because, as his daughter Josephine reminds him, he wanted "to prove there's no god. Too bad," she adds, "Nietzsche beat you to it when he said, '*Gott ist tot*' . . . 'God is dead.'"[8] Russell wanted to prove that there is no god, and ended up posing as god. This is very Nietzschean; if God is dead, Nietzsche asks, "Do we not ourselves have to become gods merely to appear worthy of it?"[9] However, as Girard points out, the collapse of the hierarchy of norms that the death of God represents does not produce a peaceful paradise. The world where human beings are "gods for each other" is rather the hell of mimeticism.[10] And unchecked mimeticism inevitably leads to violence.

A.L.I.E. and Russell represent two "ways of the world" to address the problem of violence. They both want peace. A.L.I.E., like Dostoevsky's Inquisitor, seeks peace for the sake of mankind. Its solution is the removal of desire (and with that, of human identity itself). Russell wants peace for the sake of the Primes, although he tries to convince others, and himself, that the benevolent ruling of the Primes ensures the well-being of the people. They both spread "the lie of the persecutors" to prevent the emergence of the "truth of the victim." They represent two forms of temptation: one gives up free will to avoid suffering (A.L.I.E.), the other to submit to the idolatry of the false gods of violence (Russell). Facing these temptations is an essential component of Clarke's journey of conversion. Clarke resists both the former (by destroying A.L.I.E.) and the latter temptation (as we are going to see in the next section).

"WE CAN DEFINE WHAT WE ARE. . . . THIS IS HOW WE DO BETTER"

In season 6, Octavia and Clarke undergo experiences of "possession." Girard considers possession an interpretation of the phenomenon of the monstrous double: "The subject watches the monstrosity that takes shape within him and outside him simultaneously."[11] The presence of the monstrous double signals the paroxysm of mimetic crisis, whose outcome can be destructive or redemptive.

Octavia takes a dose of "red sun toxin" and has a hallucinatory experience. In her delirium, she faces Pike, whom she killed to avenge the death of Lincoln (a friendly Grounder and Octavia's lover):

> **Pike:** One more time. What do you want?
>
> **Octavia:** Forgiveness.
>
> **Pike:** Deeper. Much, much deeper. Forgiveness is for minor offenses. You murdered people to get them to eat their friends and families. [. . .] You caused the world to be destroyed. What you want needs to be earned. Now say it!
>
> **Octavia:** Redemption.
>
> **Pike:** What's that? I can't hear you.
>
> **Octavia:** (screaming) Redemption!
>
> **Pike:** Ding ding ding! A gold star for Miss Blake. I was trying to earn mine when you put a sword through me. Which brings us to big question number two: what are you willing to do to get it?
>
> **Octavia:** What if I don't deserve it?
>
> **Pike:** Deserve's got nothing to do with it.

At this point, Octavia splits up into two personas. Her "double" is Blodreina, her dark violent self:

> **Blodreina:** Shut up, Pike. Pick up the sword and strike him down. Do what you know has to be done.
>
> **Pike:** Here we go again. Doing the same thing and expecting a different result is the definition of insanity. Einstein said that. (6.09, "What You Take With You")

Octavia realizes her need for redemption. Ethically, redemption is the state of being kept from evil or of improving morally. Girard, however, employs the term with a meaning that is closer to its use in Christian theology, where redemption describes the liberation from sin brought about through the atonement, a life marked by repentance, a changed orientation and ongoing conversion. "Conversion" comes from the Latin *convertere*, "to turn about." In the Gospels, it translates the Greek verb *metanoeite* (Mk 1:15), which means "change your way of thinking." For Girard, conversion is a combination of experience and self-reflection resulting in the ability to recognize one's own entanglement in mimeticism and propensity to violence.[12] Such ability is made possible by the revelation of the scapegoat mechanism and the "truth of the victim" in the Gospels.

Girard's view of conversion has been accused of being a combination of Gnosticism and Pelagianism, doctrines that consider salvation achievable through, respectively, the acquisition of special knowledge or the human ability to choose holiness, rather than through divine grace.[13] Girard provided an early reply to such allegations: "There is an irreducible supernatural dimension to the Gospels that I do not wish to deny or denigrate. But because of this we should not refuse the means of comprehension now available to us."[14] While never a Pelagian, in his later writings, Girard became more explicit in positively affirming the need for divine grace, identified with the divine revelation of the truth of the victim. The proclamation of the innocence of Jesus "calls for a form of religious consent that dogma says is possible only through divine grace."[15] Humans would never manage to gain access to this religious dimension "through the meager power of reason alone."[16] Therefore, "a special grace is needed," without which "there can be no redemption."[17] Christ provides access to the truth of the victim "to all human beings who are willing to let themselves be raised up by grace."[18] Grace is a gift: "Nowhere in the Gospels is divine favor deserved."[19] Once can choose to resist grace, or through the relationship with Christ, take advantage of the gift and undertake a process of conversion. "Christian conversion is our discovery that we are persecutors without knowing it."[20] In the dynamic of grace, as Kaplan remarks, "the believer, as forgiven, comes to realize the shape of this grace as more of an entry into something bigger than a conceptual grasping of something to be known discursively."[21] For Girard, conversion in a general sense does not need to be explicitly Christian. For example, "novelistic" conversions, such as Proust's, are not explicitly religious, but in Girard's view they still follow a Christian pattern.[22] To quote Kaplan again, "Revelation occurs not so much in the suddenness of an event, but in the slow and painful coming-to-understand that unifies being forgiven with becoming conscious of one's sinfulness."[23]

Consistent with Girard's view, Octavia's first step in the process of conversion is the rejection of her violent self, her monstrous double. The solution suggested by Blodreina is to resort to violence again, but Octavia symbolically kills her dark side. Like a Dostoevskian character, Octavia emerges from her hallucinatory experience converted, determined to reject violence.[24]

Clarke too confronts her "double." Russell uses her as a host and inserts the mind drive of his daughter Josephine into Clarke. Clarke's consciousness is now trapped inside her own mind, but it is not erased. The following conversation, occurring in Clarke's mind, is noteworthy:

Josephine: You like being the savior. You like playing god. You're not so different from the Primes, you know."

...

> **Josephine:** All of this is guilt for the deaths you've caused, but I don't get it. Why are you so torn up? Everything you did was to save your people. I'd do the same thing.
>
> **Clarke:** A ringing endorsement. (6.07, "Nevermind")

Clarke realizes that she did enjoy being the savior of her people. Sometimes she was so absorbed in her role as savior that she saw the sacrifice of others, reduced to the status of "collateral damages," as inevitable. The confrontation with Josephine makes Clarke consider that it is her entire way of thinking, still centered on violence (her "I have no choice" mode), that needs to change.

As a first reaction to this self-discovery, Clarke is tempted to sacrifice herself. Initially, she agrees to allow Josephine to erase her mind, in exchange for the survival of her people, who will be allowed to settle on the moon, while the sacrificial system of the Primes will go on undisturbed. At this point, however, a projection of her mind, represented by her late friend Monty, convinces her otherwise:

> **Monty:** That deal means our side gets to live, but at what cost? You're giving in to people who murder human beings to live forever.
>
> **Clarke:** That's easy to say, but in the real world, we have to do what's best for our people.
>
> **Monty:** Doing the wrong thing is never what's best. The ends don't justify the means.(6.07, "Nevermind")

Self-sacrifice, however noble it seems, is not the redemption Clarke seeks. Her sacrifice might save her people, but it would make them complicitous with the Primes. In the decisive moment of her inner crisis, Clarke's consciousness confronts Josephine's consciousness. Josephine shows some regret, blaming her traumatic past experience to justify what she has become:

> **Josephine:** I wasn't always like this.
>
> **Clarke:** Trust me, I know the feeling. . . . We can let the bad things that happened to us define who we are. Or we can define who we are. (6.10, "Matryoshka")

Clarke's claim marks her resolution to change her "way of thinking," to "think differently." Before the mind drive is extracted, Josephine's consciousness still tries to erase Clarke's mind, using this argument:

> **Josephine:** I know you, Clarke. If you came back, you'd kill everyone inside Sanctum. It's what you do" (6.10, "Matryoshka")

Having access to Clarke's memories, Josephine has reasons to believe that a free Clarke will kill everybody in Sanctum to save her people. Clarke was indeed planning the release of red sun toxin to generate uncontrolled violence in Sanctum so that her people could escape. But once Josephine's consciousness is destroyed for good, Clarke has an epiphany: "Josephine was right. This is Mount Weather all over again. That bomb won't just cause chaos. It'll cause a massacre. There has to be a better way."[25] Clarke forces herself to think differently, and comes up with an altered plan that does not involve the loss of innocent lives. They will use enough red toxin to trigger the early warning system and the evacuation of the city, which will serve as distraction, but not enough to kill innocent people. In order for the plan to work, Clarke needs to pose as Josephine to infiltrate Sanctum. Clarke's friend Bellamy tries to convince her to stick to the original plan:

Bellamy: Risking your life when we don't have to is just. . .

Clarke: . . . is how we do better.

. . .

Octavia: Bellamy, if we can spare innocent lives, we should. (6.11, "Ashes to Ashes")

Octavia and Clarke have undergone a process of conversion. "Do better" is an expression that recurs two other times in the episode. Once they get into Sanctum, they manage to get their people to safety, but other innocent lives are still at risk. Octavia says that she cannot let them die, and Echo (Bellamy's girlfriend) adds: "I guess it's time to do better." If we accept the grace of the revelation of the truth of the victim, then we have to act accordingly. Good works are also necessary. In this respect, Girard's "perspective on conversion is consistent with much of the Catholic perspective on 'operative grace.'"[26]

How would the "converted" Clarke judge her past choices in light of her new way of thinking? Does the conversion change one's way of dealing with moral dilemmas, and if so, how?

For Girard, our traditional "moral sense" "has been shaped by the history of attempts to bring consistency among moral distinctions that obscurely track the difference between good and bad violence and the difference between actions that promote the crisis and those that end it."[27] Clarke's actions at Mount Weather are consistent with this "sacrificial" moral sense, because they effectively end the crisis. However, mimetic theory points to a different moral standard, that set by Christ. As Girard writes: "If the God of victims intervenes on their behalf in the human world, then he cannot 'succeed.' All that can happen to him is what happens to Jesus and has already happened to Job and all the prophets. . . . Rather than inflict violence, the Paraclete would prefer to suffer."[28] But what does this mean, for us, in concrete? Girard wrote: "To leave violence behind, it is necessary to give up the idea of retribution. . . . Violence is always perceived as being a legitimate reprisal or even self-defence. So what must be given up is the right to reprisals and even the right to what passes, in a number of cases, for legitimate defence."[29] In *The One by Whom Scandal Comes*, Girard clarifies: "I should make it clear that I am not an unconditional pacifist, since I do not consider all forms of defense against violence to be illegitimate."[30] The two statements are not in contradiction.[31] The right to retribution, conceived as the attempt to balance the scales in the aftermath of a suffered harm, should be given up without exception (think of Lexa's renunciation to avenge the massacre). About the right to self-defense, Girard acknowledges that there are instances of legitimate self-defense as well as a "number of cases" that may be considered as self-defense but really are not. Girard supports the legitimacy of self-defense, while at the same time warning against our propensity to mystify our acts of aggression as merely defensive.

Consistent with Girard's view, the journey of conversion requires a "hermeneutics of suspicion" of the self, which moves "from misrecognition to recognition" by understanding how desire and violence work.[32] This implies renouncing the attachment to our point of view, which we tend to consider as absolute, and open up to other perspectives. This is not easy, because, as Girard warns, we humans have a striking inclination to justify our violence as self-defense "by resorting to more and more complex casuistry in order to elude the self-criticism."[33] Self-suspicion can become a solitary internal act, whose outcomes are always uncertain. It is important to underline, therefore, how one's self is truly revealed only in certain kinds of relationship with others: in Clarke's confrontation with Josephine, for example, or in Octavia's relationship with her brother. Christian thought (Augustine's *Confessions*, for example) has often emphasized the intersubjective nature of a genuine process of self-discovery.[34]

There is also an additional problem: moral dilemmas can present themselves unexpectedly and require quick response. Consider the case of Mount Weather. Clarke has no time to perform an extensive self-analysis to determine whether her violence does or does not count as self-defense. Thus, in order to live a life of continuing *metanoia*, or conversion, the hermeneutics of the self needs to be complemented by an introjected inclination to act differently and seek nonviolent solutions. In turn, this requires developing different thinking habits. There is a form of virtue ethics that is already implicit in Girard's mimetic theory.[35] Virtue ethics, in this context, means the cultivation of a set of dispositions. Such dispositions are informed by mimetic theory to help us achieve the balancing of desire and avoid violent mimeticism. They are the disposition to consider other perspectives, the disposition to self-demystification of justifications for violence, and, more importantly, the disposition to think in a different way, or "outside the box"—where the box is the traditionally violent and sacrificial way of thinking. The cultivation of such dispositions allows us to "do better" when a dilemma presents itself. The result would then be a truly practical wisdom (*phronesis*) rather than mere knowledge (*gnosis*). *Phronesis*, in this context, refers to the virtuous circle between good judgment, not blinded by mimetic rivalry but inspired by the truth of the victim, and a character constantly self-trained to come up with non-violent solutions to moral dilemmas. One can gain knowledge about the principles of action, but the embodiment of those principles requires the experience of the world, in order for one to become capable of applying them in unforeseen circumstances.

As an example, consider the story (mentioned by d'Elbee) of the officer who, during the Paris riots of 1848, received the order to evacuate a square by firing upon the "rabble." Before giving the order, he cried: "I have received the order to fire upon the rabble; but as I perceive before me many honest people, I ask them to depart so that I may execute this order." The crowd left the square.[36] Prima facie, the officer's moral dilemma only allowed a binary choice: fire upon the crowd or disobey the order. However, he came up with another, non-violent solution. Similarly, Clarke, after the enlightening experience with her "double" Josephine, modifies the plan to rescue her people from Sanctum without killing innocent lives. Could have Clarke done something similar at Mount Weather? It is difficult to say. Perhaps there was a way to announce the irradiation of the bunker ("I've done it!") without actually doing so, and Cage, knowing that the threat was not a bluff, would have changed his mind and released the prisoners. Perhaps there was a way to release only a limited amount of radiation, without killing everybody in the bunker. We cannot know, and counterfactual history is pointless (even in fiction). However, these hypotheses point to a relevant theological issue tackled by Girard: the *katechon*. This term appears in 2 Thess. 2:1–12: "The secret power of lawlessness is already at work; but the one who now holds it back [katechon] will continue to do so till he is taken out of the way." Girard interprets the katechon as referring to the mimetic victimage, which channels uncontrolled violence through sacrifice.[37] After the Christian revelation, "*katechon* still retains a little of the old order, without which nothing would stand in the way of absolute violence."[38] Katechon "holds back violence," and therefore is to some extent unavoidable because, without it, uncontrolled violence would immediately lead to total destruction. "It must be admitted," Girard argues, "that, in order to prevent violence, we cannot do without a certain amount of violence. We are therefore obliged to think in terms of least possible violence. But, as a practical matter, it's difficult to say how little the least violence would have to be."[39] This is the dilemma at the core of *The 100*.

Clarke is a leader and she bears the responsibility to protect her group. Girard wonders: "The question of *katechon* concerns all those who have the authority to act. How must they act if they know? What is the weight to be given to sacrifices in a world in which the truth has been revealed?"[40]

Girard has no ready answers to these questions, and neither has Clarke. In Sanctum, Clarke learns that the implementation of nonviolent solutions might also come at the cost of suffering tragic losses. In fact, as a consequence of Clarke's choice about Sanctum, her mother gets killed. In this context, the expression "do better" occurs for the last time:

> **Clarke:** I tried to do better. I did . . . and then I lost my mom. Tell me it was worth it. Tell me—tell me it was worth it.
>
> **Bellamy:** We did do better. I have to believe that that matters. (6.13, "The Blood of Sanctum")

There are often no solutions that are completely devoid of violence. The effort to minimize inflicted violence and the refusal to sacrifice others might result in an increase of suffered violence. Yet, this is the journey of conversion. In Girard's view, the miraculous gift of the truth of the victim is offered to us. Only through the acceptance of that gift we can undertake the journey of conversion. Then, when the obscurity of desire and violence becomes transparent, we can finally define who we are—by doing better. A life of continuing conversion is a life lived in the belief that "doing better" actually matters.

NOTES

1. *The 100* premiered in 2014 on The CW and has run for 7 seasons, ending in 2020. Developed by Jason Rothenberg, it is loosely based on the novel series of the same name by Kass Morgan. The chapter was written at the end of Season 6.
2. René Girard, *Violence and the Sacred*, trans. P. Gregory (Baltimore: Johns Hopkins UP, 1979), 20.
3. 3.01, "Wanheda: Part One."
4. Paul Dumouchel, *The Ambivalence of Scarcity and Other Essays* (East Lansing: Michigan State UP, 2014), 27.
5. René Girard, *Resurrection from the Underground: Feodor Dostoevsky*, trans. J.G. Williams (East Lansing: Michigan State UP, 2012), 61.
6. Fyodor Dostoevsky, *The Brothers Karamazov*, trans. A.R. MacAndrew (New York: Bantam, 1970), 307.
7. 6.03, "The Children of Gabriel."
8. 6.02, "Red Sun Rising."

9. Friedrich Nietzsche, *The Gay Science*, trans. J. Nauckhoff (Cambridge: Cambridge UP, 2011), 120. See René Girard, *Battling to the End*, trans. M. Baker (East Lansing: Michigan State UP, 2010), 95.

10. René Girard, *Deceit, Desire, and the Novel*, trans. Y. Freccero (Baltimore: Johns Hopkins UP, 1965).

11. Girard, *Violence and the Sacred*, 165. On possession, see Jean-Michel Oughourlian, *The Puppet of Desire: The Psychology of Hysteria, Possession and Hypnosis*, trans. E. Webb (Stanford: Stanford UP, 1991).

12. James Alison and Wolfgang Palaver, eds., *The Palgrave Handbook of Mimetic Theory and Religion* (New York: Palgrave Macmillan, 2017), 537.

13. See Paul Valadier, "Bouc émissaire et revelation chrétienne selon René Girard," *Etudes* 357 (1982): 256; George Hunsinger, *Disruptive Grace: Studies in the Theology of Karl Barth* (Grand Rapids: Eerdmans, 2000), 28.

14. René Girard, *The Scapegoat*, trans. Y. Freccero (Baltimore: Johns Hopkins UP, 1986), 162–63.

15. René Girard, *When These Things Begin: Conversations with Michel Treguer*, trans. T.C. Merrill (East Lansing: Michigan State UP, 2014), 91.

16. Ibid., 92.

17. René Girard, *The One By Whom Scandal Comes*, trans. M.B. DeBevoise (East Lansing: Michigan State UP, 2014), 94.

18. Girard, *When These Things*, 115.

19. Girard, *The One By Whom Scandal Comes*, 62.

20. René Girard, *Evolution and Conversion: Dialogues on the Origins of Culture* (London and New York: Continuum, 2007), 198.

21. Grant Kaplan, *René Girard, Unlikely Apologist: Mimetic Theory and Fundamental Theology* (Notre Dame: Notre Dame UP, 2016), 44.

22. See Scott Cowdell, "Embodiment and Incarnation," in Alison and Palaver, eds., *The Palgrave Handbook*, 196.

23. Kaplan, *René Girard, Unlikely Apologist*, 94.

24. See the role that hallucinatory phenomena have for Arkadi, the protagonist of Dostoevsky's *The Adolescent*, which I analyzed in "Secolarizzare il Male: La Teoria Mimetica e *L'Adolescente* di Dostoevskij," in P.D. Bubbio and S. Morigi, eds., *Male e Redenzione: Sofferenza e Trascendenza in René Girard* (Turin: Edizioni Camilliane, 2008), 17–39.

25. 6.11, "Ashes to Ashes."

26. John P. Edwards, "James Alison's Theological Appropriation of Girard," in Alison and Palaver, eds. *The Palgrave Handbook*, 235.

27. Paul Dumouchel, "Naturalizing Ethics: A Girardian Perspective," *Contagion: Journal of Violence, Mimesis, and Culture* 20 (1/2013): 83.

28. René Girard, *Job: The Victim of His People,* trans. Y. Freccero (London: Athlone Press, 1987), 157.

29. René Girard, *Things Hidden since the Foundation of the World: Research Undertaken in Collaboration with Jean-Michel Oughourlian and Guy Lefort* (Stanford, CA: Stanford UP, 1987), 198.

30. Girard, *The One by Whom Scandal Comes*, 131, n3. See Andrew Bartlett, "Girard and the Question of Pacifism," *Anthropoetics* 21 (2/2016): http://anthropoetics.ucla.edu/category/ap2102/.

31. For this analysis, I am indebted to a conversation with George Dunn in the "Mimetic Theory" Facebook group.

32. Jean-Marc Bourdin, "Mimetic Theory and Self-Criticism," in Alison and Palaver, eds., *The Palgrave Handbook*, 475. Cf. Paul Ricoeur, *Freud and Philosophy*, trans. D. Savage (New Haven: Yale UP, 1970), 32–36. Elsewhere, I argued that the hermeneutics of suspicion is one of the essential elements of a *Hermeneutic Mimetic Theory*. See Paolo Diego Bubbio, *Intellectual Sacrifice and Other Mimetic Paradoxes* (East Lansing: Michigan State UP, 2018), 197ff.

33. René Girard, *I See Satan Fall Like Lightning*, trans. J.G. Williams (Ossining: Orbis Books, 2001), 159.

34. I am grateful to Chris Fleming for drawing my attention to this point.

35. The use of virtue ethics in the context of mimetic theory has been previously suggested by Frank C. Richardson and Nicolette D. Manglos, in "Reciprocity and Rivalry: A Critical Introduction to Mimetic Scapegoat Theory," *Pastoral Psychology* 62 (4/2013): 423–36.

36. Pierre d'Elbee, "Obeying Bad Orders and Saving Lives: The Story of a French Officer," *Contagion: Journal of Violence, Mimesis, and Culture* 6 (1/1999): 45.

37. See Michael Kirwan, "Mimetic Theory and the Katēchon," in Alison and Palaver, eds., *The Palgrave Handbook*, 363-9.

38. Girard, *The One By Whom Scandal Comes*, 98.

39. Ibid.

40. Ibid.

BIBLIOGRAPHY

Alison, James and Palaver, Wolfgang, eds. *The Palgrave Handbook of Mimetic Theory and Religion*. New York: Palgrave Macmillan, 2017.

Bartlett, Andrew. "Girard and the Question of Pacifism." *Anthropoetics* 21 (2/2016): http://anthropoetics.ucla.edu/category/ap2102/.

Bourdin, Jean-Marc. "Mimetic Theory and Self-Criticism." In *The Palgrave Handbook of Mimetic Theory and Religion*, edited by James Alison and Wolfgang Palaver, 471–77. New York: Palgrave Macmillan, 2017.

Bubbio, Paolo Diego. *Intellectual Sacrifice and Other Mimetic Paradoxes*. East Lansing, MI: Michigan State University Press, 2018.

———. "Secolarizzare il Male: La Teoria Mimetica e L'Adolescente di Dostoevskij." In *Male e Redenzione: Sofferenza e Trascendenza* in René Girard, edited by Paolo Diego Bubbio and Silvio Morigi, 17–39. Turin: Edizioni Camilliane, 2008.

Cowdell, Scott. "Embodiment and Incarnation." In *The Palgrave Handbook of Mimetic Theory and Religion*, edited by James Alison and Wolfgang Palaver, 193-200. New York: Palgrave Macmillan, 2017.

d'Elbee, Pierre. "Obeying Bad Orders and Saving Lives: The Story of a French Officer." *Contagion: Journal of Violence, Mimesis, and Culture* 6 (1/1999): 45–54.

Dostoevsky, Fyodor. *The Brothers Karamazov*. Translated by A. R. MacAndrew. New York: Bantam, 1970.

Dumouchel, Paul. *The Ambivalence of Scarcity and Other Essays*. East Lansing, MI: Michigan State University Press, 2014.

———. "Naturalizing Ethics: A Girardian Perspective." *Contagion: Journal of Violence, Mimesis, and Culture* 20 (1/2013): 77–86.

Edwards, John P. "James Alison's Theological Appropriation of Girard." In *The Palgrave Handbook of Mimetic Theory and Religion*, edited by James Alison and Wolfgang Palaver, 233–39. New York: Palgrave Macmillan, 2017.

Girard, René. *Battling to the End*. Translated by M. Baker. East Lansing, MI: Michigan State University Press, 2010.

———. *Deceit, Desire, and the Novel*. Translated by Y. Freccero. Baltimore, MD: Johns Hopkins University Press, 1965.

———. *Evolution and Conversion: Dialogues on the Origins of Culture*. London and New York: Continuum, 2007.

———. *I See Satan Fall Like Lightning*. Translated by J. G. Williams. Ossining, NY: Orbis Books, 2001.

———. *Job: The Victim of His People*. Translated by Y. Freccero. London: Athlone Press, 1987.

———. *The One by Whom Scandal Comes*. Translated by M.B. DeBevoise. East Lansing, MI: Michigan State University Press, 2014.

———. *Resurrection from the Underground: Feodor Dostoevsky*. Translated by J. G. Williams. East Lansing, MI: Michigan State University Press, 2012.

———. *The Scapegoat*. Translated by Y. Freccero. Baltimore, MD: Johns Hopkins UP, 1986.

———. *Things Hidden since the Foundation of the World: Research Undertaken in Collaboration with Jean-Michel Oughourlian and Guy Lefort*. Stanford, CA: Stanford University Press, 1987.

———. *Violence and the Sacred*. Translated by P. Gregory. Baltimore: Johns Hopkins University Press, 1979.

———. *When These Things Begin: Conversations with Michel Treguer*. Translated by T.C. Merrill. East Lansing, MI: Michigan State University Press, 2014.

Hunsinger, George. *Disruptive Grace: Studies in the Theology of Karl Barth*. Grand Rapids, MI: Eerdmans, 2000.

Kaplan, Grant. *René Girard, Unlikely Apologist: Mimetic Theory and Fundamental Theology*. Notre Dame, IN: Notre Dame University Press, 2016.

Kirwan, Michael. "Mimetic Theory and the Katēchon." In *The Palgrave Handbook of Mimetic Theory and Religion*, edited by James Alison and Wolfgang Palaver, 263–69. New York: Palgrave Macmillan, 2017.

Nietzsche, Friedrich. *The Gay Science*. Translated by J. Nauckhoff. Cambridge: Cambridge University Press, 2011.

Oughourlian, Jean-Michel. *The Puppet of Desire: The Psychology of Hysteria, Possession and Hypnosis*. Translated by E. Webb. Stanford, CA: Stanford University Press, 1991.

Richardson, Frank C. and Manglos, Nicolette D. "Reciprocity and Rivalry: A Critical Introduction to Mimetic Scapegoat Theory." *Pastoral Psychology 62* (4/2013): 423–36.

Ricoeur, Paul. *Freud and Philosophy*. Translated by D. Savage. New Haven, CT: Yale University Press, 1970.

Valadier, Paul. "Bouc émissaire et revelation chrétienne selon René Girard." *Etudes 357* (1982): 251–60.

Chapter 8

Mercy, Honor, and Girardian Conversion in *The Karate Kid* **and** *Cobra Kai*

Ryan Smock

John G. Avilsen's *The Karate Kid* was, in Roger Ebert's words, "one of the nice surprises of 1984—an exciting, sweet-tempered, heart-warming story with one of the most interesting friendships in a long time."[1] Released with accolades and quickly becoming a staple underdog movie, it was hailed as the story of a poor "new guy" named Daniel LaRusso rising up against school bullies to gain self-respect, social status, and the affections of a pretty girl—all because he was taught karate by quirky old Mr. Miyagi. The performances of Ralph Macchio and Pat Morita immortalized certain moments of the film, turning Daniel's training scenes into instructional models and Miyagi's mantra "wax on, wax off" into a well-known trope. But *The Karate Kid*'s influence did not end with the box office. The film's success spawned three feature-length sequels, a Nintendo game, and the contemporary YouTube series *Cobra Kai*. The series has also received academic attention, including from theologians. Recent articles have addressed links between martial arts and masculinity, specifically referencing *The Karate Kid* and *The Next Karate Kid*,[2] while theological writers have focused on Daniel's and Miyagi's disciple-sage relationship.[3] But while the educational link between Miyagi and Jesus Christ has been discussed,[4] the spiritual and ethical aspects of *The Karate Kid* and *Cobra Kai* remain largely unexplored. Interestingly, it is these aspects that reveal overtones of a deeper tragedy in this saga of ostensible success and achievement, especially when considered in the context of René Girard's idea of mimetic desire.

"DON'T TOUCH IT, PUNK!": HOW MIMETIC DESIRE PERVERTS GODLY LOVE

Daniel has just moved from Newark, New Jersey to Reseda, California, so that his mother can take a new job. Although he seems to quickly make friends, his initial welcome is short-lived. While playing soccer at a beachfront bonfire party Daniel notices Ali Mills sitting nearby. They exchange lingering looks and finally come together later in the evening. The two seem to bond, taking turns knee-bumping a soccer ball as many times as possible and eventually collapsing on the sand together in a laughing heap. Lost in romantic frivolity, neither notice Ali's ex-boyfriend Johnny Lawrence drive up on his motorcycle with his gang in tow.

"Brew time, man!" shouts one of the gang. "Who's for a warm one? Here you go."

Johnny refuses the beer. "No, I pass, man."

"Who are you kidding? You're still the ace degenerate."

"No," Johnny corrects him, "ex-degenerate, man. Eight a.m. tomorrow, I'm a senior. I've got one year to make it all work. That's what I'm gonna do. Make it work. All of it, right?"

"Hey, you must be a trendsetter, Johnny. Looks like everyone's doing something new. Take a right. Check it out."

Enraged at seeing Ali with someone else, Johnny guns his engine and races onto the beach to confront her. His gang, meanwhile, relays brief but necessary exposition. In addition to Johnny being the local bad boy, Ali was "his" until only recently, and their breakup seems to have been one-sided: "she did, he didn't." We know that Johnny wants to turn his life around because of his comments and by refusing to drink. The desperation with which he pleads to "just talk" with Ali during their confrontation, though, indicates that fixing his relationship may be a significant part of his plan to "make it all work." But Ali never caves. Every time Johnny speaks she blasts her radio to drown out his voice.

Johnny, frustrated and angry, snatches the radio and throws it to the ground.

Daniel reaches for it.

"Don't touch it, punk!" Johnny shouts.

Daniel picks up the radio anyway and, as he hands it back to Ali, Johnny rips it away. For a moment the two boys taunt each other, and then Daniel is shoved hard into the sand. Awash with rage, Daniel picks himself up and rushes in with fists swinging.

In *Deceit, Desire and the Novel*, René Girard first introduces his idea of mimetic desire, whereby one's desire is determined not by the self but through a triangular relationship with a model. For now, let us assume the desiring subject is Johnny, the model is Daniel, and the desire-object is Ali. When Johnny is alerted to Daniel's presence, he sees a model in possession of an object and forms certain *tutelary beliefs*—beliefs about the model which may or may not be true.[5] The beliefs in this case seem clear: (1) Daniel has won Ali's affection and (2) that affection is reciprocated. For Johnny, the belief that Daniel desires Ali suddenly enflames his own desire. His past relationship with Ali no doubt augments this feeling and contorts it to resemble the love they once shared. But then something weird happens: Johnny switches the logical and chronological order of his desiring, so that he believes his desire for Ali preceded Daniel's.[6] Daniel is now transformed into a rival, someone whom Johnny sees as trying to steal *his* girl. Since desire here is *internally mediated*—meaning Daniel is within Johnny's social sphere, thus close enough for them to compete over the same object—Johnny seeks to eliminate Daniel from the newly-formed love triangle.[7] His insistent pleading to "just talk" is a farce. By redirecting Ali's attention away from Daniel, Johnny moves to possess her once again.

When we consider Daniel's perspective, however, a new triangle appears. Daniel is the desiring subject, Johnny the model-rival, and Ali the desire-object. It is important to note here that when Ali sees Johnny tearing down the hillside she kicks away the soccer ball, forcing Daniel to retrieve it. This sets Daniel up as an outsider, for when he returns Johnny and Ali are already engaged in their confrontation. Now, Daniel could let the two quarrel and catch up with Ali later, but he doesn't. This is because, just like Johnny, Daniel thinks he is "in love."

The first time they see each other Daniel and Ali experience *erotic* feelings, but their connection is a far cry from the lustful attraction most associate with the term. For C.S. Lewis, eros or romantic love is part of God's natural programming. It is a pure or noble love in which people see each other "most intensely" as admirable in themselves, "important far beyond" their relation to lovers' selfish needs.[8] Nowhere does the film depict Daniel and Ali simply wanting sex from each other. Instead, they take genuine joy in the other's presence, showing deep concern for each other throughout the film and longing after and revering each other as persons. Whenever Johnny enters the picture, however, mimetic rivalry contaminates this contemplative and considerate love.

While strange to consider, negative attention is still attention. Each time Daniel sees Johnny talking with Ali throughout the film, he perceives that what should be *his* attention is now being given to someone else. Johnny therefore becomes Daniel's model and Daniel develops similar tutelary beliefs: (1) Johnny has Ali's attention and (2) Johnny desires Ali. And as before, the model quickly becomes a rival. So when Daniel witnesses Johnny throwing the radio to the ground, he is not just being a nice guy by returning it. Seeing an opportunity to insert himself between Johnny and Ali, Daniel takes full advantage of it.

This Girardian reading reveals there is no good guy or bad guy in *The Karate Kid*, as each boy believes himself to be the hero and the other to be the villain. Unknowingly implicated in the mimetic process, however, both are perhaps morally culpable for reducing Ali to a mere object. This is seen most clearly when her radio, ordinarily a meaningless item, becomes her surrogate for the two boys to fight over. No longer valued as a person, Ali functions only to serve their selfish need to prevail over one another. Because of this, and despite the overwhelming romantic cuteness of their date at Golf 'N' Stuff, Daniel is ultimately unable to stay "in love" with Ali. Now that the boys have locked horns, Daniel has eyes only for Johnny. Natural and wholesome eros is therefore first contaminated by imitative desire and then in short order twisted and perverted into obsessive hatred.[9]

"LOOK FOR REVENGE THAT WAY, START BY DIGGING TWO GRAVES": THE WHIRLWIND OF RECIPROCAL HATE

Reciprocity—the reciprocal imitation of imitated desire—is a central element of internal mediation that drives and escalates rivalrous conflict. Girard writes:

> This person who is a mediator without realizing it . . . will be tempted to copy the copy of his own desire. What was for him in the beginning only a whim is now transformed into a violent passion. We all know that every desire redoubles when it is seen to be shared. Two identical but opposite triangles are thus superimposed on each other. Desire circulates between the two rivals more and more quickly, and with every cycle it increases in intensity like the electric current in a battery which is being charged.[10]

Johnny's motivation to make things right with Ali is likely just a whim at first, a teenager's optimistic daydream, but seeing Daniel play with her on the beach transforms that whim into a raging desire. Likewise, the erotic feelings Daniel initially has for Ali mushroom the moment Johnny enters the picture. By imitating each other's perceived desire for Ali the boys generate a whirlwind of fury and ignorantly become what Girard calls the "mediator-subject" and "subject-mediator."[11] Their respective opposing triangles superimpose as soon as the radio is picked up, and each displays aggression toward the other. For Girard this aggression is fueled by *hatred*, the consumptive emotion we experience when someone "prevents us from satisfying a desire which he himself has inspired in us."[12] And as each boy shows his hate for the other, the other is increasingly vilified.

Ordinarily we like to think hatred divides, that two people who hate would prefer to avoid one another; but for Girard the opposite is the case. Mutual enmity unites Daniel and Johnny in obsessing over each other's downfall and fuels continually escalating conflicts throughout the remainder of the film. When Daniel meets with Ali during a gym class, Johnny responds by humiliating him in front of her. When Daniel hatches his plan to learn karate, thinking he can use it to defeat his rival, Johnny drives him off a road into a ditch. And when Daniel reciprocates the humiliation at a Halloween dance, Johnny gathers his friends to gang up on Daniel and savagely beat him. One of the group protests that they have done enough, that they should stop, yet Johnny argues "the enemy deserves no mercy" and aims a brutal jumping kick at Daniel's head. If not for the timely appearance of Miyagi, Daniel might have been killed right then.

"I PROMISE TEACH KARATE ... YOU PROMISE LEARN": CHRIST, BUDDHISM, AND MARTIAL ARTS

Despite the negative focus Girard usually places on mimetic desire, he maintains it is intrinsically good.[13] "The best way of preventing violence," he writes, "does not consist in forbidding objects . . . but in offering to people the model that will protect them from mimetic rivalries."[14] For him, Christ provides such a model, inviting us to imitate his desire to be a "perfect image of God."[15] What does it mean, though, to be an image of God? One example Girard gives is "detached generosity," being kind and freely giving of oneself without favoritism or prejudice.[16] "If we imitate the detached generosity of God," writes Girard, "then the trap of mimetic rivalries will never close in on us."[17] Whereas internal mediation directs subjects to think in terms of material possession and/or various forms of prestige, Christ counters this by modeling unconditional compassion and care for everyone he meets. Girard quotes Mathew 5:45, where Jesus urges his followers to follow the example of God, who "makes the sun rise on the evil and the good."[18] What is presented as an ethical injunction in the biblical text is also modeled by Jesus in practice, as he heals, preaches to, and otherwise supports anyone who approaches him, not just those in good standing. By freely showing kindness toward everyone and sharing what we have, we can stymie mimetic rivalry and violence before they can get a foothold. In one of his most extended discussions of the imitation of Christ, Girard associates it with a kind of "withdrawal"—"leaving the mimetic giddiness of worldly existence," with its "ups and downs," in which our too great identification with others draws us inexorably into rivalry with them.[19]

In Miyagi's religion of Buddhism,[20] the concepts of *Right Thought* and *Right Action* maintain approximately the same position. Zen Master Seung Sahn describes Right Thought as "not becoming attached to any views, not holding our opinion and condition and situation, and only keeping a before-thinking mind that spontaneously wants to help all beings."[21] This means we should not cling to our labels of "good" and "evil" or "with us" and "against us," as such thinking inevitably leads to divisive action. We begin preferring to benefit only ourselves and our friends and to harm (or at least hinder) our enemies. And when thought and action become divisive, the mimetic process has already taken control, for every evil we visit upon our enemies is returned. Right Action, then, first aims to act without discrimination, and then aims to abstain from taking life, stealing, lying, or committing any action which results in suffering.[22] Girard notes that the exact same abstinence is required by Mosaic commandments six through nine,[23] all of which were intended to prevent mimetic conflict. Another parallel with Christianity can be found in the concept of "Ignatian Indifference," which charges Christians to "use created things insofar as they help towards our [Christly] end, and free ourselves from them insofar as they are obstacles."[24]

Miyagi attempts to model such understandings and actions from the moment he begins teaching Daniel, which incidentally is not the famous car scene in which they officially become sensei and student. After an early encounter between Daniel and Johnny, Miyagi invites Daniel to trim a bonsai tree, telling him to clear his mind of everything but the tree and to trust the image he spontaneously creates. One lesson to be learned here is that action should not be fettered by preconception, but instead be done to promote health, growth, and beauty. This teaching is reinforced later by the deceptively menial chores Miyagi assigns to be completed at his house in the middle of a junkyard. Daniel must wash and wax dirty cars, paint a fence and house which had both fallen into disrepair, and sand a newly installed deck. Viewers and even characters within the YouTube series *Cobra Kai* misconstrue the work as muscle memory exercises, but their understanding is not entirely misplaced. Miyagi does confirm that the peculiar hand and arm motions he makes Daniel perform correspond to various defensive moves. However, as Christopher Richardson notes, all of Miyagi's teachings have multiple layers, and we are meant to pay very close attention to them.[25] The nature of the exercises, and therefore of karate itself, is neither offensive nor defensive but *restorative* and *transformative*. Daniel's various tasks do not merely strengthen his muscles and teach defense; they slowly change Miyagi's backyard—now a shared space in which both characters train—into a beautiful garden. The symbolism here cannot be ignored: Miyagi leads

Daniel through a conversion process, attempting to rid mimetic clutter and cultivate something verging on the divine. Like the practice of imitating Christ, the practice of martial arts is meant to lathe the soul.

An obvious critique is the charge that martial arts is inherently violent, that it specifically teaches people to fight. This is not a new accusation and it cannot be readily dismissed. Alex Channon notes that when it became "modernized" after World War II, martial arts became less a vehicle for philosophical education and more a means of masculinized competition. Further, he states, "sport karate" was specifically developed for competitive fighting due to its strong similarity to other Western practices such as boxing.[26] In *The Karate Kid*, John Kreese, the sensei of Johnny's Cobra Kai dojo, clearly champions this aspect. He leads students to chant that they study the "way of the fist," the way of striking first, striking hard, and showing no mercy. He then instructs them that any man who confronts them on the street or in competition is the enemy and deserves no mercy. Even Daniel conflates the martial arts with combat, as we learn in a scene where he practices balance by standing on the prow of a small boat.

"Karate's fighting," says Daniel, "you train to fight."
"That what you think?" Miyagi asks, looking quizzical.
"No," Daniel stammers, caught off guard.
"Then why train?" asks Miyagi.
". . . So that I don't have to fight," Daniel says.
"Ah," Miyagi laughs, "Miyagi have hope for you."

The answer to the charge is simple: Kreese's karate, as well as other "sport" arts specifically geared for fighting, are needlessly violent. Miyagi's karate is different.

One way to understand the nature of Miyagi's karate is perhaps to connect it with another spiritual art. Morihei Ueshiba, the founder of aikido, teaches his students in *The Art of Peace* that victory over oneself is the primary goal of training and that their focus should be on the spirit rather than the form.[27] Victory over oneself can be understood as overcoming what Seung Sahn calls "selfish desire,"[28] the root of human suffering which occupies in Buddhism roughly the same place as acquisitive mimesis in Girard.[29] Ueshiba echoes this understanding, warning aikido students away from materialistic thinking and telling them to cleanse the various body parts which can all give rise to "evil desires." The more these senses are contaminated, he states, the more disorder is created in the world, which is the greatest evil of all.[30] Girard's own thinking reflects this idea, as seen when he quotes Jesus's command to cut off the hand and put out the eye that causes one to sin.[31] Miyagi would agree. In one powerful scene he points to Daniel's head and chest, telling Daniel each time, "karate here." Then, pointing to his stomach, he says, "but karate never here." The lesson is that karate must never be used as a tool for satisfying selfish desires.

Since martial arts as Miyagi understands it is a way of thinking about and interacting with the world and its phenomena, its practice should become part of a person's essence. "Living karate" is therefore a kind of discipleship in which students imitate their masters and ancestors the same way disciples imitate Christ. "I say, you do," Miyagi tells Daniel, underscoring this very point. Masters fulfill a similar function as Christ, motivating their students to desire what they desire. If the desire for peace is modeled and cultivated, students will seek nonviolent solutions to conflicts. Ueshiba expresses such sentiment in his own teaching:

> Material martial arts fixate on physical objects. That kind of martial art is a source of endless contention because it is based on the opposition of two forces. A spiritual martial art views things on a higher level. Its base is love, and it looks at things in their totality. It is formless, and never seeks to make enemies.[32]

It is notable that Miyagi never refers to Daniel, Johnny, and the other boys as enemies, but only as friends. While some might attribute this way of speaking to ignorance or an outright denial of the relationship dynamics, we need to remember that identifying people as friends avoids the polarization—the opposition of two forces—inherent in mimetic conflict. Furthermore, by persuading the boys to limit their fighting to the karate tournament, a place governed by rules that minimize the risk of injury, Miyagi minimizes the violence they would inflict upon each other. But his best modeling is perhaps seen in *The Karate Kid: Part II*. In this film Miyagi calls his rival Sato "old friend" despite being on the receiving end of his violent behavior. Miyagi seeks reconciliation rather than conflict and even saves Sato's life when he could easily have left Sato to die.

Unfortunately, as Girard points out, even Christ's disciples initially fail to undergo the conversion from violence to peacemaking, for they are so inured to the mimetic cycle that they cannot hear his message.[33] As *The Karate Kid* approaches the inevitable showdown, one of Kreese's students illegally attacks Daniel, who is carried to a locker room where his injury can be assessed. In this climactic scene, we might expect Daniel to reveal what he learned from Miyagi and show how martial arts training helped him grow. The doctor commends him for doing so well, his mother says that she couldn't be prouder, Ali is with him rather than with Johnny, and even Miyagi acknowledges that he had a good chance to win. Daniel has every reason to feel accomplished and let the rivalry die. But he is distraught.

"Can you fix my leg, you know, with that thing you do?" he asks.

"No need fight anymore," says Miyagi, "you prove point."

"What point, that I can take a beating?" says Daniel, raising his voice. "I mean, every time I see those guys they're gonna know they got the best of me. I won't have balance that way. Not with them, not with Ali . . . not with me."

We might interpret his attitude as revealing his perseverance through hardship, his emergence from tribulation, yet that is not what it is. He is too preoccupied with what others think ("*they're* gonna know") to appropriate fully Miyagi's teachings. Even though he says he wants "balance," it is questionable whether his definition of the term matches Miyagi's. If we understand Daniel's use of the word to mean "feeling content," then of course he wouldn't have balance. No person who is enthralled by a rivalry could feel content when the scales have shifted in favor of his rival. Daniel believes at this point that he can only regain his sense of "balance" by fighting and winning against Johnny, but the victory he achieves is empty. Daniel has learned to fight, but he has not learned karate.

"I FEEL LIKE, LATELY, I'VE LET MY ANGER TAKE CONTROL": COBRA KAI AND SATANIC INFLUENCE

Cobra Kai, YouTube's sequel series to *The Karate Kid*, centers on Johnny rather than Daniel and takes place roughly thirty years later. Chronologically, however, we first see Johnny after the tournament in *The Karate Kid: Part II* when he argues with Kreese. Johnny insists he did his best, but Kreese becomes furious and locks him in a stranglehold. Although Miyagi intervenes and saves his life, Johnny cannot bear to offer thanks. He sits on the ground, hanging his head in silent shame. The next time we see Johnny is at the outset of *Cobra Kai's* pilot episode. Waking up alone in a messy studio apartment, he breakfasts on stale beer and pan-seared bologna, then gets dressed for his job as a harried fix-it man. Johnny has become the "ace degenerate" he swore he would never be. While driving to work he notices a billboard advertising the LaRusso Auto Group: "You've gotta be kidding me," he groans, "not another one."

In his analysis of Max Scheler, Girard distinguishes *hatred*, *jealousy*, and *envy*. We have already seen that hatred forms when someone models a desire that he then prevents us from satisfying. Jealousy arises when seeing our rival possess the desire-object. As for envy, Girard quotes Scheler's observation that it "occurs only when our efforts to acquire it fail and we are left with a feeling of impotence."[34] The rest of *Cobra Kai's* first episode depicts Johnny being fired, picked on by a gang of high schoolers, arrested for beating them, insulted by a stepfather who loathes him, and victimized in a hit-and-run. The various shots of Johnny trying to cope by reliving happier times are all quashed by Daniel in some way. A LaRusso Auto commercial interrupts a song on the radio. A LaRusso TV spot interrupts Johnny's favorite movie. Daniel's daughter Samantha is a passenger in the hit-and-run. Finally, adding insult to injury, Johnny's totaled Firebird is towed to a nearby LaRusso Auto retailer where Daniel works. Tyrannized by his rival's success and his own failure, Johnny boils with hatred but is powerless to do anything in response. Until, that is, Daniel accidentally reveals a weakness.

Upon seeing Johnny in his store, Daniel cannot help falling back into rivalrous aggression. It does not matter that Ali has long since fallen out of the picture: Daniel is still so obsessed with seeing Johnny defeated that he calls over two employees just to gloat in front of them. When Johnny responds in kind, though, one of the employees quickly steps in to calm things down. In an epic display of insincere graciousness, Daniel offers to cover the repairs, gives Johnny a bonsai tree, and presumes to forgive him for their past conflict. "I don't blame you for what happened back in the day," Daniel says, "I know that wasn't you. It was Cobra Kai. We're all better off without it, am I right?" By revealing a distaste for Cobra Kai, Daniel provides the means by which he can be defeated and Johnny seizes the opportunity. This time, however, Miyagi cannot mitigate their reciprocal escalation. The Christ figure has died, leaving Satanic influence to fill the void.

Satan for Girard is not a tangible being but rather a "presence" representative of the mimetic cycle. As the antithesis of Christ, Satan is the *seducer* who encourages us to override our moral scruples in pursuit of objects of desire, the *adversary* we encounter as we are drawn into mimetic rivalry and become each other's obstacles, and the *accuser* who enables us to resolve the resulting crisis, offering us salvation through the sacrifice of a single victim or *scapegoat*.[35] In the absence of a Christ figure to reveal our mimetic folly and provide a nonrivalrous model, this process repeats itself without end, consigning us to what might be called a "Girardian Hell."

The overall narrative of *Cobra Kai* follows this path. Season One rekindles the dormant rivalry between Daniel and Johnny, which later evolves into scandal and crisis. Daniel begins this new cycle by gloating over his victory. To spite Daniel, Johnny reopens the Cobra Kai dojo and posts adverts in a nearby high school. Incensed, Daniel drives Johnny away with threats. Johnny's reprisal is once again to resort to public humiliation, this time by painting a gigantic penis on one of Daniel's billboards. Daniel hits back twice as hard by conspiring to raise Johnny's rent. In the episode "Molting," however, their escalating conflict becomes contagious. Rather than peace or love, the two "masters" model hatred and conflict for their children to imitate. Daniel calls Cobra Kai "monsters" in front of his daughter Samantha and takes Johnny's son Robby as a pupil. Meanwhile, Johnny warns Miguel—his star student—away from any LaRussos by casting them as bullies. The children initially resist thinking badly of each other, but because they have already internalized their masters' teachings, several dubious events seem to confirm the other's evil nature.

While the reciprocal conflict remains contained in Season One, as their mutual aggression is once again channeled into a karate tournament, in Season Two the children become openly hostile toward one another. Slander and libel are weaponized, a "brainwashing karate cult" develops in the kids' school, and private properties are vandalized as each dojo's student body seeks to overpower and defeat the other's. In the finale, "No Mercy," reciprocal violence swirls out of control as the children explode into a brutal all-against-all melee, leaving some of them in critical condition.

"I'M TRYING TO CHANGE COBRA KAI": MERCY, HONOR, AND THE COST OF CONVERSION

Somehow, amidst the chaos and mayhem of *Cobra Kai*'s heavily webbed character arcs, it is Johnny and not Daniel who begins to rise above and turn away from the mimetic cycle. Lacking a figure such as Christ, Ueshiba, or Miyagi to reveal the Satanic mechanism and provide a model which "saves" him from the consequences of rivalry, however, it is not an easy or pleasant journey. As Johnny recruits more students the sheer weight of his responsibility becomes a catalyst for self-improvement. Miguel provokes him to clean up and fly straight(ish), and another student forces him to abandon antifeminine attitudes in favor of more accepting practices. The inclusion of "nerds" and "rejects" in his classes—the kinds of people he mocks and derides—causes Johnny to reflect critically on his own childhood and adjust his teaching style to accommodate them. So when petitioning that Cobra Kai be readmitted into the All-Valley karate tournament in Season One, Johnny truthfully asserts that his students have mediated a desire for growth and change. After his son Robby is injured by one of the Cobra Kai, though, Johnny's eyes are truly opened to the terrible ramifications of the "strike first, strike hard, no mercy" creed he teaches.

From childhood Kreese had instilled in Johnny the idea that mercy is something an enemy, understood in Girardian terms as the rival opposing the subject, never deserves. Neither the movies nor the show ever define what is meant by their use of the word "mercy." Mercy as Christians understand it means showing forgiveness, kindness, and benevolence when they are undeserved. For our purpose it would be like Johnny talking to Daniel about their situation and working out a peaceful compromise, rather than continually escalating things without regard for the consequences—especially those which affect and influence their children. But Johnny's and Kreese's view of mercy is founded on combat rather than on love, and it therefore departs significantly from this theological view. Given Johnny's and Kreese's attitudes about the word, we can perhaps extrapolate that mercy—for them—is the decision not to strike the final blow which ends the conflict.[36] It is the decision, to borrow Johnny's own language, that "pussies" make because they don't have the "balls" to finish the fight. It is the decision to allow and enable a rival to further thwart the subject's mission to take and possess what he rightfully desires. Therefore, it is, along their understanding, a notion deeply rooted in mimetic conflict, where Satanic influence urges retribution against the adversary. There is nothing Christlike about mercy as Johnny understands it. Rather than restoring or generating peace, it instead presents a devilish dilemma. On the one hand, showing an opponent mercy only propagates reciprocal escalation. But on the other hand, not showing mercy brings the Satanic cycle to completion and sets it up to be renewed.

During the Season One finale, "Mercy," Miguel's and Robby's final bout forces Johnny to face such a dilemma. As the fight goes back and forth Johnny becomes disturbed to see Miguel repeatedly target Robby's dislocated arm and leverage it to score points. Concern ripples across Johnny's face, and he pointedly ignores Miguel when he looks back for support. Johnny is too focused on his son to cheer for his student. Robby recovers after a moment, though, and lands a double-legged kick which sends Miguel sprawling to the floor. But when Robby offers to help him up, rather than take the outstretched hand, Miguel rips at the dislocated arm yet again. This agonizes Robby, and the two boys are sent to the sidelines while the injury is assessed.

"I found his weakness, sensei," Miguel says excitedly. "It's his shoulder."

"Look," says Johnny, slowly and deliberately. "I know we want to win, but it's got to be the right way. We don't have to fight dirty."

"Dirty? There's nothing dirty about winning, sensei. You taught me that."

Johnny, horrified, cannot speak.

"Don't worry," says Miguel. "I got this. No mercy."

Miguel and Robby enter the ring again and, as before, Miguel hacks away at the weakened arm. Within seconds the match is over. A trophy is presented to Cobra Kai, and everyone raises a joyous clamor. Johnny, however, looks as though the most somber funeral would be more festive.

At the outset of his next class Johnny rebukes Miguel for attacking the opponent's weakness. He then instructs that Cobra Kai is about defeating the opponent when he is at his strongest—"not when his back is turned, not when he's injured!"—and that from now on cheating and fighting dirty are "pussy moves." To punctuate his teaching, Johnny demotes all his students back to white belts (the entry-level rank in American karate) and announces, "we're starting over." Miguel, perplexed and frustrated, stays after class to question his sensei. But when Johnny tries to explain that he's teaching a lesson, Miguel only becomes more confused.

"I just don't understand," he says. "You had no problem with us attacking anyone else. Why take pity on Robby Keene?"[37]

"Look," Johnny explains, "I wasn't taught the difference between mercy and honor, and I paid the price for it. If I'm extra hard on you, it's only because you have the potential to be better than I ever was."

It seems that in witnessing Robby's suffering, Johnny finally learns to distinguish between "mercy" and "honor." While the series doesn't exactly define this loaded term either, there is nevertheless something to be said about it. While Johnny's understanding of mercy roots itself in hatred and conflict, his understanding of honor seems founded on showing respect for the other. A good bit of Christian philosophy holds that we should love and respect each other as persons, and the same idea is reflected across numerous religions and disciplines including Buddhism and aikido. It is perhaps not a far stretch to presume showing respect entails that people, even the fiercest of enemies, share certain basic truths. As it applies to *Cobra Kai*, one such truth might be the moral prohibition against continuing to beat opponents when they are down. By shifting his students' focus away from "no mercy" and toward having honor, Johnny essentially tries to do what Miyagi did so long ago: limit their violence and provide an alternative model which stops reciprocal escalation.

Johnny's attempt to revise his educational philosophy and transmit his newfound knowledge is, sadly, too little too late. Kreese reappears in Season Two and seduces most of the students into maintaining their violent interpretation of Johnny's creed, then bolsters their adversarial relationship with Daniel's dojo. Only Miguel accepts Johnny's new direction and grows along with him. But in a stunning upset, it is Miguel's choice to *not* escalate reciprocal violence during the school-wide battle in the final episode that leaves him critically harmed. Kreese uses this loss to goad the remaining students into blaming Johnny for the fracas. "Miguel's in the hospital because of you," says one student. "He showed mercy to Robby Keene because of you. If he dies, that's on you." Then, as a unified group, the students and Kreese exile Johnny and drive him from his own dojo.

Devastated that teaching honor caused Miguel's spinal injury and reeling from his expulsion, Johnny would normally have been at his most violent in this pivotal scene. It is here, however, that he finally turns away from the mimetic cycle altogether. Despite having a prime opportunity to lash out at Kreese and take vengeance on the traitorous students (as when he beat the teenagers in Season One), Johnny renounces all ties to Cobra Kai and the creed he once espoused. "This was a mistake," he says. "You want Cobra

Kai, it's yours." Johnny's conversion is reconfirmed by a final encounter with Daniel, who in the closing moments of Season Two still seems enthralled by their conflict. As the two share one last elevator ride before the credits roll, Daniel continually looks to Johnny as though he wants something to happen. Johnny, however, fixes his gaze forward. He wants nothing to do with Daniel.

GIRARDIAN LESSONS IN THE KARATE KID AND COBRA KAI

The spiritual and ethical teachings embedded in *The Karate Kid* and *Cobra Kai* are consonant with the lessons of mimetic theory and, as we have seen, they provide a surprising bridge linking Christianity, as understood by Girard, with the martial arts. Just as Don Quixote fixed his mind on Amadis of Gaul in the opening of *Deceit, Desire, and the Novel*, so too must the Christian fix his mind on Christ and the martial artist fix his mind on peace. While Johnny is finally able to do this by the end of *Cobra Kai* Season Two, because he never had a good master his new perspective comes only by suffering the fallout from modeling violence. Johnny learns, painfully and at great personal cost, to turn away from mimetic conflict and cultivate universal desires like benevolence and honor. Daniel, by contrast, had a good master but never finds peace because self-victory is more important to him than victory over the self. Even though he experiences moments of clarity where Miyagi's teachings seem to shine through, Daniel continually fails to follow his master's example and allows himself to be led by acquisitive desires like money and prestige. This ruins his relationship with Ali, causes him to misappropriate and misapply Miyagi's karate, and helps propagate the violent scandals in which all characters become immersed. "Daniel-san," Miyagi had once admonished, "never put passion before principle. Even if win, you lose." Could the lessons of mimetic theory be stated more elegantly?

NOTES

1. Roger Ebert, "The Karate Kid movie review & film summary (1984)," *rogerebert.com*, January 1, 1984.

2. U.B.A.H.N. Perera, "The Female Athlete Engaged in 'Masculine Sports'; A Study of the Depiction of Female Athleticism in Post-Title IX Western Sports Films," Department of English Language Teaching, Sabaragamuwa University.

3. Keiko Nitta, "An Equivocal Space for the Protestant Ethnic: US Popular Culture and Martial Arts Fantasia," *Social Semiotics*, 2010, 20 (4): 377–92.

4. Christopher Richardson, "The Miyagi Method: A New Vision for Religious Educators." *Journal of Beliefs & Values: Studies in Religion & Education*, 1998, 19 (2): 219.

5. Livingston, Paisley. "What is Mimetic Desire?" *Philosophical Psychology*, 7(3), 291–305. 1994. Livingston uses this term to describe beliefs which inform the subject's selection of a model. These beliefs then "determine which attributions of desire are relevant to [his] own motivation." So Johnny's beliefs about Daniel here motivate him to choose Daniel as his model. In addition to those mentioned, Johnny could very well have the beliefs that (1) "Ali will like me if I have my life together," and (2) "Ali likes Daniel, so he must have his life together." Just like Iago's belief that Othello slept with his wife Emilia, Johnny's beliefs need not be true. They only need to be conceived as true to have their effect.

6. René Girard, *Deceit, Desire, and the Novel: Self and Other in Literary Structure*. Baltimore: Johns Hopkins University Press, 1965, 11.

7. Girard, *Deceit*, 10–11.

8. C. S. Lewis, *The Four Loves* (San Francisco: HarperOne, 2017), 122.

9. Girard's interpretation of eros or romantic love seems to diverge from Lewis's. Girard often expresses skepticism of the possibility of a "natural" eros uncontaminated by mimetic desire, treating it as a "romantic myth." For Lewis, however, under the right circumstances erotic desire can be continuous with divine love: "Spontaneously and without effort we have fulfilled the law (towards one person) by loving our neighbour as ourselves. It is an image, a foretaste, of what we must become to all if Love Himself rules in us without a rival. It is even (well used) a preparation for that" (*Four Loves*, 146).

10. Girard, *Deceit*, 99.

11. Girard, *Deceit*, 99–100.

12. Girard, *Deceit*, 10–11.

13. René Girard, *I See Satan Fall Like Lightning*. Maryknoll: Orbis Books, 2001, 14; René Girard, *Evolution and Conversion: Dialogues on the Origins of Culture*. New York: Continuum International Publishing, 76.

14. Girard, *I See Satan*, 14.

15. Ibid., 13.

16. Ibid.

17. Ibid., 14.

18. Ibid.

19. René Girard, *Battling to the End: Conversations with Benoît Chantre*, trans. Mary Baker (East Lansing: Michigan State University, 2017), 123

20. While it is never clear to which specific branch of Buddhism Miyagi belongs, his comment "Buddha provide" at the All-Valley tournament indicates clearly this religious preference.

21. Seung Sahn, *The Compass of Zen*, Boston: Shambhala, 2012, Kindle ed., loc. 2049.

22. Sahn, *Compass*, 2085.

23. Girard, *I See Satan*, 7.

24. James Torrens, "The Ignatian Goal Line," *Human Development*, 2013, 34 (1), 42–43.

25. Richardson, "The Miyagi Method."

26. Alex Channon, "Western Men and Eastern Arts: The significance of Eastern martial arts disciplines in British men's narratives of masculinity," *Asia Pacific Journal of Sport and Social Science*, 2012, 1 (2).

27. Morihei Ueshiba, *The Art of Peace*, Boston: Shambhala, 2011, 86–87.

28. Sahn, *Compass*, 101–102.

29. Leo Lefebure points out this similarity in "The Roots of Violence: Society and the Individual in Buddhism and Girard," published in *Mimetic Theory and World Religions*. He draws further connection to Girard by pointing out the Buddhist focus on interconnectivity in all things, and by illustrating that desire arises specifically in relation to others.

30. Ueshiba, *Art of Peace*, 57–58.

31. Girard, *I See Satan*, 17. Some would claim Girard uses Jesus's (possibly hyperbolic) statement here to press the importance of guarding against scandal—the situation resulting from one or more people having their desires thwarted because they cannot overcome the rival, or because everyone in a group prevents each other from getting the desire-object. But such scandal only results from the "disorder," understood as rivalrous conflict, created by acquisitive mimesis. It is this disorder which propels Daniel and Johnny into scandal.

32. Ueshiba, *Art of Peace*, 31–32.

33. Girard, *I See Satan*, 16–17.

34. Girard, *Deceit*, 12–13.

35. Girard, *I See Satan*, 31–33.

36. Johnny's and Kreese's view of mercy is founded on combat rather than love, and it therefore departs significantly from the theological view of mercy shared by many Christians. Mercy as Christians understand it is the showing of forgiveness, kindness, and benevolence particularly when they are undeserved. For our purpose it would be like Johnny talking to Daniel about their situation and working out a peaceful compromise, rather than continually trying to one-up Daniel without regard for the consequences.

37. Miguel does not know at this point that Robby is Johnny's son.

BIBLIOGRAPHY

Channon, Alex. "Western Men and Eastern Arts: The Significance of Eastern Martial Arts Disciplines in British Men's Narratives of Masculinity," *Asia Pacific Journal of Sport and Social Science 1*, no. 2-3 (2012): 111–127.

Ebert, Roger. "The Karate Kid Movie Review & Film Summary (1984)," rogerebert.com, January 1, 1984. https://www.rogerebert.com/reviews/the-karate-kid-1984.

Girard, René. *Battling to the End: Conversations with Benoît Chantre*. Translated by Mary Baker. East Lansing: Michigan State University, 2017.

———. *Deceit, Desire, and the Novel: Self and Other in Literary Structure*. Baltimore: Johns Hopkins University Press, 1965.

———. Evolution and Conversion: Dialogues on the Origins of Culture. New York: Continuum International Publishing.

———. I See Satan Fall Like Lightning. Maryknoll, NY: Orbis Books, 2001. Kindle.

Lefebure, Leo. "The Roots of Violence: Society and the Individual in Buddhism and Girard," *Mimetic Theory and World Religions*. East Lansing: Michigan State University Press, 2018.

Lewis, C. S. *The Four Loves*. San Francisco: HarperOne, 2017.

Livingston, Paisley. "What Is Mimetic Desire?" *Philosophical Psychology* 7, no. 3 (1994): 291–305.

Nitta, Keiko. "An Equivocal Space for the Protestant Ethnic: US Popular Culture and Martial Arts Fantasia." *Social Semiotics* 20, no. 4 (2010): 377–392.

Perera, U.B.A.H.N. "The Female Athlete Engaged in 'Masculine Sports': A Study of the Depiction of Female Athleticism in Post-Title IX Western Sports Films," *Department of English Language Teaching*, Sabaragamuwa University.

Richardson, Christopher. "The Miyagi Method: A New Vision for Religious Educators." *Journal of Beliefs & Values: Studies in Religion & Education 19*, no. 2 (1998): 219–230.

Sahn, Seung. *The Compass of Zen*. Boston: Shambhala, 2012.

Torrens, James. "The Ignatian Goal Line," *Human Development* 34, no. 1 (2013): 42–43.

Ueshiba, Morihei. *The Art of Peace*. Boston: Shambhala, 2011.

Chapter 9

The Pleasures and Perils of Revenge

Sons of Anarchy *and Girard*

George A. Dunn

The destructive fury of revenge, with its unforeseen and often-disastrous consequences, is one of the principle themes of *Sons of Anarchy*, the critically-acclaimed television series created by Kurt Sutter, which ran for seven seasons on the FX network. From 2008 to 2014, *Sons of Anarchy* portrayed the moral travails of Jackson "Jax" Teller, initially vice-president and later president of the outlaw Sons of Anarchy Motorcycle Club, Redwood Original, often referred to by its acronym SAMCRO. The drama is set in the fictional Southern California town of Charming, where the club has solicited the good will of their fellow citizens by protecting the town from outsiders and less public-spirited local criminals. Meanwhile, they dominate most of the town's public servants through a combination of intimidation and graft. The club generates much of its income through a lucrative but perilous gun-running and smuggling business, which routinely brings it into conflict with both law-enforcement agencies and rival gangs and MCs (motorcycle clubs). Over the course of the show's run, Jax works diligently and, in the end, successfully to extricate SAMCRO from the volatile world of illegal gun-running, finally securing its long-term financial security through the less dicey revenue stream the club receives from its legitimate pornography and escort businesses.

The criminal underworld SAMCRO inhabits is one of blood feuds and deadly contests of honor. It resembles the archaic world in which René Girard believes our ancestors lived before the creation of legal systems to adjudicate their conflicts, a world constantly "haunted by the specter of vengeance."[1] To the extent SAMCRO leaves behind this violent world and sets up shop in the hedonistic precincts of carnal pleasure and bourgeois profiteering, we might applaud their moral progress. Measured against the recent arc of history, SAMCRO may be just catching up with the rest of us. According to Girard, our liberal market society, with all of the legal protections it affords us, rescued us from the violent world of our ancestors with its blood-soaked battles for glory, redirecting mimetic rivalry along more benign channels, such as economic competition.[2] The love of lucre and the pursuit of tawdry pleasures may be less noble than risking life and limb for glory, but they're also less likely to get us killed. On one level, then, *Sons of Anarchy* might be viewed as a parable about finding a path to peace by building on what the political philosopher Leo Strauss called the "low but solid ground" of our baser passions.[3] But, alas, the story isn't that simple.

JAX'S NOT-SO-DULL REVENGE

Transitioning from guns to porn might seem like a "happy ending" for SAMCRO—if you will forgive the double entendre—but the story is in fact a tragedy, incorporating elements from both William Shakespeare and classical sources to tell the tale of a man whose infatuation with violence seals his doom. Sutter has acknowledged drawing inspiration from Shakespeare's classic tale of murder and revenge, *The Tragedy of Hamlet, Prince of Denmark*, prompting some to christen the show "*Hamlet* on Harleys." Early seasons established Jax as an updated version of the gloomy Danish prince, haunted by the ghost of his murdered father John "J. T." Teller, the former president of the club who had tried unsuccessfully to pivot the club away from outlaw enterprises toward more legitimate occupations. *Sons of Anarchy*'s Claudius-figure is Clay Morrow, Jax's stepfather and J.T.'s successor as SAMCRO president. Clay married Jax's mother Gemma Teller Morrow after the two of them murdered J.T.

In another parallel with *Hamlet*, Jax receives regular dispatches from the "other side" through reading J.T.'s unpublished manuscript, *The Life and Death of Sam Crow: How the Sons of Anarchy Lost Their Way*, which Jax accidentally finds in storage in the pilot episode. Over the next several seasons, Jax learns the truth about his father's death and in due course avenges his murder. In the final scene of *Hamlet*, the prince runs his sword through King Claudius, punishing the man who usurped the kingdom. Most of the other characters also bite the dust along the way and as the curtain falls the stage is littered with bodies, including Hamlet's, collateral damage of his own vengeance. True to the Shakespearean script, Jax also racks up a staggering body count on his way to exacting revenge on J.T.'s murderer. But, unlike Hamlet's killing of Claudius, Jax didn't execute Clay solely as an act of private revenge but as an agent of the club, which had unanimously voted for this meeting between Clay and Mister Mayhem, the club's euphemistic expression for murder. And, in another departure from *Hamlet*'s dramatic template, Jax survives this showdown, which occurs near the end of season six, to paint the final season in even more blood. The final episode of the penultimate season, "A Mother's Work," determines the course of the final season, as the murder of Jax's beloved wife Tara Knowles sets him again on a path of vengeance.

In his essay "Hamlet's Dull Revenge," Girard argues that Shakespeare had a "double goal in mind" in writing *Hamlet*. While crafting a crowd-pleasing tale of vengeance to achieve "the dramatic success that is necessary to his own career as a dramatist," he also sought to "denounce revenge theatre and its works with the utmost daring."[4] The sheer length and, on Girard's view, "tedium" of the play, resulting from Hamlet's endless vacillations and delays in carrying out the directives of his father's ghost, reflects Shakespeare's own distaste for the conventions of revenge theater. With its long run of seven seasons, *Sons of Anarchy* also postponed the death of its villain for what seemed to some like an inordinate length of time, but there were always enough car chases and gunfights to ensure it never became "dull." In fact, it was the rare action-oriented television series that was not only emotionally riveting but also intellectually stimulating.[5] And, like Shakespeare's *Hamlet*, one of the things it was capable of stimulating was philosophical and theological reflection on the pleasures and perils of revenge.

In the standard revenge tragedy, vengeance was required of the protagonist as an inexorable moral imperative, a sacred duty owed to the innocent victim. Everything else, including the demands of self-preservation and the hero's qualms about shedding blood, were expected to take a backseat to his overriding obligation to become heaven's chosen instrument for punishing the guilty. Even when his single-minded pursuit of his mission left a trail of carnage in its wake, the hero could still count on the audience's sympathy so long as everything done was in obedience to the imperative of vengeance. But revenge can cloak itself in the mantle of justice only if a couple of crucial conditions are met: first, the victim whose death is being avenged must really be innocent and, second, the alleged perpetrator must really be guilty. Absent these conditions, the act of revenge can't offer the audience the emotional and moral catharsis that comes from witnessing a grave moral wrong being redressed. It is timeless truth, one that explains the enduring appeal of tales of revenge, that retaliatory violence often feels right and can even be relished when framed as a straightforward case of good versus evil—but less so otherwise. And it's precisely this sort of relish that Sutter, following in Shakespeare's footsteps, denied his audience in the final season of *Sons of Anarchy*.

Shakespeare violates the first of these conditions, the innocence of the victim. As Girard points out, "It cannot be without a purpose that Shakespeare suggests that the old Hamlet, the murdered king, was a murderer himself. However nasty Claudius may look, he cannot look nasty enough if he appears in the context of previous revenge."[6] If the one whose death must be avenged isn't simply the innocent victim of pure, unprovoked malice, but rather someone who, from the perpetrator's point of view, had it coming, then the act of vengeance begins to look less like righting a grievous wrong and more like perpetuating an ongoing cycle of violence. In Girard's analysis, Hamlet has such a notoriously hard time warming to his task precisely because he's burdened with insights that make it impossible for him to frame the conflict in terms of the simplistic dichotomy of good versus evil that ordinarily gives the demand for vengeance its moral urgency. As Girard writes, "the crime by Claudius looks to [Hamlet] like one more link in a long chain, and his own revenge will look like still another link, perfectly identical to all the other links."[7]

Whereas Hamlet suffers from a crippling surfeit of insight, Jax's problem when he sets out to avenge Tara is just the opposite—he warms to his task too quickly. From a moral perspective, an even bigger problem is that Sutter violates the second condition that must be met for a revenge tragedy to deliver a satisfying moral catharsis, the necessity that the target of the revenge be really guilty of the crime for which he's being punished. Jax believed gangster Henry Lin, head of the Lin Triad, ordered the hit on Tara. However, though Lin is guilty of some truly horrible atrocities—like virtually everyone else that SAMCRO deals with on a regular basis and, indeed, the members of the club themselves—sending his henchman to kill Tara is *not* one of them. Flouting the conventions of the revenge tragedy in these ways strips away the moral sheen that beautifies what is otherwise an ugly deed. But to understand how violence can acquire this beautiful luster in the first place, we need to turn from Shakespeare to the Bible, specifically to the biblical book of Leviticus.

THE EYE OF REVENGE

"Anyone who maims another shall suffer the same injury in return: fracture for fracture, eye for eye, tooth for tooth; the injury inflicted is the injury to be suffered" (Leviticus 24: 19–20). So says the *lex talionis*, the law of retaliation, which is often expressed in the more compressed formula of "an eye for an eye" to accent its gruesomeness.[8] It's unlikely that Jax Teller ever read Leviticus, yet he seems to have a solid instinctive grasp of the underlying principle that the ideal punishment should be a perfect mirror of the crime. Perhaps that's because the *lex talionis* is not unique to the biblical tradition but shows up in many ancient legal codes, an indication of its universal, intuitive appeal.[9] According to Jewish tradition, the lex talionis is part of the law given by God to the Jewish people through the prophet Moses, so no doubt the writers thought it would be a delicious irony for the prophet's own namesake and SAMCRO enemy Moses Cartwright to find himself on the receiving end of "eye for an eye" justice as doled out by SAMCRO. In the seventh season episode "Faith and Despondency," SAMCRO ambushed Moses and his crew, mowing them down in a hail of bullets that left only Moses alive. Jax then grabbed Moses by the throat and proceeded to unleash some "Old Testament justice" on him,[10] ripping one of Moses's eyes from its socket in retaliation for the eye he took from SAMCRO member Bobby Munson. Then, as other members of the club pinned Moses to the ground, Chibs Telford sawed off the fingers of Moses's left hand, once again mirroring what he had done to Bobby. Finally, to cap off this showcase of poetic justice, Jax put a bullet through Moses's skull, ending his life in the same way Bobby's ended.

This episode offers a graphic—indeed literal—enactment of the *lex talionis*. There's no evidence that the biblical traditions ever consistently favored such a literal interpretation of the law of retribution, but neither SAMCRO nor the outlaw world to which they belong have ever been known for casuistic subtlety. And this episode is not the first time that SAMCRO or its members have been the agents of some punishment that was intended to mimic perfectly the crime. In the final episode of season three, Opie Winston placed Agent June Stahl in the driver's seat of her vehicle, instructing her to put her hands on the wheel so that she would be in the same position as his wife Donna when she died from a bullet to the back of her head as a direct result of Stahl's actions. "This is how she felt," he tells Stahl, before splattering her brains on the windshield ("NS").

Jax also wants the ones he holds responsible for the death of his own wife, Tara Knowles, to experience exactly the same pain they inflicted. "What you did to her, how you did it—I'm going to make sure you feel that," Jax told Chris Dun, the Lin Triad member whom Jax mistakenly believed had murdered Tara. After torturing Dun for a while, Jax finished him off with a carving fork thrust into the back of his head, the same utensil used to deliver the same fatal wound that Tara suffered—a gruesomely literal compliance with the Leviticus 24:19 dictate: "Anyone who maims another shall suffer the same injury in return" ("Black Widower"). And the crowning finish of Jax's original plan to destroy Henry Lin was for him to experience the same devastating grief that Jax had suffered when he lost the love of his life. After ruining Lin's business, Jax planned to "look around his table, his men, his family, ask him who he wants spared. First person he points to, that's who I'm killing. And then everyone else he cares about. I'm going to let him live in the agony of that for a little while. And then I'm going to end him, as slowly and painfully as possible" ("Toil and Till").

Lin got wind of Jax's plans before he could carry them to completion, which was enough to unleash Lin's own crew of Furies against the club. After SAMCRO orchestrated an attack on a Lin Triad whorehouse, roughing up both clients and staff, Lin sent his men to slaughter the girls of Diosa Norte, the escort service owned by SAMCRO friend and business associate Nero Padilla. A whore for a whore. The title of this episode, "Poor Little Lambs," implicitly identifies these innocent victims with the Paschal Lamb sacrificed at the first Passover, whom the apostle Paul later compared to Christ.[11] But this brutal act wasn't the first time innocent victims on *Sons of Anarchy* had been substituted for the eyes and teeth that the lex talionis demands as payment. When Agent Stahl killed Cameron Hayes's son Edmund and framed Gemma for the murder, the anguished father flew to Jax's house in a grief-stricken rage. Threatening Jax's infant son Abel with a kitchen knife, Cameron mused out loud: "A son for a son seems about right" ("Na Trioblóidí"). And, finally, there's Damon Pope, another SAMCRO nemesis, whose daughter Veronica was accidentally killed by member Tig Trager. "Now you feel my pain," he told Tig before immolating his daughter Dawn and forcing him to witness the holocaust ("Sovereign"). A daughter for a daughter. All of these horrific episodes exhibit, in addition to *lex talionis*, a kind of "penal substitution," in which one person is made to suffer a penalty that rightfully ought to fall on another. It's how many American Protestants interpret the significance of Christ's crucifixion,[12] but Girard protests that such an interpretation stands truth on its head, since sacrificing innocents is what human beings do, not what God does.[13] As the Girardian theologian Michael Hardin observes, to accept such a view of God makes us "little different from archaic sacrificial devotees of Moloch," the Canaanite god associated with child sacrifice.[14] Moloch would feel right at home in Charming.

THE BEAUTIFUL SYMMETRY OF REVENGE

It would be crude in the extreme to take *Sons of Anarchy*'s many direct and indirect biblical allusions as the basis for our theology, but it would also be naïve to deny that the Bible is saturated in retributive violence, cover to cover, in a way that brings it uncomfortably close to the world of *Sons of Anarchy*. For Girard, the apparent contradiction between the biblical praises of "mercy"—a theme that runs from the Pentateuch to the Psalms to the

Gospels—and the stream of blood that runs through so many of its narratives reflects the Bible's emergence from a violent archaic world, the same world in which nearly all human beings lived for most of our history. Perhaps we moderns have not strayed as far from that world as we'd like to believe. Though we in the modern West may associate "eye for an eye" justice with the dark side of a biblical tradition that we in our sophistication have superseded, Girard reminds us that "the law of retribution is very real; it has its origins in the reality of human relationships."[15] The Bible, he argues, is "a process underway, a text in travail; it is not a chronologically progressive process, but a struggle that advances and retreats."[16] And what it is struggling against is an archaic worldview whose traces and lineaments can be discerned on its own pages, giving voice to a morality that upholds violence as the ultimate currency in which all debts must be paid.[17] The outlaw subculture to which SAMCRO belongs is an atavistic enclave of that same archaic world within the more peaceful precincts of modernity, a reminder of what our world would be like were our own archaic instincts not institutionally restrained. Like it or not, Jax Teller's blood flows in all of our veins, shaping our moral sensibilities in ways we may find uncomfortable to acknowledge.

As ugly and barbaric as the *lex talionis* may be when innocents become substitutionary victims, many still find something deeply satisfying about the symmetry and balance that the Levitical principle of "eye for an eye" represents. After all, it's not for nothing that Jax chose to take out Moses's eye, rather than inflict an equivalent amount of pain in some other manner. There's something about such a punishment that feels fitting and right to many people, even as it makes us squirm. Only the most naïve psychological theory would deny what a little honest introspection reveals—that we find retribution satisfying, all the more so when the punishment gives culprit a "taste of his own medicine." It seems unlikely that the pleasure we derive from payback that bears the signature of the original offense is reducible to some utilitarian calculus focused solely on its deterrent effect. The satisfaction we experience feels *morally* right—think of Immanuel Kant's term *Selbstzufriedenheit*, which denotes the feeling of being pleased with oneself for acting in accord with the moral law—even though we normally judge the infliction of harm or injury on others to be morally wrong.[18]

For Girard, punitive retaliation is just a special case of the universal human practice of reciprocity, rooted in our natural and often irresistible reflex to imitate others. Reciprocity makes social cooperation on a wide scale possible by giving content to our moral emotions of anger and gratitude, which regulate many of our most important dealings with others. It is our mimetic proclivities and the patterns of reciprocity they establish that make us naturally inclined to reward favors and requite harms.[19] What Girard calls "good reciprocity" is displayed when Jax hands Sheriff Vic Trammel an envelope containing his usual bribe fattened with "a little gratitude bump, a 'thank you'" for having helped SAMCRO in a particularly sticky situation ("AK-51"). Not only its cozy relationship with the local sheriffs, but most of the other alliances that allow SAMCRO to survive in its dangerous world are maintained through such ongoing practices of "good reciprocity." Indeed, as Girard reminds us, "There would be no society at all if there were not a lot of good reciprocity"—and that includes the society of criminals. But, unlike the overt palm-greasing that goes on between SAMCRO and their corrupt accomplices in the local constabulary, most good reciprocity is "not readily visible."[20] We often take pains to disguise it as something else, making it appear more like an exchange of gifts than a payment for services, since, according to Girard, we instinctively fear that good reciprocity could devolve into revenge, its "bad" twin, if openly avowed.[21] "In revenge," on the other hand, "you try to make it as visible as possible." You want the person on the receiving end to know exactly what's happening to him and *why*—and nothing makes that more palpable than giving back just what he dished out in the very same coin.

When the punishment almost perfectly mirrors the crime, we often refer to it as "poetic justice," which suggests that there's something not only morally gratifying but also aesthetically pleasing about the right punishment delivered in just the right way. It's not entirely unlike the satisfaction we derive from a well-proportioned piece of art, such as the Grim Reaper tattoo emblazoned on Jax's back. In both cases, the elements are beautifully balanced and symmetrical, related to each other in a way that feels orderly and right. Both the Reaper and "eye for an eye" retribution are grim, but that doesn't mean they can't both in their own ways be sources of pleasure.

No doubt the idea of deriving aesthetic pleasure from a well-executed act of vengeance strikes many as barbaric, though the writers of *Sons of Anarchy* probably haven't misread the aesthetic sensibilities of their audience if they've concluded that hoisting villains on their own petards is a crowd-pleaser. But isn't it a sordid pleasure that civilized people should renounce? If so, then we would also have to renounce Dante Alighieri's *Divine Comedy*, the original "scared straight" field trip, which features a grisly compendium of poetic justice that would probably make even self-mutilating SAMCRO member Otto Delany squirm a little bit. The barbarity of the justice is necessitated by the horror of the crimes. And, edifying tours of hell aside, the ideal of making the punishment "fit" the crime is in fact at the heart of our ordinary conception of justice. Like the rabbinic tradition that softened the *lex talionis* by allowing other forms of compensation,[22] we don't often literally demand an eye for an eye, but our criminal justice system does prescribe certain ranges of penalties for certain types of crimes, scaled according to the gravity of the offense. Even if we can't replicate all of the specifics of the pain and injury the perpetrator inflicted on his victim, we at least want him to experience something of proportionate intensity. In this way, a just punishment is said to restore the "balance" disrupted by the crime, an idea represented in the familiar image of Lady Justice holding aloft her scales, symmetrically arrayed when the punishment is just as weighty as the offense. Justice, wrote Kant in *The Philosophy of Law*, "is just the principle of equality, by which the pointer on the scale of justice is made to incline no more to one side than to the other."[23]

But can we really compare the bloody vengeance dished out by SAMCRO and other denizens of their outlaw world with our exalted ideal of justice? No doubt the various federal, state, and local law-enforcement agencies with which SAMCRO has tangled have an opinion on the matter. Their own violence, they would surely claim, is just and legitimate because it has the lawful sanction of the state, whereas SAMCRO's outlaw vengeance, lacking any such sanction, is unjust and criminal. Such a view comes very close to Girard, for whom law is based on "the always arbitrary but culturally real distinction between legitimate and illegitimate violence,"[24] though the agents of law enforcement might be reluctant to admit that the distinction is arbitrary. Girard's main point, however, is that even though justice and revenge may fall on opposite sides of the law, they still obey the same logic. "Our penal system operates according to principles of justice that are in no real conflict with the concept of revenge," he insists. "The same principle is at work in all systems of violent retribution. Either the principle is just, and justice is therefore inherent in the idea of vengeance, or there is no justice to be found anywhere."[25] Disconcerting as this claim may be, *Sons of Anarchy* gives us reasons to believe it's right.

THE REVENGE OF THE LAW

Some philosophers want to draw a hard line with retributive justice on one side and outlaw revenge on the other. Revenge, in their minds, has nothing to do with just retribution, for only the latter is guided by a concern for proportion and balance. "Retribution sets an internal limit to the amount of the punishment, according to the seriousness of the wrong," writes Robert Nozick, "whereas revenge internally need set no limit to what is inflicted."[26] In contrast to the rational and dignified Lady Justice with her scales that measure out penance in the right proportions, Nozick seems to imagine the agent of vengeance as driven by an insatiable, uncontrollable, and utterly reckless desire to inflict a limitless amount of harm on his adversary. The image that comes to mind is a rampaging Tig Trager crashing his car full-speed into an outdoor café full of bystanders in an attempt to kill the rival gang leader whom he held responsible for an attack on SAMCRO's president, Clay Morrow. Nozick concedes that "the revenger may limit what he inflicts for external reasons"[27]—such as the need to hightail it to safety in the aftermath of the aforementioned crash—but he claims that the limits of what one might do in pursuit of revenge are never set by the nature of the offense, only by other extraneous considerations.

But while Nozick's description of the revenge-seeker may be a good fit for emotionally overwrought types like Tig, there are plenty of instances when members of SAMCRO sought revenge in ways that were constrained by a sense of measure. Clay slept with Cherry to punish Half-Sack Epps for his ill-considered testimonial to Gemma's womanly allure ("Clay's old lady gave me a serious MILF chubby"), a punishment that was, in Clay's mind at least, proportionate to the offense and sufficient to settle the score ("Patch Over"). And it even had a bit of an "eye for an eye" quality to it, since it involved paying back in kind what Clay undoubtedly felt was a disrespectful trespass on his own sexual domain. It was certainly an act of revenge, but Clay didn't seek to do unlimited harm to Half-Sack. Contrary to Nozick's belief that a concern for balance and proportion is entirely foreign to the desire for revenge, one can seek revenge as Clay did, with very specific goals in mind and without tossing every inhibition to the wind.

Nozick rightly insists that revenge, unlike the impersonal administration of justice by the courts, is usually fueled by a passion that derives pleasure from the suffering of its target, but even that's not always true. The pursuit of revenge can be experienced as a disagreeable burden or even as an abhorrent duty, as we witness in the final episodes of *Sons of Anarchy*. Having learned that it was *not* Lin's henchmen, but rather his own mother Gemma who killed Tara and then concocted a lie that not only led to the mutilation and death of Bobby Munson but seriously imperiled the club's very existence, Jax felt a sacred duty to Tara and his club to avenge what had been done—even if resulted in a self-inflicted "wound that's too deep to heal," as Nero warned him. There could be no repeat of the personal satisfaction that Jax took in bringing down Lin. In the end, Sutter's final season dramatic template turned out not to be Hamlet after all, but rather Euripides' tragedy of *Orestes*, whose eponymous protagonist kills his mother Clytemnestra to avenge the death of his father and is then driven mad by the horror of his deed. The pleasure people may take in revenge must not blind us to the fact that it can also be felt as a painful, even odious, moral responsibility. It is for this reason that Girard speaks of "the terrible obligations of vengeance," from which our legal system relieves us by taking that obligation upon itself.[28]

Still, despite its commonalities with the justice dispensed by the courts, denizens of the modern world have become extremely uncomfortable with the idea of vengeance being doled out by some private individual. It can't be because revenge is wholly irrational, lacking all limit and proportionality, which we've seen is not true. There are, of course, the innocent casualties, who have made a substantial contribution to the body count on *Sons of Anarchy*, but perhaps some of that bloodshed could have been avoided if the avengers had directed their wrath at the responsible parties rather than blameless bystanders. But what about the other problem illustrated by *Sons of Anarchy*, namely, that without the safeguards afforded by due process, it's too easy to go after the wrong guy? That's undoubtedly true, but our judicial system also makes mistakes, prosecuting the innocent (such as Tara Knowles, who's hounded by the law for a crime she didn't commit) and protecting the guilty (such as Agent Josh "Stalker-Boy" Kohn, who suffers no legal consequences for his obstinate defiance of the protection order to stay away from Tara). Often, the victim is in a better position than the courts to identify the real offender, though admittedly SAMCRO has a pretty poor track record on that score.

Girard helps us to identify the real danger of private vengeance. "Why does the spirit of revenge, whenever it breaks out, constitute such an intolerable menace?" he asks. "Vengeance professes to be an act of reprisal, and every reprisal calls for another reprisal."[29] When both parties to a conflict feel they're in the right, as they nearly always do, the act whereby one party seeks to settle the score becomes for his adversary a new source of grievance. As philosopher Elizabeth Wolgast has put it, the two sides employ "different arithmetics," so, though both may be aiming at symmetry, the result is simply a steady escalation of violence.[30] However, when a legal system is in place to punish on behalf of victims and has enough violence at its disposal to deter any retaliation, then "an act of vengeance is no longer avenged; the process is terminated, the danger of escalation averted."[31] Those of us who live under the protection of the law can hardly imagine what life was like in archaic societies that didn't enjoy its benefits—or in those present-day islands of the archaic world represented by the criminal underworld.

FROM REVENGE TO SACRIFICE AND BEYOND

Sons of Anarchy depicts one way the danger of escalation was averted in the archaic world—through scapegoating, which Girard believes evolved into the practice of ritual sacrifice that seems to have been a feature of every archaic religion. He observes that sacrifice can be an effective way of safely discharging the community's violence, since "sacrifice is primarily an act of violence without risk of vengeance," sharing with legal retribution the fact that it is an act of the community as a whole.[32] That's precisely why Jax's revenge on Clay did not have the same catastrophic consequences for SAMCRO as

Hamlet's revenge on Claudius had for Denmark. The entire club had a hand in dispatching their former president, making this act of vengeance more closely resemble another one of Shakespeare's memorable murders, the assassination of Julius Caesar in the play that bears his name. The collective murder of the Roman dictator by a band of conspirators exemplifies the workings of what Girard calls the "scapegoat mechanism," in which a beleaguered and splintered community finds renewed unity and purpose by directing all of its pent-up hostility against a single individual, a hapless "scapegoat" saddled with the blame for all of their troubles. "Nothing unites men like a common enemy," he writes,[33] while emphasizing that a collective murder can reconcile a community only when everyone is on board with it, there is unanimous agreement as to the scapegoat's guilt, and the victim has no allies who could emerge later to avenge his murder.

Clay's murder satisfies every item on the checklist, making him an ideal scapegoat for a club that had recently gone through hell and needed an outlet for its anger. Jax may not have ever read *Julius Caesar* or even heard of Girard, but he clearly orchestrated the killing of Clay in a deliberate fashion to serve as a watershed for SAMCRO, a cathartic repudiation of what it had become under its former leadership. Embodying all that had gone wrong with the club, Clay was offered up as a ritual sacrifice whose execution served as a cleansing purgative and a prelude to a new beginning. Like the slaying of the Roman tyrant, it was designed to be a "founding murder" that would inaugurate a new order.[34] And it almost worked.

Sacrifice and scapegoating are the archaic (or outlaw) methods of tamping down the social conflagrations that unrestrained vengeance always threatens to ignite. Retributive justice impersonally administered by the courts is their more civilized successor. However, these punitive measures don't exhaust our options for addressing conflict. There is yet another possibility, though it is most conspicuous in *Sons of Anarchy* by its absence. In his book, J.T. had lamented the spiritual toll the outlaw life had taken on him, reporting that it had robbed him of "basic human graces. The most obvious was forgiveness. If I was wronged, by anyone, in or out of the club, I had to be compensated—money or blood. There was no turning the other cheek" ("Smite"). Turning the other cheek, forgoing the right to retaliation, is explicitly introduced by Jesus in his Sermon on the Mount as a new commandment, superseding the Mosaic *lex talionis* (Matthew 5: 38–39).[35] Of such forgiveness, Girard writes:

> Without ever leaving its narrative framework the biblical account pursues a reflection on violence whose radicalism is revealed at the point where pardon replaces the obligatory vengeance. It is only this pardon, this forgiveness, that is capable of stopping once and for all the spiral of reprisals, which of course

are sometimes interrupted by unanimous expulsions, but violently and only temporarily.[36]

Though forgiveness is commanded only in the New Testament, even in some of the oldest books of the Bible, the ones where the archaic world is most starkly on display, this possibility of forgoing revenge in favor of pardon is showcased. Sold into slavery by his resentful brothers but then, through a wild roller coaster ride of narrative twists, rising to the rank of vizier of Egypt, the Jewish patriarch Joseph finds himself in a position to punish his brothers but pardons them instead, even weeping with joy at being reunited with then.[37]

Alas, that's normally not an option for an outlaw like Jax Teller. Lacking Joseph's power as a head of state, Jax has much more to fear from his enemies and thus more to risk in extending forgiveness. As J. T. reminds us in his manuscript, "once you move your life off the social grid, you give up the safety that society provides" ("Seeds"). Consequently, Jax's survival is bound up with an internalized code of honor that requires him to project an image of strength and bravado that signals he's nobody's chump. On the plus side, this code dictates being trustworthy and brave, qualities that make him someone others will seek out as a reliable ally. For without such allies, there's no way to survive in a lawless world. On the other hand, honor demands a swift reprisal to any insult or injury. You *must* punish any show of disrespect to restore your tarnished honor, for otherwise you not only invite further abuse, but also send a message that it would be worthless to enter an alliance with a you.[38] For Jax to relinquish completely his right to revenge would be tantamount to surrendering his life to his enemies—at least as long he remains a part of the archaic or outlaw world.

The forgiveness Jax can't extend to others is also the forgiveness he sees himself as ineligible to receive. "This is who I am. I can't change," he confesses in a final soliloquy spoken to his departed father ("Papa's Goods"), declaring himself beyond redemption and echoing Gemma's words in the moments before he shot her in the back of the head: "You have to do this. It's who we are, sweetheart" ("Red Rose"). The message of the gospel, on the other hand, is just the opposite. It says that we need not be prisoners of our past, that the freedom our bad choices have stolen from us can be restored. It offers something more beautiful than the unforgiving symmetry of revenge, which imprisons us in an eternal cycle of violent retaliation. It promises the sublimity of a new creation.

Jax explicitly rejects that message. Still, the series ends on a note suggesting that the light of the gospel still flickers in his dark world of violence and offering a hint that Sutter's ultimate template may have been neither Shakespeare nor Euripides nor Leviticus, but the kenotic event of the Passion.

After all of the mayhem and madness Jax has inflicted on his club, he comes to realize that the survival of SAMCRO now depends on him exiting the picture for good—not like Clay as an unwilling victim of a collective murder, but as someone who out of love lays down his life for his friends. The final image of the final episode is a piece of bread discarded by the side of the highway, with Jax's blood pooling next to it, an unmistakable allusion to the Eucharist. The final word spoken by anyone in the series is "Jesus." And the look of serenity on Jax's face as he surrenders his life, arms outstretched in cruciform fashion, suggests that maybe, just *maybe*, he has in these very last moments of his life moved beyond tragedy and even beyond the closed system of the law to partake in the reality signified by that image and that name.

NOTES

1. René Girard, *Violence and the Sacred*, trans. Patrick Gregory (Baltimore: Johns Hopkins University Press, 1977), 15.

2. See René Girard, *Things Hidden Since the Foundation of the World*, trans. Stephen Bann and Michael Mettteer (Stanford: Stanford University Press, 1987), 295: "All that capitalism, or rather our liberal society that allows capitalism to flourish, does is to give mimetic phenomena a freer rein and to direct them into economic and technological channels. For religious reasons that are far from simple, capitalism is capable of doing away with the restraints that archaic societies put on mimetic rivalry."

3. Leo Strauss, *Natural Right and History* (Chicago: University of Chicago Press, 1999), 247.

4. René Girard, *A Theater of Envy: William Shakespeare* (New York: Oxford University Press, 1991), 273.

5. So intellectually stimulating in fact that a collection of philosophical essays about the show was published a few years ago. See *Sons of Anarchy and Philosophy: Brains Before Bullets*, edited by George A. Dunn and Jason T. Eberl (Hoboken: Wiley-Blackwell, 2013).

6. *A Theatre of Envy*, 273.

7. Ibid.

8. For a thoughtful historical and philosophical study of *lex talionis*, see William Ian Miller, *Eye for an Eye* (Cambridge: Cambridge University Press, 2007).

9. The underlying principle of the *lex talionis* is "getting even," exacting a punishment that is proportionate in severity to the crime, rather than an insistence on body parts as payment. The statement often attributed to Mohandas Gandhi—"an eye for an eye makes the whole world blind"—misses the point by interpreting the formula too literally. Within the rabbinic tradition, the literal meaning of the text (*peshat* פשט) is often set aside in favor the general principle, so that monetary compensation may be considered a suitable substitute for maiming someone who has caused another to lose an eye or a tooth. Needless to say, the exegetical sophistication of the rabbinic

tradition, with its attempt to soften some of the implications of the *lex talionis*, is foreign to members of the outlaw subculture to which SAMCRO belongs, for whom physical pain is the only currency in which certain debts can be paid.

10. The phrase "Old Testament justice" typically denotes punishment that is harsh, merciless, or meted out in strict obedience to the *lex talionis*. The Old Testament, the first of two collections of writings included in the Christian Bible, roughly corresponds to the canonical collection of sacred texts that Jews call the Tanakh or sometimes the Hebrew Bible. Though some have insisted that designating those book as the "Old Testament" necessarily carries supersessionist connotations, Girard, like many other scholars both Christian and non-Christian, routinely used that term without any such anti-Jewish intention. See *Things Hidden*, 141 and *passim*. It should be noted, however, that the abundant examples of mercy in the Old Testament/Tanakh make the phrase "Old Testament justice" somewhat misleading. See Clifford S. Fishman, "Old Testament Justice," *Catholic University Law Review*, 51, 2 (2002): 405–423.

11. "Clean out the old yeast so that you may be a new batch, as you really are unleavened. For our paschal lamb, Christ, has been sacrificed" (1 Corinthians 5:7). It would be a gross misreading of this text to imagine that Paul is blaming the Jews for the sacrifice of Jesus. Paul is using an extended metaphor that would have been immediately understood by readers familiar with the rituals surrounding the Jewish commemoration of Passover. In preparation for the festival, Jews would scour their homes to remove any trace of yeast, a reminder of the unleavened bread the Hebrew slaves were obliged to carry due to the haste of their exodus from Egypt, which allowed no time for the bread to rise (Exodus 12:15). Paul is urging his readers in the church at Corinth likewise to purify their ranks of the "yeast" of sinful conduct that he fears could "leaven" the community in harmful ways. His identification of Christ with the Paschal Lamb completes the Passover metaphor, since the sacrifice of a year-old lamb was also part of the Passover ritual at the time. This sacrifice commemorated the slaughter of those lambs whose blood protected the Hebrews from the angel sent by the LORD to strike dead the first born of the Egyptians on the eve of the Exodus (Exodus 12: 1–12). Paul's *clear* meaning is that the sacrifice made by Christ affords the church blessings, such as freedom from bondage to sin, that are somehow analogous to what the LORD did for Israel at the first Passover. Largely because of this passage, references to Christ as the Paschal Lamb have become a standard part of Christian devotion. Again, Paul is in *no way* blaming the Jews for the sacrifice of Jesus. Such a reading is not only tendentious, but it betrays a woeful ignorance of the context of Paul's use of this trope.

12. In should be noted that penal substitution is just one theory of atonement. Other theories were prevalent before the Reformation and are still taught by many Roman Catholics, Orthodox Christians, and even some Protestants in the post-Reformation era. Among the most influential of these is the ransom theory, according to which the death of Christ was a ransom paid to Satan to release human beings from the debt they had incurred due to their sins.

13. We could easily devote three full paragraphs or *more* to explicating Girard's thoughts on the subject of penal substitution and atonement theory, but that would surely be overwhelming in this context. In place of a too-long digression from the

main topic under discussion, the reader interested in learning more is urged to look at chapters 2 and 3 of Book II of Girard's magnum opus *Things Hidden Since the Foundation of the World*, respectively titled "A Non-Sacrificial Reading of the Gospel Text" and "The Sacrificial Reading of Historical Christianity" (180–262). For a book-length Girardian critique of the doctrine of penal substitution, the reader can consult Anthony Bartlett, *Cross Purposes* (Harrisburg: Trinity Press, 2001). Mark S. Heim also develops a Girardian theology of atonement in *Saved from Sacrifice: A Theology of the Cross* (Grand Rapids: Wm. B. Eerdmans Publishing Company, 2006).

14. Michael Hardin, "Practical Reflections on Non-Violent Atonement," in *Violence, Desire, and the Sacred, Volume 2: René Girard and Sacrifice in Life, Love, and Literature*, ed. Scott Cowdell, Chris Fleming, and Joel Hodge (New York: Bloomsbury Academic, 2014), 248.

15. Girard, *Violence and the Sacred*, 260.

16. René Girard, "Generative Scapegoating," in *Violent Origins: Walter Burkert, René Girard and Jonathan Z. Smith on Ritual Killing and Cultural Formation*, ed. Robert G. Hamerton-Kelly (Stanford: Stanford University Press, 1987), 141.

17. Though traces of what Girard call "the violent sacred" are found throughout the Old Testament/Tanakh, he seems to have concluded, after overcoming some initial misgivings concerning the book of Hebrews, that it is absent from the New Testament except as an object of criticism. For a dissenting view, see Robert M. Price, "Sacred Scapegoat?" in *Deconstructing Jesus* (Amherst: Prometheus Books, 2000), 169–212.

18. For an excellent study of how violence and even taking pleasure in violence can be morally motivated, see Alan Page Fiske and Tage Shakti Rai, *Virtuous Violence: Hurting and Killing to Create, Sustain, End, and Honor Social Relationships* (Cambridge: Cambridge University Press, 2014).

19. To quote a famous formula for justice proposed in Plato's *Republic*, "Justice is doing good to friends and harm to enemies." See Plato, *Republic*, trans. Allan Bloom (New York: Basic Books, 2016), 8 (332d). Socrates rejects this definition of justice, however, in favor of one not bound to reciprocity.

20. These quotes and the ones that follow in this paragraph are from a lecture Girard delivered at the Center for International Security and Arms Control at Stanford University in 1993. Titled "Revenge," it can be streamed at https://cornerstone-forum.org/?page_id=905. Accessed 3/10/2020.

21. Though Girard never fully explains why good reciprocity carries this risk, Aristotle may have supplied a clue. He points out that "friendships of use," that is, friendships based primarily on exchanging benefits, are prone to give rise to complaints and hard feelings, since both parties tend to believe they gave more than they got in return. See Aristotle, *Nicomachean Ethics*, trans. Joe Sachs (Indianapolis: Focus Philosophical Library, 2002), 160–161 (1162b-1163a). This pitfall of good reciprocity could be seen as the flip side of the problem of "different arithmetics" discussed by Elizabeth Wolgast in *The Grammar of Justice* (Ithaca: Cornell University Press, 1987), which drives escalating cycles of vengeance because the antagonists can never come to an agreement about when the scales are even.

22. See endnote 9 above.

23. Immanuel Kant, *The Philosophy of Law: An Exposition of the Fundamental Principles of Jurisprudence as the Science of Right*, trans. William Hastie (Union: The Lawbook Exchange, 2002), 196.

24. *Things Hidden*, 128.

25. *Violence and the Sacred*, 16.

26. Robert Nozick, *Philosophical Explanations* (Cambridge: Belknap Press, 1983), 367.

27. Ibid.

28. *Violence and the Sacred*, 21.

29. *Violence and the Sacred*, 15.

30. Elizabeth Wolgast, *op. cit.*

31. *Violence and the Sacred*, 16.

32. Ibid., 13.

33. *A Theater of Envy*, 186.

34. Ibid., 201.

35. Of course, we should bear in mind that the *lex talionis* is at its heart a principle of restraint—the punishment should not exceed the crime in severity. An eye for an eye—but *no more* than an eye for an eye! Interpreted in this way, the Mosaic Law leaves open the possibility of an even greater exercise of restraint, the possibility of leniency or even forgoing punishment altogether.

36. René Girard, *I See Satan Fall Like Lightning* (Maryknoll: Orbis Books, 2001), 111.

37. Girard discusses the story of Joseph in *Evolution and Conversion*, pointing out that "traditional Christianity sees in Joseph a *figura* of Christ" (202).

38. For more on the importance of reputation within the outlaw biker world, see George A. Dunn, "SAMCRO versus the Leviathan: Laying Down the (Motor)Cycle of Violence," in *Sons of Anarchy and Philosophy*, 53–64.

BIBLIOGRAPHY

Aristotle. *Nicomachean Ethics*. Translated by Joe Sachs. Indianapolis: Focus Philosophical Library, 2002.

Bartlett, Anthony. *Cross Purposes*. Harrisburg: Trinity Press, 2001.

Dunn, George A. and Jason T. Eberl, editors. *Sons of Anarchy and Philosophy: Brains Before Bullets*. Hoboken: Wiley-Blackwell, 2013.

Dunn, George A. "SAMCRO versus the Leviathan: Laying Down the (Motor)Cycle of Violence," in *Sons of Anarchy and Philosophy: Brains Before Bullets*. Hoboken: Wiley-Blackwell, 2013.

Fishman, Clifford S. "Old Testament Justice." *Catholic University Law Review*, 51, 2 (2002): 405–423.

Fiske, Alan Page, and Tage Shakti Rai. *Virtuous Violence: Hurting and Killing to Create, Sustain, End, and Honor Social Relationships*. Cambridge: Cambridge University Press, 2014.

Girard, René. "Generative Scapegoating," in *Violent Origins: Walter Burkert, René Girard and Jonathan Z. Smith on Ritual Killing and Cultural Formation*. Edited by Robert G. Hamerton-Kelly. Stanford: Stanford University Press, 1987.

———. *I See Satan Fall Like Lightning*. Maryknoll: Orbis Books, 2001.

———. "Revenge." 1993. https://cornerstone-forum.org/?page_id=905.

———. *A Theatre of Envy*. New York: Oxford University Press, 1991.

———. *Things Hidden Since the Foundation of the World*. Translated by Stephen Bann and Michael Mettteer. Stanford: Stanford University Press, 1987.

———. *Violence and the Sacred*. Translated by Patrick Gregory. Baltimore: Johns Hopkins University Press, 1977

Hardin, Michael. "Practical Reflections on Non-Violent Atonement," in *Violence, Desire, and the Sacred, Volume 2: René Girard and Sacrifice in Life, Love, and Literature*. Edited by Scott Cowdell, Chris Fleming, and Joel Hodge. New York: Bloomsbury Academic, 2014.

Heim, Mark S. *Saved from Sacrifice: A Theology of the Cross*. Grand Rapids: Wm. B. Eerdmans Publishing Company, 2006.

Kant, Immanuel. *The Philosophy of Law: An Exposition of the Fundamental Principles of Jurisprudence as the Science of Right*. Translated by William Hastie. Union: The Lawbook Exchange, 2002.

Miller, William Ian. *Eye for an Eye*. Cambridge: Cambridge University Press, 2007.

Nozick, Robert. *Philosophical Explanations*. Cambridge: Belknap Press, 1983.

Plato. *Republic*. Translated by Allan Bloom. New York: Basic Books, 2016.

Price, Robert M. *Deconstructing Jesus*. Amherst: Prometheus Books, 2000.

Strauss, Leo. *Natural Right and History*. Chicago: University of Chicago Press, 1999.

Wolgast, Elizabeth. *The Grammar of Justice*. Ithaca: Cornel University Press, 1987.

Chapter 10

Exorcising Blame through
A Contract with God
A Girardian Analysis of Will Eisner's Graphic Novel

Daniel DeForest London

Considered by many to be the first graphic novel,[1] *A Contract with God* was written and illustrated by one of the great figures in comic book history, Will Eisner, who described his creation of the book as "an exercise in personal agony."[2] He wrote,

> My only daughter, Alice, had died of leukemia eight years before the publication of this book. My grief was still raw. My heart still bled. In fact, I could not even bring myself to discuss the loss. [The main character's] anguish was mine. His argument with God was also mine. I exorcised my rage at a deity that I believed violated my faith and deprived my lovely 16-year-old child of her life at the very flowering of it.[3]

Growing up in a Jewish household, with a mother who assured him that God rewarded people for their good deeds,[4] Eisner had adopted what William Morrow calls a "Deuteronomic" theology, which explains suffering as the consequence of sinful behavior.[5] When confronted with his daughter's undeserved suffering, Eisner admitted that, although he would like to believe in a benevolent and personal "supreme intelligence," he remained deeply troubled by God's apparent violation of the Deuteronomic contract.[6] When confronted with his own emotional suffering in the midst of tragic loss, Eisner found only one way to constructively process his grief: through drawing and writing comics. "Drawing," he said, "has been a great savior for me emotionally. I have been able to use it as a way of living through very difficult times."[7] Although Eisner's act of drawing served as his "great savior," I argue that another element helped him through his grief and rage: the Jewish tradition of protest against God, which pervades his graphic novel.

In this essay, I employ the insights of René Girard to explore the ways in which *A Contract with God* can function for readers today as an effective outlet for pain, anguish, and rage. Furthermore, I demonstrate the ways in which *A Contract with God* draws from the literary tradition of protest against God and can thus serve as a popular gateway into this rich tradition of prayer and literary expression that has helped Jews and Christians cope with suffering in prayerful and nonviolent ways.

MIMESIS ON DROPSIE AVENUE

Eisner's *Contract* begins with a preface titled "A Tenement in the Bronx" that describes the setting of the story: a 1930s tenement on Dropsie Avenue in the Bronx, overcrowded with recent American immigrants. He describes the tenants as "intent on their own survival, busy with breeding their young and dreaming of a better life they knew existed 'Uptown.'"[8] The image that accompanies these words depicts two women hanging laundry out to dry on clotheslines between two tenement buildings. Both women look strained and overwrought as they mingle with one another from windows of separate buildings that seem claustrophobically close. The tenement buildings in the background form a triangle with the apparent "uptown" at the top and the two women at the two bottom vertices. From a Girardian perspective, this image and the accompanying words depict the triangular nature of desire and the potential for internal mediation between the two neighboring women, which is enhanced by the activity in which they are both mimetically engaged: hanging their laundry on the clothesline.[9] Such an activity is not insignificant since one of the most visible indicators of one's social status and participation in the coveted "better life" is sartorial display. From a Girardian perspective, these two tenement women represent humanity's susceptibility to mimetic rivalry and potential violence, which is often successfully halted by a social "brake" that Girard calls the scapegoat mechanism. In the very next line of the preface, Eisner seems to intuit this scapegoat mechanism perfectly well when he writes, "What community spirit there was, stemmed from their hostility toward a common enemy—the landlord!"[10]

In *Violence and the Sacred*, Girard explains how mimetic rivalry is placated through the scapegoating of a common enemy, who bears the brunt of the tension and animosity between the subject and model. This scapegoat mechanism has allowed humanity to survive without wiping itself out completely in a Hobbesian all-against-all war.[11] Therefore, the human compulsion to scapegoat and blame has grown in lockstep with the human impulse to survive. So the tenants of Dropsie Avenue discharge the tension that accumulates in their rivalry with one another by unleashing their hostility towards their common enemy: the landlord.

"THE BIG LIE"

In order to persist in this scapegoating, humanity has repressed culpability for collective hostility by creating stories that illustrate the victim's responsibility for the hatred in the first place, thereby justifying the blaming of the victim. In Eisner's extended 2004 preface, he adds that the surrogate superintendent also fell into the role of scapegoat,[12] explaining that "the super was . . . blamed for any unusual happening, real or imagined."[13] Girard calls these imagined stories that blame scapegoats "myths" and argues that they pervade all human cultures. These myths are essentially lies that humans tell themselves in order to maintain group identity and to justify the excluding and scapegoating of innocent victims.

Toward the end of his career, Eisner used his artistic and literary gifts to dismantle myths that scapegoated innocent victims.[14] In his final graphic novel, which was published posthumously, he explored the alluring power of a pernicious "myth" known as the *The Protocols of the Elders of Zion*, a fabricated text intended to stir anti-Semitic hatred and violence. In his graphic novel titled *The Plot*, he exposes the mythic nature of *The Protocols* and writes, "Whenever one group of people is taught to hate another, a lie is created to inflame the hatred and justify a plot. The target is easy to find because the enemy is always the other."[15] In his introduction to Eisner's *The Plot*, Umberto Eco identifies Girardian "myth" as the "Big Lie" when he writes, "It is not the Protocols that produce antisemitism, it is people's profound need to single out an Enemy that leads them to believe in the Protocols. I believe that—in spite of this courageous, not *comic* but *tragic* book by Will Eisner— the story is hardly over. Yet it is a story very much worth telling, for one must fight the Big Lie and the hatred it spawns."[16] Just as the Gospels of the New Testament expose the "myth" that fuels violent scapegoating (according to Girard) so too does Eisner's story in *The Plot* expose the "Big Lie" expressed in *The Protocols*.[17] From a Jewish perspective, Eisner's work is inspired by prophetic Judaism, which Sandor Goodhart argues is "Girardianism before the fact" as it exposes and critiques the violence of archaic religions.[18] However, even when the violence of scapegoating is exposed and critiqued, humanity still has to confront what Eco calls our "profound need to single out an Enemy," be it a race or tribe or class of people sharing a particular profession, such as landlords. Although the fictional landlords and superintendents of Dropsie Avenue were certainly flawed human beings as Eisner illustrated graphically in his stories,[19] they still became victims of blame within the myths and plots and "Big Lies" told by tenants who felt compelled to discharge their resentment toward someone, as they endured the sordid challenges of urban life, miles away from uptown.

PROTEST AGAINST GOD: BLAMING THE DIVINE LANDLORD

René Girard argues that this human compulsion to scapegoat and blame others (including landlords and superintendents) actually helps prevent humanity from destroying itself by providing concentrated outlets for anger, aggression, and violence.[20] This ubiquitous compulsion to blame has fueled theological projects called theodicies, which attempt to defend an omnipotent and omnibenevolent God in the face of evil and suffering.[21] By refusing to hold God accountable, many Christian theodicies have historically held particular groups of people responsible for suffering, thus offering theological justification for violence toward innocent victims, especially women, heretics, Muslims, and Jews.[22] However, within the margins of the Jewish and Christian literary traditions, there has been another outlet for this compulsion to blame, which does not require violence towards innocent victims: the tradition of lament and protest against God.[23] In this tradition, human aggression is directed toward God, in the context of prayer and literary expression. With roots in the Psalms and Job, this tradition of arguing with God persists in Judaism and Christianity. In the Christian tradition, protest against God has persisted in authors such as Augustine of Hippo, Julian of Norwich, Teresa of Avila, and C. S. Lewis who passionately interrogate God, whose justice seems absent or unfathomable in the midst of suffering.[24] The tradition prevails even more robustly within Judaism, which includes many clever and choleric arguments with God in the Talmud (particularly *Bava Metzi'a*),[25] midrash (particularly *Lamentations Rabbah*),[26] the tales of Rabbi Levi Yitzhak of Berditchev,[27] and the writings of Zvi Kolitz, Elie Wiesel, and David Blumenthal, to name a few.[28] In these disputes with the divine, the Torah is often utilized as a tool (or weapon) for argumentation with a God who can be held accountable to the ethics and terms of the covenant (i.e., contract).[29] This same strategy of using a contract to argue with God is employed by the main character of Will Eisner's graphic novel.

In the tradition of protest against God, the resentment that had been directed towards various scapegoats such as the landlord or the superintendent is directed, so to speak, against the "divine landlord." In fact, there is a story from a Jewish midrash on Genesis in which Abraham observes a building on fire and learns, after inquiring, that the landlord is God.[30] Although there are a variety of ways to interpret this story, one may read it as an indictment against the divine, who appears to be a questionable and irresponsible landlord whose property is in shambles. The idea of a divine landlord who may deserve our resentment and blame for the apparently pitiful and dangerous conditions of his property (creation) permeates throughout Eisner's graphic novel, thus offering fuel for quarrel with God.

"THIS IS NOT A FUNNY STORY"

After the preface, *A Contract* continues with one of Eisner's famous opening splash pages.[31] As early as 1940, Eisner used the title page as an opportunity to experiment with the interweaving of words, font, architecture, landscape, and dimensionality. Each splash page sets the tone for the story like a book's epigraph or opera's overture. On the title page of *A Contract,* a person (whom we later learn is the main protagonist Frimme Hersh) walks dismally along a city street through pouring rain as a heavy stone tablet hovers overhead with the following words inscribed in Hebraic and condensed Roman lettering, reading, "A Contract with God."[32] The cracks on the tablet, the downpour of rain, and the wet and miserable condition of the person below suggests that someone has broken their part of the contract, thus resulting in a state of betrayal and despair.

It is also worth noting the fire hydrant beside the clearly dejected pedestrian. Although this may simply be an indication to the reader that the man is walking in an urban setting, it adds a touch of irony: a fire hydrant, containing water, becomes relatively useless in the midst of such a downpour. The image of a fire hydrant in the rain may suggest that much of life and even God can seem useless and meaningless in the midst of a downpour of suffering. In this way, the novel may already be subtly implicating and accusing God on the title page. The title page conveys through image what another title page from one of Eisner's previous comics expresses through words. On the splash page of "The Story of Gerhard Shnobble" from his syndicated comic *The Spirit,* Eisner writes, "This is not a funny story!! . . . Please . . . no laughter." After telling the tragic story of an innocent man with supernatural gifts becoming the target of human aggression and violence, he writes, "Shed a tear for all mankind."[33] The title page of *A Contract* also communicates to the reader that "this is not a funny story" and that tears may be shed, but the target of human aggression and violence will not be a human, but God.

ARGUING WITH GOD AS ROLE OF JEWISH PROPHET

Although Eisner utilizes water and nautical imagery throughout the preface with references to a "ship afloat on concrete,"[34] a "flood of immigrants,"[35] and a "ship board fellowship of passengers,"[36] it is his reference to Noah's ark that can be seen as a foreshadowing of the novel's climax: "The tenement at No. 55 Dropsie Avenue seemed ready to rise and float away on the swirling tide. 'Like the ark of Noah,' it seemed to Frimme Hersh as he sloshed homeward."[37] Eisner's explicit reference to Noah can be interpreted as an implicit reference to a passage in the Zohar in which God chastises Noah for *not* protesting against him when he first learned of the destructive flood's imminence.[38] Unlike Abraham and Moses who challenged God when other peoples' lives were at stake (Genesis 18:16–33; Exodus 32:9–14), Noah remained disturbingly silent and submissive after learning that God's judgment would result in the destruction of many human lives. Part of the Jewish prophet's role is to remind both parties involved of their commitment to the covenant (i.e. the contract). Often the prophet needs to remind humanity, but sometimes the prophet must remind God, especially when people's lives are at stake.[39] According to the Zohar, Noah only challenges God *after the flood*, which proves to be too little too late for God who says, "I lingered with you and spoke to you at length so that you would ask for mercy for the world! But as soon as you heard that you would be safe in the ark, the evil of the world did not touch your heart. You built the ark and saved yourself. Now that the world has been destroyed you open your mouth to utter questions and pleas?"[40] For the reader familiar with the Jewish tradition of protest against God, Eisner's evocation of Noah suggests that the currently downcast and docile Frimme Hersh will later be hurling "questions and pleas" against the Almighty, even though it may be too late.

The reader quickly learns that the reason for Frimme's misery is because his beloved daughter Rachele grew ill and died suddenly "in the springtime of her life."[41] The narrator explains that, although these human tragedies occur rather frequently, this particular tragedy "should not have happened to Frimme Hersh because [he] had a contract with God!"[42] The comic then flashes back to a 19th century Russian Jewish shtetl named Piske, where the protagonist was born and given the name Frimmehleh, which is likely derived from the Yiddish word for "pious": *frum*.[43] In Piske, young Frimmehleh performed many righteous deeds and was often told by others, "God will reward you."[44] As a result of the anti-Semitic pogroms that followed the assassination of Tsar Alexander II, the Jewish elders of Piske decided to send their beloved Frimmehleh to the United States. As he traveled to the United States with a rabbi, Frimmehleh learned that God is indeed a just God who rewards the righteous and punishes the wicked. Inspired by the rabbi's wisdom, Frimme wrote a contract with God and inscribed it upon a stone tablet. Although the terms of the contract are not detailed, the reader can infer that it promised divine reward for righteous behavior. True to his name, Frimme "faithfully and piously . . . adhered to the terms of his contract with God."[45]

The year of Frimmehleh's birth is 1882, which Eisner presents as the same year of Tsar Alexander II's assassination. Although historically inaccurate,[46] the reader familiar with Jewish history may recall 1882 as the year of the Balta Pogrom in which 1,200 Jewish houses and shops were pillaged by anti-Semitic Russians. It is also the year that the Song of the Balta Pogrom was written, which includes the searing words: "Shout Jews, shout loud as you can, / So loud your shout reaches on high / And wakes up the Old Man."[47] Less than 10 pages after referencing the year 1882, Eisner portrays Frimme, in the climax of the comic, shouting as loud as he can at the divine "Old Man." For five solid pages, Frimme shakes his fist, spits, and shouts so loud that the entire tenement trembles at his words of accusation against the divine: "You violated your contract!"[48] After shouting at God, Frimme eventually says, "Enough," spits on the stone tablet contract, and then hurls it out the window into the rain-soaked alley. Through these five pages, the reader not only gets a sense of Eisner's own anger toward God and cathartic release, but also receives permission to bring his or her own honest vitriol toward God in prayer.

"IS NOT ALL RELIGION A CONTRACT BETWEEN MAN AND GOD?"

After accusing God of violating the contract, Frimme sits *shiva* and then prays morning prayer, much like the Jews whom Elie Wiesel witnessed in Auschwitz who convicted God as guilty of their horrific suffering and then consequently prayed evening prayer.[49] However, for Frimme, this is the last time he will ever pray morning prayer because he then proceeds to shave off his beard, dress like a Gentile, and soon become a successful real estate tycoon. As a landlord, Frimme treats his tenants unjustly by raising their rent, cutting their heat and then refusing to entertain any complaints. In this way, Frimme becomes the very person whom his previous fellow tenants tend to scapegoat and despise. Moreover, he seems to become the monster whom he believes God to be: an unjust landlord who makes conditions dangerous for his tenants and seems to turn a deaf ear to any complaints. To use Girardian terms, Frimme's mimetic model is a monstrous God whom Frimme strives to become. Girard argues that all desire is a desire for being and that the subject's desire for the mediator's being stems from a profound self-hatred, explaining, "The wish to be absorbed into the substance of the Other implies an insuperable revulsion of one's own substance."[50] Although the Other into whom Frimme wishes to be absorbed is God, Frimme clearly holds a dangerously oversimplified understanding of God. As a result, Frimme develops a "black hole inside" that makes him feel so profoundly empty that he eventually returns to the synagogue, where he asks the elders to write him a new contract with God.[51] Although initially resistant, the elders eventually agree, asking themselves, "Is not all religion a contract between man and God?"[52] Their question reveals the give-and-take nature of prayer as well as the push-and-pull dynamic of the biblical event from which Israel receives its name: Jacob wrestling with the divine (Genesis 32:22–32). Frimme returns to his home, immensely pleased with his new contract which he insists God will not violate. However, moments later, he suffers a severe heart attack that leaves him dead on the floor with the new contract crumpled in his hand, as lightning strikes and an angry wind swirls through the tenements.

The story concludes with an Epilogue about a young Hasidic boy named Shloime Khreks who demonstrates heroic bravery by saving people from a tenement fire on Dropsie Avenue and then subsequently receives assurances from his neighbors that God will reward him. Soon after the fire, three young bullies mock and threaten to hurt Shloime, but he responds by hurling stones at them. As the bullies run away, Shloime notices that one of the stones he picked up has writing on it and realizes it is a contract with God, a contract into which he decides to enter by signing his name, right below that of Frimme Hersh.

A CONTRACT WITH GOD **AS "VIOLENCE-OUTLET"**

In the above summary and analysis of *A Contract with God*, one can see that Eisner was not only exorcising his personal rage by drawing, but also by drawing *from* the Jewish tradition of protest against God, whether consciously or not. Jeremy Dauber observes: "Naturally, Eisner references larger theological issues, as well as previous literary treatments of this issue: Frimme Hersh's insistence on the rabbi's creating a contract with God recalls the Hasidic tales surrounding Rabbi Levi Yitzach of Berdichev, for example."[53] Although many other significant allusions to the Jewish tradition of protest against God can be identified in Eisner's graphic novel, it is worth reflecting, with Girard, on the ways that *A Contract* can serve as a healthy outlet for readers today to exorcise anger, pain, and the compulsion to blame.

"Violence," Girard writes, "is not to be denied, but it can be diverted to another object, something it can sink its teeth into."[54] Girard then suggests that the reason why Cain murdered his brother Abel was because he did not have a "violence-outlet" at his disposal.[55] According to Girard, Abel was never tempted to murder his brother because he had found an effective "violence-outlet" in animal sacrifice. I contend that *A Contract with God* can function as an effective and healthy "violence-outlet" for readers today who, like Eisner, may feel betrayed by God and overwhelmed with grief and rage toward a God who sometimes seems to be a monstrous landlord. Eisner wrote, "The format of comics presents a montage of both word and image" which provides the reader with both visual and verbal stimulation.[56] By reading the graphic novel, readers can unleash their own frustration toward God through the vitriol of Frimme Hersh, which is expressed verbally through his accusations and questions, followed by Hebraic style question marks, and illustrated visually through his hyperbolized body language. I posit that a reader can engage *A Contract with God* prayerfully, much like the way one might engage the Psalms of Lament or the Book of Job or other expressions of protest against God. A reader can lodge a host of honest complaints before God, with the awareness that "complaint does not exclude hope."[57] By doing so, a reader may not only discover a nonviolent outlet for rage but also a God who responds, sometimes through a storm theophany, sometimes through wind and lightning, and sometimes through a glimmer of light in the darkness. According to the rich tradition of protest against God (from which *A Contract* draws and of which it is indeed a recent expression), the heavenly response often reveals a God who is willing to be blamed, eager to be challenged, and always open to receiving and thus transforming our most violent selves. By reading *A Contract with God* in light of Girard's insights, the graphic novel can become a powerful tool and catalyst for raw, contentious, and ultimately redemptive prayer.

NOTES

1. Although Eisner himself described *A Contract with God* as a graphic novel when it was first published in 1978, some have challenged this appellation since it is, in fact, an anthology of four short stories. The first of these short stories is titled "A Contract with God," which will be the subject of this essay. The full title is *A Contract with God and Other Tenement Stories*. The other tenement stories include "The Street Singer," "The Super" and "Cookalein." For more on *A Contract* as graphic novel,

see Scott McCloud, "Introduction to the Centennial Edition," *A Contract with God: Centennial Edition* (New York: W.W. Norton, 2017), ix–xiv.

2. Eisner, *Contract with God*, xvi

3. Eisner, *Contract with God*, xvi.

4. Eisner's mother "referred to God constantly, promising that if Eisner did the right things, God would reward him." Bob Andelman, *Will Eisner: A Spirited Life* (Raleigh NC: TwoMorrows, 2015), 168.

5. William Morrow, *Protest Against God: The Eclipse of a Biblical Tradition* (Sheffield, UK: Sheffield Phoenix Press, 2007), 208.

6. Andelman, *Will Eisner: A Spirited Life*, 168.

7. Andelman, *Will Eisner: A Spirited Life*, 169.

8. Eisner, *Contract with God*, xxxiii.

9. Laundry hanging on the clothesline can also be a way of illustrating how, in tenement neighborhoods, everyone's personal laundry was exposed: clean and otherwise.

10. Eisner, *Contract with God*, xxxiii.

11. Thomas Hobbes, *Leviathan*, ed. Hermann Klenner (Hamburg: Meiner Verlag, 2005), 673.

12. Eisner, *Contract with God*, xxv.

13 Eisner, *Contract with God*, xxvii.

14. Will Eisner explores antisemitic themes in *The Dreamer* (New York: W.W. Norton, 2008), *To the Heart of the Storm* (New York: W.W. Norton, 2008) and *Fagin the Jew* (Milwaukie OR: Dark Horse Comics, 2013). In the latter, Eisner challenges the problematic portrayal of the Jewish character Fagin in Dickens's *Oliver Twist* while also acknowledging his own problematic portrayal of a young African-American superhero sidekick named Ebony White who appeared in his syndicated newspaper comic book *The Spirit* in 1940–1949. In the Introduction, he confesses, "I was . . . feeding a racial prejudice with this stereotype image." Eisner, *Fagin the Jew*, 3.

15. Will Eisner, *The Plot: The Secret Story of the Protocols of the Elders of Zion* (New York: W.W. Norton, 2005), 5–6.

16. Umberto Eco, *The Plot*, trans. Alessandra Bastagli, vii.

17. Not only does Girard claim that "the resurrection of Christ crowns and finishes both the subversion and the unmasking of mythology," he also boldly asserts that "the Gospels reveal everything that human beings need to understand their moral responsibility with regard to the whole spectrum of violence in human history." René Girard, *I See Satan Fall Like Lightning*, trans. James G. Williams (Maryknoll, NY: Orbis, 2001), 125.

18. Sandor Goodhart, "Judaism and the Exodus from Archaic Religion: Reading René Girard among the World Religions" in *Mimetic Theory and World Religions*, ed. Wolfgang Palaver and Richard Schenk (East Lansing MI: Michigan State University Press, 2018), 385–399.

19. Eisner explores the misery of a superintendent in the short story "The Super." Eisner, *Contract with God*, 93–122.

20. See René Girard, *Violence and the Sacred*, trans. Patrick Gregory (Baltimore, MD: Johns Hopkins University Press, 1972), *The Scapegoat*, trans. Yvonne Freccero

(Baltimore, MD: Johns Hopkins University Press, 1989) and *I See Satan Fall Like Lightning*.

21. The term theodicy was coined by 18th century German philosopher Gottfried Wilhelm von Leibniz. It is a combination of two Greek words: *theos* which means "God" and *dikē* which means "trial" or "judgement." The etymology of the word implies that God is on trial. Gottfried Wilhelm von Leibniz, *Theodicy: Essays on the Goodness of God, the Freedom of Man, and the Origin of Evil*, trans. E. M. Huggard (La Salle, IL: Open Court, 1993).

22. See Joseph F. Kelly, *The Problem of Evil in the Western Tradition: From the Book of Job to Modern Genetics* (Collegeville, MN: Liturgical Press, 2002), 68–74.

23. See David Roskies, *The Literature of Destruction: Jewish Responses to Catastrophe* (Philadelphia, PA: Jewish Publication Society, 1989); Anson Laytner, *Arguing with God: A Jewish Tradition* (Matwah, NJ: Jason Aronson, 1990); Daniel London, "Judging God: Learning from the Jewish Tradition of Protest Against God" in Journal of Comparative Theology Vol. 6. Issue 1, June 2016, 15–31.

24. For examples of protest against God in these authors, see Gordon Mursell, *Out of the Deep: Prayer as Protest* (London: Darton Longman and Todd, 1989); Daniel London, "'Pray Interly': Julian of Norwich's Spirituality of Prayer" in *Compass: A Review of Topical Theology* Spring 2015, Vol 45 (1), 14–24; Daniel London, *Theodicy and Spirituality in the Fourth Gospel: A Girardian Perspective* (Lanham, MD: Lexington Books/Fortress Academic, 2020). Since the relatively recent rediscovery of lament psalms by Claus Westermann and Walter Brueggemann, the Christian tradition of protest against God has become more widespread.

25. *Bava Metzia* 59b.

26. *Eichah Rabbah*, in *The Literature of Destruction: Jewish Responses to Catastrophe*, edited by David G. Roskies (Philadelphia: Jewish Publication Society, 1989), 53.

27. Samuel H. Dresner, *Levi Yitzhak of Berditchev: Portrait of a Hasidic Master* (New York: Hartmore House, 1974), 81.

28. Zvi Kolitz, *Yossel Rakover Speaks to God* (New York: Random House, 1999); Elie Wiesel, *Trial of God (as it was held on February 25, 1649, in Shamgorod)* (New York: Schocken Books, 1995); David Blumenthal, *Facing the Abusing God: A Theology of Protest* (Louisville, KY: Westminster John Knox Press, 1993).

29. Laytner, *Arguing with* God; London, "Judging God."

30. *Bereishit Rabbah* 39: 1–2.

31. "Unlike other artists, Eisner didn't rely on a set logo every time, a practice that was unheard of in comic books, newspapers, or magazines. To put what he did in context, imagine the *New York Times* changing its front-page logo every day." Andelman, *A Spirited Life,* 32.

32. Laurence Roth identifies the tablet as "a none-too-subtle redrawing of the *shnei luchot ha-berit*, the two tablets of the covenant given to Moses and Israel at Mt. Sinai." Laurence Roth, "Drawing Contracts: Will Eisner's Legacy." *Graven Images: Religion in Comic Books and Graphic Novels,* edited by A. David Lewis and Christine Hoff Kraemer (New York: Continuum, 2010), 44–62, 46. Eisner himself describes this title page when he writes, "The meaning of the title is conveyed by the employment of

a commonly recognized configuration of a tablet. A stone is employed—rather than parchment of paper, for example, to imply permanence and evoke the universal recognition of Moses' Ten Commandments on a stone tablet. Even the mix of the lettering style—Hebraic vs. a condensed Roman letter—is designed to buttress this feeling." Will Eisner, *Comics and Sequential Art: Principles and Practices from the Legendary Cartoonist* (New York: W.W. Norton, 2008), 4.

33. Will Eisner, "The Story of Gerhard Shnobble (Original publication date: September 5, 1948)" in *The Best of the Spirit* (Broadway, NY: DC Comics, 2005), 83.

34. Eisner, *Contract with God*, xxv.

35. Eisner, *Contract with God*, xxxi.

36. Eisner, *Contract with God*, xxxii–xxxiii.

37. Eisner, *Contract with God*, 5.

38. Daniel Chanan Matt, trans. *The Zohar: The Book of Enlightenment* (Mahwah NJ: Paulist Press, 1988), 57–59. I am indebted to Suzanne Guthrie for sharing this passage with me.

39. Yochanan Muffs, *Love and Joy: Law, Language and Religion in Ancient Israel* (Cambridge, MA: Harvard University Press, 1992), 9–48

40. Matt, *The Zohar*, 58.

41. Eisner, *Contract with God*, 22.

42. Eisner, *Contract with God*, 12.

43. Harry Brod, *Superman Is Jewish?: How Comic Books Superheroes Came to Serve Truth, Justice, and the Jewish-American Way* (New York: Simon & Schuster, 2012), 115.

44. Eisner, *Contract with God*, 15, 16.

45. Eisner, *Contract with God*, 19.

46. Alexander II was assassinated on March 13, 1881.

47. "Song of the Balta Pogrom" from David G. Roskies, *The Literature of Destruction*, 121. This era also coincides with a revival of the Jewish tradition of protest against God. Regarding this time period in Jewish history, Roskies writes, "Now, for the first time, writers who shared the burden of suffering refused to buy into the system. Instead, they issued a call for Jewish self-determination. To drive the message home, they began to use the archetypes of destruction as a warning and a threat." Roskies, *The Literature of Destruction*, 118.

48. Eisner, *Contract with God*, 24.

49. The story is retold by Robert McAfee Brown in his Introduction to Elie Wiesel, *Trial of God (as it was held on February 25, 1649, in Shamgorod)* (New York: Schocken Books, 1995), vii.

50. René Girard, *Deceit, Desire & the Novel: Self and Other in Literary Structure*, trans. Yvonne Freccero (Baltimore: Johns Hopkins University Press, 1965), 54.

51. Eisner, *Contract with God*, 39.

52. Eisner, *Contract with God*, 48.

53. Jeremy Dauber, "Comic Books, Tragic Stories: Will Eisner's American Jewish History." *The Jewish Graphic Novel: Critical Approaches,* ed. Samantha Baskind and Ranen Omer-Sherman (New Brunswick, NJ: Rutgers University Press, 2010), 22–42,

29. See "The Deal" in Martin Buber, *Tales of the Hasidim* (New York: Schocken Books, 1991), vol. 1: 209–210.
54. Girard, *Violence and the Sacred*, 4.
55. Girard, *Violence and the Sacred*, 4.
56. Eisner, *Comics and Sequential Art*, 2.
57. Gustavo Gutiérrez, *On Job: God-Talk and the Suffering of the Innocent*, trans. Matthew J. O'Connell (Maryknoll, NY: Orbis, 2009), 98. Black liberation theologian James Cone also highlights the interwoven nature of hope and complaint in African-American spirituals and blues. "Black music," he writes, "is unity music. It unites the joy and the sorrow, the love and the hate, the hope and the despair of black people; and it moves the people toward the direction of total liberation." James H. Cone, *The Spirituals and the Blues: An Interpretation* (New York: Seabury Press, 1972), 5.

BIBLIOGRAPHY

Andleman, Bob. *Will Eisner: A Spirited Life*. Raleigh, NC: TwoMorrows, 2015.

Blumenthal, David. *Facing the Abusing God: A Theology of Protest*. Louisville, KY: Westminster John Knox Press, 1993.

Brod, Harry. *Superman Is Jewish?: How Comic Books Superheroes Came to Serve Truth, Justice, and the Jewish-American Way*. New York: Simon & Schuster, 2012.

Buber, Martin. *Tales of the Hasidim*. New York: Schocken Books, 1991 (original work published in 1947).

Cone, James H. *The Spirituals and the Blues: An Interpretation*. New York: Seabury Press, 1972.

Dresner, Samuel H. *Levi Yitzhak of Berditchev: Portrait of a Hasidic Master*. New York: Hartmore House, 1974.

Dauber, Jeremy. "Comic Books, Tragic Stories: Will Eisner's American Jewish History." In *The Jewish Graphic Novel: Critical Approaches*, edited by Samantha Baskind and Ranen Omer-Sherman. New Brunswick, NJ: Rutgers University Press, 2010.

Eisner, Will. *Comics and Sequential Art: Principles and Practices from the Legendary Cartoonist*. New York: W.W. Norton, 2008 (original work published in 1985).

———. *A Contract with God: Centennial Edition*. New York: W.W. Norton, 2017 (original work published in 1978).

———. *The Dreamer*. New York: W.W. Norton, 2008. (Original work published in 1985).

———. *To the Heart of the Storm*. New York: W.W. Norton, 2008 (original work published in 1991).

———. *Fagin the Jew*. Milwaukie, OR: Dark Horse Comics, 2013 (original work published in 2003).

———. *The Plot: The Secret Story of the Protocols of the Elders of Zion*. New York: W.W. Norton, 2005.

———. "The Story of Gerhard Shnobble." In *The Best of the Spirit*. Broadway, NY: DC Comics, 2005 (original work published in 1948).

Girard, René. *Deceit, Desire & the Novel: Self and Other in Literary Structure*. Translated by Yvonne Freccero. Baltimore, MD: Johns Hopkins University Press, 1965.

———. *I See Satan Fall Like Lightning*. Translated by James G. Williams. Maryknoll, NY: Orbis, 2001.

———. *The Scapegoat*. Translated by Yvonne Freccero. Baltimore, MD: Johns Hopkins University Press, 1989.

———. *Violence and the Sacred*. Translated by Patrick Gregory. Baltimore, MD: Johns Hopkins University Press, 1972.

Goodhart, Sandor. "Judaism and the Exodus from Archaic Religion: Reading René Girard among the World Religions." In *Mimetic Theory and World Religions*, ed. Wolfgang Palaver and Richard Schenk, 385–399. East Lansing, MI: Michigan State University Press, 2018.

Gutiérrez, Gustavo. *On Job: God-Talk and the Suffering of the Innocent*. Maryknoll, NY: Orbis, 2009.

Hobbes, Thomas. *Leviathan*, ed. Hermann Klenner. Hamburg: Meiner Verlag, 2005. (Original work published in 1651).

Kelly, Joseph F. *The Problem of Evil in the Western Tradition: From the Book of Job to Modern Genetics*. Collegeville, MN: Liturgical Press, 2002.

Kolitz, Zvi. *Yossel Rakover Speaks to God*. New York: Random House, 1999.

Laytner, Anson. *Arguing with God: A Jewish Tradition*. Mahway, NJ: Jason Aronson, 1990.

Leibniz, Gottfried Wilhelm von. *Theodicy: Essays on the Goodness of God, the Freedom of Man, and the Origin of Evil*. Edited by Austin Farrer. Translated by E. M. Huggard. La Salle, IL: Open Court, 1993.

London, Daniel. "Judging God: Learning from the Jewish Tradition of Protest Against God." *Journal of Comparative Theology.* Vol. 6, issue 1 (June 2016): 15–31.

———. "'Pray Interly': Julian of Norwich's Spirituality of Prayer." *Compass: A Review of Topical Theology* Vol. 45 no. 1 (Spring 2015), 14–24.

———. *Theodicy and Spirituality in the Fourth Gospel: A Girardian Perspective*. Lanham, MD: Lexington Books/Fortress Academic, 2020.

Matt, Daniel Chanan. *The Zohar: The Book of Enlightenment*. Mahwah, NJ: Paulist Press, 1988.

McCloud, Scott. *Understanding Comics: The Invisible Art*. New York: HarperCollins, 1993.

Morrow, William. *Protest Against God: The Eclipse of a Biblical Tradition*. Sheffield, UK: Sheffield Phoenix Press, 2007.

Muffs, Yochanan. *Love and Joy: Law, Language and Religion in Ancient Israel*. Cambridge, MA: Harvard University Press, 1992.

Mursell, Gordon. *Out of the Deep: Prayer as Protest*. London: Darton Longman and Todd, 1989.

Roskies, David. *The Literature of Destruction: Jewish Responses to Catastrophe*. Philadelphia, PA: Jewish Publication Society, 1989.

Roth, Laurence. "Drawing Contracts: Will Eisner's Legacy." In *Graven Images: Religion in Comic Books and Graphic Novels*, edited by A. David Lewis and Christine Hoff Kraemer, 44–62. New York: Continuum, 2010.

Wiesel, Elie. *Trial of God* (as it was held on February 25, 1649, in Shamgorod). New York: Schocken Books, 1995.

Chapter 11

Unmasking the Theological Shell
A Girardian Reading of Jonathan Hickman's Secret Wars

Matthew Brake

From 2012 to 2015, the Avengers main comic book title was helmed by Jonathan Hickman, who told an epic, universe-ending tale over the course of three years, covering *Avengers* #1–44 and *New Avengers* #1–33 as well as the event comics *Infinity* #1–6 and *Secret Wars* #1–9. The events in *Secret Wars* take place after the entire Marvel multiverse has been destroyed in a series of incursions, when the Earths of the multiverse collide into each other, taking their entire individual universes with them. In a last-ditch effort to preserve the Marvel universe, Dr. Doom is able to harness enough power to create a world hodge-podged together from the various Earths of the multiverse—Battleworld. On Battleworld, Doom establishes himself as god of the universe and recreates and claims his archnemesis Reed Richards's family as his own. Unbeknownst to Doom, however, Richards has survived and plans to repair the universe.

 René Girard wrote that "the great writers apprehend intuitively and concretely, through the medium of their art . . . the system in which they were first imprisoned together with their contemporaries."[1] At the time of this writing, superheroes are more popular than they have ever been, but comic books, particularly those about superheroes, still have to argue for their place as a genuine human art form with something meaningful to say about human life. This essay continues my argument[2] that Jonathan Hickman is a great writer according to Girard's criteria, and Hickman's superhero writing casts light upon the human situation. As Pierpaolo Antonello says regarding Girard's novelistic criteria, "the successful novel is either a magnifier of the pitfalls of metaphysical desire or [it] is ultimately uninteresting."[3] The discussion of metaphysical desire relates to Girard's theory that human desires do not spontaneously arise from the autonomous subject. Rather, they arise mimetically, by imitating the desires of others. Such mimetic desires eventually breed conflict, and conflict eventually escalates to an unending cycle of violence and revenge. It is here that Girard sees the origins of religion and culture as a whole developing through the sacrifice of an innocent scapegoat, which ends the cycle of violence and establishes the myth that obscures this bloody foundation of a new peaceful order. This order remains in place as long as the myth remains viable, but should the myth be questioned and lose its efficaciousness, a sacrificial crisis will result and mimetic tensions will rise again. To restore peace, a new meaning system or myth must be established.[4]

A Girardian lens illuminates ways in which *Secret Wars* contains key features of a theological reflection on the human situation. One can see Girard's theological anthropology at play in Dr. Doom's own personal myth about being god on Battleworld, his mimetic conflict with Reed Richards, and the sacrificial crisis that brings Battleworld to an end. If great writers uncover the mimetic nature of human interaction, then Hickman demonstrates artistic excellence in a story that illustrates Girard's view of mimesis and the role and function of religion in society.

IT BEGAN WITH A SACRIFICIAL CRISIS . . .

Secret Wars begins with the end of one myth and the establishment of a new myth. Hickman's run on the *Avengers* begins by establishing a myth—the myth of the Avengers World, an expanded roster of heroes established by Iron Man and Captain America. This myth, however, was built on the lie of Cap's betrayal by a secret group of superhero leaders called the Illuminati. It turns out that Iron Man helped Captain America build an expanded roster to make up for that betrayal. When this came out, the Avengers institution fell apart, and Hickman's last issue of *Avengers* features a fight between the two men in which both die as the final incursion between the main Marvel universe and the Ultimate Marvel universe[5] destroys the last remaining remnants of existence.[6]

Girard speaks of the sacrificial crisis as "the disappearance of the sacrificial rites," which he equates with "a crisis of distinctions . . . a crisis affecting the cultural order. This cultural order is nothing more than a regulated system of distinctions in which the differences among individuals are used to establish their 'identity' and their mutual relationships."[7] When the meaning system, myth, or "religious framework of a society starts to totter . . . the whole cultural foundation of the society is put in jeopardy. The institutions lose their vitality; the protective façade of the society gives way; social values are rapidly eroded, and the whole cultural structure seems on the verge of collapse."[8] It is with the loss of differences that order collapses into "violence and chaos."[9] One might recall Mircea Eliade, who discusses the order and differentiation brought about by religion and the sacred as a way of breaking up the chaos of homogeneous nondifferentiation.[10] Girard notes the same theme in "primitive religion," asserting that it is our differences that define our identities.[11] Without them, we are "reduced to indefinite objects, 'things' that wantonly collide with each other like loose cargo on the decks of a storm-tossed ship. . . . In this situation, no one and nothing is spared; coherent thinking collapses and rational activities are abandoned."[12]

This is what we see at the end of Hickman's *Avengers* run and in the first issue of *Secret Wars*—the breakdown of the Avengers organization, the universe, and even the distinctions between right and wrong.[13] Hero and villain alike fight simply to fight. The violence that is unleashed escalates to the extreme; the Marvel universe collapses and dies in chaotic, violent confusion. But waiting in the wings is Dr. Doom, who, with the help of Stephen Strange and Owen Reece the Molecule Man, has obtained the power to remake the universe, and with a new universe, a new mythology is born.

THE MYTH OF GOD-DOOM

Hickman's run on the *Avengers* began like the story of a creation myth: "There was nothing. Following by everything. . . . And then we raced to the light."[14] This myth signified the founding of the Avengers expanded roster. That myth lost its efficacy and the world of which it was a part was destroyed. *Secret Wars* #2 begins with a new myth on Battleworld: "There was nothing. Followed by everything. Swirling, burning specks of creation that circled life-giving suns. God Doom . . . created the light."[15] Gone is any knowledge of the multiverse that existed before Battleworld. In its place is a construct created by Doom after he stole the power from the Beyonders, the original orchestrators of the previous multiverse's destruction. In this new world, Dr. Doom is god, Stephen Strange his sheriff, and the Molecule Man the secret source of Doom's power. All people know is the myth, not the destruction of the previous order. The myth functions to preserve the status quo.

In the myth of Battleworld's creation and the beginning of the religion of Doom, we can see Girard's understanding of myth play out: "Myths are the retrospective transfiguration of sacrificial crises, the reinterpretation of these crises in the light of the cultural order that has arisen from them."[16] As

Grant Kaplan points out, "myths attempt to conceal founding violence."[17] People need their myths to prevent the unleashing of mimetic violence, but as Girard notes:

> Violence will come to an end only after it has had the last word and that word has been accepted as divine. The meaning of this must remain hidden. . . . For religion protects man as long as its ultimate foundations are not revealed. . . . To remove men's ignorance is only to risk exposing them to an even greater peril. The only barrier against human violence is raised on misconception.[18]

On Battleworld, the inhabitants are unaware of the world and social order that came before. All they know is Battleworld, and all they know is God-Doom.

MYTH AND THE SCAPEGOAT

For Girard, at the foundation of every myth is a scapegoat, the unfortunate victim who ends the sacrificial crisis by taking the brunt of the community's violence. Battleworld, whose order is upheld by a myth, contains its own myths within myths and its own history of mini-sacrificial crises. In *Secret Wars* #3, readers discover that in the history of Battleworld, Johnny Storm stood against God-Doom, and as punishment, Doom made him into Battleworld's sun. On Battleworld, any type of schism, blasphemy, or other heresy, dissension, or break from the religion of God-Doom is silenced. As we have seen from our brief discussions of Girard, it can be dangerous when the meaning-structure of a society breaks down because a sacrificial crisis can be unleashed. Violence then overtakes the community; however, these violent impulses are diverted through the sacrifice of a scapegoat. The sacrifice of a scapegoat quells the violence and "all the dissensions, rivalries, jealousies, and quarrels within a community. . . . The purpose of the sacrifice is to restore harmony to the community, to reinforce the social fabric."[19] Johnny Storm becomes that sacrifice that reinforces the social fabric of Battleworld. In order to bring violence to an end, violence must have a victim to blame and "must be deflected to some individual."[20] It is "a matter of pinning the responsibility for the troubled state of the community on some individual."[21]

However, something peculiar happens after the execution or expulsion of the victim. Peace is restored to the community and violence is banished.[22] Girard writes, "Because human thought has never succeeded in grasping the mechanism of violent unanimity, it naturally turns toward the victim and seeks to determine whether he is not somehow responsible for the miraculous consequences of his own death or exile."[23] The result of the quelling of violence through the sacrifice is thus attributed to "the victim himself."[24]

Because his death causes the end to violence (the violence he is blamed for), the scapegoat is now heralded as a savior and even a divine being.[25] Likewise, even though Johnny Storm's fate is a punishment for inciting rebellion, his expulsion to the sky brought peace and he is worshiped as a god. As Girard writes later in his career, "The myth is the *lie* that hides the founding lynching, which speaks to us about the gods, but *never about the victims that the gods used to be*."[26]

A bigger and more relevant example of the relationship between myth and the scapegoat in Hickman's work can be glimpsed in *Secret Wars* #5, entitled, "Owen Reece Died For Our Sins." Owen Reece, or the Molecule Man, is a character that first appeared in 1963 in *Fantastic Four* #20. Before Hickman's use of him in his run, Molecule Man had played important roles in each of Marvel's *Secret Wars* events, events which usually featured the Beyonders.[27] In *Secret Wars* #5, readers are treated to a brief recap of what they learned in *New Avengers* #33 prior to *Secret Wars*. In a bit of retroactive continuity, Hickman reveals that Owen Reece himself is a bomb created by the Beyonders to destroy the entire multiverse, and it wasn't that there were different Molecule Men in each reality. Rather, as Molecule Man says in *New Avengers* #33, "I was constructed as a singular being across all of space and time. . . . A single consciousness shared throughout all my infinite selves." Here, we can see another example of the obfuscation caused by myth, with Molecule Man stating that his origin, as it was generally taken to be for over 40 years of Marvel continuity, was a fiction covering over a disturbing truth, a fiction that came to be "accepted as real." In fact, this fiction concealed the Beyonders' plan to set off all the Molecule Men at once in order to cause "the simultaneous death of everything in the multiverse."[28]

To thwart the Beyonders' plans, Molecule Man takes Dr. Doom 25 years into the past of another universe, to Owen's origin. Molecule Man, with the consent of his doppelganger, kills this version of himself. As he explains to Doom in *New Avengers* #33:

Molecule Man: (speaking about the Beyonders) They lit my fuse, and now I—all of me—am terminal. And when I die . . . I'll take my universe with me. And they [the Beyonders] want to see what happens when we all go off at once.

Dr. Doom: But that isn't what occurred. You died and nothing happened.

Molecule Man: Sure it did. But that me—one of an infinite number of me's—died early, in fact. If we're going to thwart their plan, you're going to have to kill a whole lot more of me . . . and soon.

Dr. Doom balks at Reece's suggestion, wondering how one man could accomplish something so vast. Molecule Man's answer is that Doom must start a religion. Here, Girardian parallels become apparent, particularly in Molecule Man's speech to Doom:

> It all comes down to you, so you must protect your own anonymity—no one must guess who the great destroyer really is. . .and how it is that he knows what to do. Become a myth. Become a legend. Become a murderer . . . a serial killer who only kills one person.[29]

Over time, as Doom kills more and more Molecule Men, he gains followers, the Swans, who carry on his mission with him. An ever greater number of Molecule Men are killed and, unchecked and unrivaled, violence escalates and spreads.

Notice the Girardian parallels. There is, first of all, the solitary sacrificial victim whose death is meant to stave off the annihilation of everything. There is also the obfuscation of myth to hide the true reason for killing the sacrificial victim. The Swans don't know the reason their god wants to kill the many manifestations of the Molecule Man. They simply do it. Girard writes about this obscuring function:

> The sacrificial process requires a certain degree of *misunderstanding*. The celebrants do not and must not comprehend the true role of the sacrificial act. The theological basis of the sacrifice has a crucial role in fostering this misunderstanding. It is the god who supposedly demands the victims . . .[30]

The sacred myth obscures the true function of sacrifice, to divert the violence and destruction that would otherwise consume the community. This brings us back to *Secret Wars*. In issue #3, readers see a statue of Molecule Man in God-Doom's private garden. As noted, the victims who are initially seen as the cause of the sacrificial crisis, are retrospectively honored, and sometimes even divinized. While Owen Reece was the victim that had to be sacrificed to save the multiverse (a plan which ultimately fails) and was quite literally the cause of the conflict with the Beyonders, he is remembered fondly after the fact.

In the end, Doom, Dr. Strange, and the Molecule Man defeated the Beyonders by creating additional Molecule Men of their own, destroying the Beyonders and allowing the final remaining Molecule Man to channel the Beyonders power into Doom, who then created Battleworld, whose myth of God-Doom covered over the true foundation of the world. In *Secret Wars* #5, we find out that Molecule Man is still alive and hidden underneath of the statue commemorating him, and that he is the source of Doom's power. Doom's divinity is thus bestowed by Owen Reece, and in the upcoming sacrificial crisis of Battleworld, that divinity becomes, in the words of Girard, "a prize in the struggle between two rivals."[31]

DR. DOOM, REED RICHARDS, AND MIMETIC RIVALRY

The rivalry between Reed Richards, aka Mr. Fantastic, and Victor von Doom is a storied affair in the history of Marvel Comics. The two men were rivals in college, with Reed eventually warning Doom about a miscalculation in an experiment. Doom ignored Richards' advice, ruining his own experiment and destroying his own face. Nevertheless, Doom blamed Reed for the accident, and this led to Doom's lifelong pursuit of vengeance against Reed.

Anyone reading the stories about Dr. Doom knows that the accident that disfigured him is merely a pretense for his jealousy of Reed Richards. Human desire is learned and mediated through others. When we see that someone else wants an object, this signals to us that this particular object is desirable, and so we want it, too. When two people want the same object, this is bound to produce rivalry. Dr. Doom, like any victim of mimetic desire, says that "it is the mediator [Reed Richards] who is responsible for the rivalry."[32] The truth, however, is that it is Dr. Doom who desires what Reed has. In *Secret Wars*, Doom has made Reed's family his own. Sue Richards, the Invisible Woman, is his wife, and Franklin and Valeria Richards are his children. As Reed will later exclaim to Doom, "You stole my family!"[33] Doom has all of this, and total dominion of the universe, a goal he could never obtain because Reed was always in his way.

And yet, as Girard writes, "The moment [he] takes hold of the desired object its 'virtue' disappears like gas from a burst balloon. The object has been suddenly desecrated by possession and reduced to its objective qualities, thus provoking the . . . exclamation: 'Is that all it is?!'"[34] Scott Cowdell acknowledges:

> what Girard came to call acquisitive mimesis is revealed to be at best partial. . . . the real focus of acquisition is the being of [the] model—that is why acquiring an object typically fails to satisfy because this or that object is only ever a proxy for the being of the model, which remains elusive.[35]

And God-Doom is nothing if not dissatisfied by his life on Battleworld. In *Secret Wars* #3, Doom is discontent and almost bored with his life on Battleworld. As his sheriff, Dr. Strange, reads off reports from across Battleworld, Doom interrupts him:

God-Doom: Why do you bother with this, Stephen?

Dr. Strange: What do you mean?

Dr. Doom: You know full well what I mean. This banality . . . this tedious record-keeping of minor transgressions.

This issue drives Doom's discontent home even further in a section entitled, "The Disquiet Heart of God." In this issue, Doom has a conversation with Susan, describing himself as the one flaw in this world he has created: "There is no flaw in the world—it is the world I wanted. But my people are restless because I fail to properly inspire them. I am a poor god. . . . I'm beginning to think that in my perfect world . . . *I* am the one flawed thing." While Susan assures him that that is not so, Girard would agree with Doom's assessment. For so long, Doom thought ridding himself of Reed Richards would allow him to get what he really wants: power, godhood, and apparently Reed's family. Yet having attained those things, Doom is still incomplete.

The objects Doom attained in Battleworld with the power of the Beyonders are ultimately superfluous. What mimetic rivals actually desire is "being." Girard writes:

> [M]an is subject to intense desires, though he may not know precisely for what. The reason is that he desires *being*, something he lacks and which some other person seems to possess. The subject thus looks to that other person to inform him of what he should desire in order to acquire that being. If the model . . . desires some object, that object must surely be capable of conferring an even greater plenitude of being.[36]

Doom's attitude and actions reflect the fact that what he ultimately wants from Reed Richards are not Reed's possessions, but Reed's very being. He wants to *be* Reed. This would explain Doom's hatred of Reed. Girard writes:

> Only someone who prevents us from satisfying a desire which he himself has inspired in us is truly an object of hatred. The person who hates first hates himself for the secret admiration concealed by his hatred. In an effort to hide this desperate admiration from others, and from himself, he no longer wants to see in his mediator anything but an obstacle.[37]

When Reed Richards reappears on Battleworld in *Secret Wars* #4, he indeed draws Doom's eye. Doom appears on the battlefield and confronts Reed, giving him a chance to surrender and bow before Doom. Stephen Strange casts a spell sending Reed away, knowing full well that Reed would not yield to Doom, and that Doom would kill Reed. Doom demands that Strange bring Reed back, but Strange refuses. Doom, however, recognizes that Reed and the others will try to restore the world to the way it was. Reed is an obstacle that must be brought into submission or destroyed. But Strange digs deeper, telling Doom, "Even with all this power. You're still afraid of him. Well, you know what, old friend? I think you should be." With that, Doom disintegrates Strange as the comic book produces a menacing close up of his eyes. It isn't that Reed is just an obstacle—he is the Girardian mediator, who Doom hates because of an admiration he won't admit to himself.

This admiration does indeed exist. In Doom and Reed's final confrontation in *Secret Wars* #9, Reed confronts Doom for stealing his family and creating a world that he controls too tightly. In reply, Doom exclaims:

> "I understand now—I know what this is. It's the same thing it's always been between you and I . . . you think you are better than I am. . . . If you had this power, you think you could have solved it all—solved everything . . . you think you could have done so . . . much . . . better . . . don't you? Don't you?!"

Reed's reply is simple: "Yes. And we both know it. Don't we?" Likewise, Doom's reply is not surprising if you understand Girard's account of metaphysical desire: "Yes. Damn you . . . now die!" We will return to the end of this conflict in the next section.

YET ANOTHER SACRIFICIAL CRISIS, THE BATTLE FOR DIVINITY, AND THE ETERNAL RETURN

With the appearance on Battleworld of those who remember the previous Marvel multiverse, a new sacrificial crisis is initiated. As Girard writes, "For religion protects man as long as its ultimate foundations are not revealed. . . . To remove men's ignorance is only to risk exposing them to an even greater peril. The only barrier against human violence is raised on misconception."[38] Doom, with the help of Stephen Strange, built up an entire world and religion around himself. Any discrepancies that were discovered that would have undone this myth were carefully monitored by Strange. As Girard says regarding the criticisms of religion, "Religion . . . is far from 'useless.' Religious misinterpretation is a truly constructive force, for it purges man of the suspicions that would poison his existence if he were to remain conscious of the crisis as it actually took place."[39] When the religious misconception is removed, the results can be disastrous. Girard tells us, "The withering away of the transcendental influence means that there is no longer the slightest difference between a desire to save the city and unbridled ambition, between genuine piety and the desire to claim divine status for oneself."[40] And Reed and the others do nothing if not try to unravel the myth of God-Doom.

In *Secret Wars* #6, we find Reed and his young, evil doppelganger from the Ultimate Marvel universe discussing their plans for beating Doom. The presence of two Reeds has an interesting parallel with Girard's thought as well, since Girard asserts that twins "*epitomize the entire* [sacrificial] *crisis*."[41] As noted earlier, if the sacrificial crisis consists of the breakdown of myth and the societal distinctions it helps to forge, then twins represent "a fear that their extreme resemblance [signifies] the advent of acute conflict."[42] While Ultimate Reed has unleashed a "prophet" on Doom's world to call into question his godhood, Reed attempts to find the source of Doom's power, eventually discovering that it is the Molecule Man (which leads to the encounter spoken about at the end of the last section). The unraveling of Doom's myth leads to all the forces of Battleworld descending on Doom's castle in a war of all against all in *Secret Wars* #7.[43]

In a very literal way, Battleworld falls apart as multiple combatants battle for divinity, which Girard says is the prize to be attained during the sacrificial crisis.[44] Thanos confronts Doom and speaks disparagingly against his godhood. Black Panther, now the lord of the dead, shows up on the battlefield with an army of the undead, ready to fight Doom using an Infinity Gauntlet (giving him the might of a god). Realizing that Black Panther is a distraction, Doom confronts Reed in the Molecule Man's underground room. Molecule Man allows the two men to fight, no longer channeling the Beyonders' power into Doom. When Doom admits that Reed could have done a better job than him, Molecule Man says, "Okay, then. If you both agree. . . ." This sets off a detonation, ending Battleworld and rebooting the Marvel universe. Reed seems to win this contest. We then see Reed and his family rebuilding the multiverse, and we see Doom is in Latveria with a healed face.

The cycle now begins again, a possibility that can exist in the Marvel universe although, Girard thinks, not in our own. For Girard, religion served to temper what he calls "the escalation to extremes," of unlimited violence that could end humanity itself.[45] This apocalyptic element in Girard's thought appears as a part of his own interpretation of Christian revelation. The death of Jesus Christ reveals the innocence of all victims, and in revealing their innocence, lays bare all the mythological misconceptions that conceal this fact, thus robbing religion of the efficacy it once enjoyed.[46] As Cowdell writes, "[I]t challenges the pagan eschatology of the eternal return, disrupting a cyclical view of time that runs on sacrificial blood."[47] It is just such a "pagan eschatology" that the Marvel universe finds itself a part of. Al Ewing's *Ultimates* #1 follows up on some of the threads from Hickman's *Secret Wars*, noting that Hickman's story affected the entire "omniverse" and indicating that it has moved from a seventh to an eighth iteration. For Girard, it may no longer be possible to witness the eternal return in our world, but the world of the Marvel universe gives us an opportunity to engage in such a thought experiment.

An argument could be made that Reed Richards acts as the revelatory agent, exposing the myth for the lie that it is. After all, it is Reed's appearance on Battleworld that begins to unravel and expose Doom's myth. Reed is also a man of science, who is not interested in replacing one myth with another. Girard, in a comment that opens him up to criticisms of ethnocentrism, believes that it is the demystification that Christianity brings to bear on religion that destroys "the ignorance and superstition that are indispensable" to religions that rely on sacrifice and the obfuscation of myth.[48] Christianity "made possible an advance in knowledge" and allowed for the invention of "science, technology and all the best and worst of culture."[49] For Girard, Reed would be a product of the effects of Christian revelation. Would this, then, make him a Christ figure?

Yes and no. On the one hand, while there might be resonances between Reed and Christ as revelatory agent, Reed is still very much bound by mimetic violence, becoming the violent twin of Doom. As the two begin to battle each other, Owen Reece notes that the two are now equal in his eyes. Christ's revelatory power, by contrast, consists in completely abstaining from retaliatory violence, something Reed cannot claim. In fact, engaging in violence in a world where sacrifice has been demystified is dangerous, for there is no longer a braking mechanism for the cycle of retaliation.[50] Additionally, Reed does not bring an end to the eternal return. On the other hand, whereas Girard describes the mimetic cycle as only ending when one party strikes the killing blow,[51] Reed refrains from doing so when given the Molecule Man's power. Instead of destroying his enemy and erasing him from existence, Reed heals Doom's face, which was damaged in an accident that Doom always blamed Reed for. And what more Christ-like action could there be than loving and healing one's enemies?

CONCLUSION

Although comics are often viewed as a frivolous medium, I have maintained for some time the excellence and Girardian nature of Jonathan Hickman's three-year Avengers tale with its culmination in *Secret Wars*. That Hickman's narrative lends itself to such a reading without, presumably, having any of Girard's influence on his thought illustrates Girard's point, that great literature indicates the mimetic nature of humanity with all of its accompanying accoutrements such as religion, myth, and the sacrificial victim. The Girardian lens brings to light dynamics that resonate with and reinforce theological reflection about violence, human interaction, and Christology. Far from imposing an interpretation, this way of reading the text discloses hitherto neglected dynamics, rendering Hickman's work intensely interesting, not least of all for the theologically attuned reader.

NOTES

1. René Girard, *Deceit, Desire, and the Novel: Self and Other in Literary Structure*, translated by Yvonne Freccero (Baltimore, MD: Johns Hopkins University Press, 1965), 3.

2. See my forthcoming essay in *The Ages of the Black Panther: Essays on the King of Wakanda in Comic Books*, edited by Joseph J. Darowsky (Jefferson, NC: McFarland and Company, Inc., Publishers, 2020); Matthew Brake, "Mythology, Mimesis, and Apocalypse in Jonathan Hickman's *Avengers*," *Theology and the Marvel Universe*, edited by Gregory Stevenson (New York: Lexington Books/Fortress Academic, 2020).

3. Pierpaolo Antonello, "The Novel, Deviated Transcendency, and Modernity," *Religion and Literature*, vol. 43, no. 3 (2011): 168, cited in Scott Cowdell, *René Girard and the Nonviolent God* (Notre Dame, IN: University of Notre Dame Press, 2018), 11.

4. René Girard, *Battling to the End: Conversations with Benoît Chantre*, translated by Mary Baker (East Lansing, MI: Michigan State University Press, 2010), 13.

5. The Ultimate Marvel universe was a comics line launched in 2000 that depicted an alternate take on many of Marvel's characters. The multiversal designation for Marvel's main continuity was Earth-616, while the Ultimate universe Earth was designated Earth1610.

6. I go into this extensively in my essay for *Theology and the Marvel Universe*.

7. René Girard, *Violence and the Sacred*, translated by Patrick Gregory (Baltimore, MD: Johns Hopkins University Press, 1977), 49.

8. Ibid. 49.

9. Ibid. 51.

10. Mircea Eliade, *The Sacred and the Profane: The Nature of Religion*, translated by Willard R. Trask (New York: Harcourt, Inc., 1987), 21–22.

11. Girard, *Violence and the Sacred*, 51.

12. Ibid. 51.

13. Ibid. 51.

14. Jonathan Hickman, *Avengers* #1.

15. Jonathan Hickman, *Secret Wars* #2.

16. Girard, *Violence and the Sacred*, 64.

17. Grant Kaplan, *René Girard, Unlikely Apologist*, cited as epigram in Cowdell, *René Girard and the Nonviolent God*, 26.

18. Girard, *Violence and the Sacred*, 135.

19. Ibid. 8.

20. Ibid. 78.

21. Ibid. 78.

22. Ibid. 85.

23. Ibid. 85.
24. Ibid. 85.
25. Ibid. 85–87.
26. Girard, *Battling to the End*, 22.
27. "Owen Reece (Earth-616)." Marvel Database. https://marvel.fandom.com/wiki/Owen_Reece_(Earth-616) (retrieved December 26, 2019).
28. Jonathan Hickman, *New Avengers* #33.
29. Ibid.
30. Girard, *Violence and the Sacred*, 7.
31. Ibid. 129.
32. Girard, *Deceit, Desire, and the Novel*, 11.
33. Jonathan Hickman, Secret Wars #9. The original text doesn't include an exclamation mark, but instead provides exclamation by bolding the text.
34. Girard, *Deceit, Desire, and the Novel*, 88.
35. Cowdell, *René Girard and the Nonviolent God*, 10.
36. Girard, *Violence and the Sacred*, 146.
37. Girard, *Deceit, Desire, and the Novel*, 10–11.
38. Girard, *Violence and the Sacred*, 135.
39. Ibid. 134–135.
40. Ibid. 135.
41. Ibid. 63.
42. René Girard, *The One By Whom Scandal Comes*, translated by M.B. DeBevoise (East Lansing, MI: Michigan State University, 2014), 12.
43. It is a bit difficult to distinguish Secret Wars 7–9 in the collected edition that I'm using. While the earlier chapters are broken up and numbered, these final issues simply run into each other in the collected edition.
44. Girard, *Violence and the Sacred*, 151.
45. Girard, *Battling to the End*, 20.
46. Ibid. 103.
47. Cowdell, *René Girard and the Nonviolent God*, 133.
48. Girard, *Battling to the End*, xiii–xiv.
49. Ibid. xiv.
50. Ibid. xiv–xv.
51. Girard, *Violence and the Sacred*, 26.

BIBLIOGRAPHY

Academic Resources

Cowdell, Scott. *René Girard and the Nonviolent God*. Notre Dame, IN: University of Notre Dame Press, 2018.

Eliade, Mircea. *The Sacred and the Profane: The Nature of Religion*. Trans. Willard R. Trask. New York: Harcourt, Inc., 1987.

Girard, René. *Battling to the End: Conversations with Benoît Chantre*. Trans. Mary Baker. East Lansing, MI: Michigan State University Press, 2010.

———. *Deceit, Desire, and the Novel: Self and Other in Literary Structure*. Trans. Yvonne Freccero. Baltimore, MD: Johns Hopkins University Press, 1965.

———. *The One By Whom Scandal Comes*. Trans. M.B. DeBevoise. East Lansing, MI: Michigan State University, 2014.

———. *Violence and the Sacred*. Trans. Patrick Gregory. Baltimore, MD: Johns Hopkins University Press, 1977.

Comics

Avengers #1. 2012. Written by Jonathan Hickman. Illustrated by Jerome Opeña. New York: Marvel Comics.

New Avengers #33. Written by Jonathan Hickman. Illustrated by Mike Deodato. New York: Marvel Comics.

Secret Wars #2. Written by Jonathan Hickman. Illustrated by Esad Ribic. New York: Marvel Comics.

Secret Wars #9. Written by Jonathan Hickman. Illustrated by Esad Ribic. New York: Marvel Comics.

Chapter 12

From Autonomy to Annihilation
The Monstrous Truth of the Romantic Lie

Robert Grant Price

René Girard's ideas have wide appeal because they have inside them, burning like an ember, an elemental truth that allows a reader to touch them against almost any text and set a fire. His well-known mimetic theory resonates because it helps to explain human nature and the art we make. His theory, briefly, says that humans model ourselves after others so completely that we imitate their desires. This desire for a common object—whether land, love, or lucre—leads to competition that culminates in violence. Even more profoundly—and perhaps more disturbingly—we desire not only what the other possess but also the very being of the other.[1]

Literature gives us a window onto the tragedies brought about by desire. In a sense, every tragedy warns us to choose our models wisely and to think carefully about what we desire. The person who desires ultimate power should note well what has happened to those people who reached for that same power.

This essay applies Girard's theories of mimetic desire and the scapegoat mechanism to the stories of three closely related characters: Dr. Victor Frankenstein, the namesake of Mary Shelley's novel *Frankenstein*; Dr. Henry Jekyll, the tragic figure in Robert Louis Stevenson's novella *The Strange Case of Dr. Jekyll & Mr. Hyde*; and Dr. Bruce Banner, the alter ego of comic book superhero—and monster—the Hulk. More specifically, this essay discusses how these characters who live "the romantic lie" undergo "novelistic conversion." By romantic, Girard was referring to the Romantic era, a period of artistic and intellectual growth during the 1800s that glorified the individual—and not just the individual, but the heroic individual, the self-created person set apart from all others, unique unto themselves. Girard, who saw mimetic desire as the key feature of human activity, regarded the notion of the self-created person as delusional, a lie. As Robert Doran explains, people seduced by the romantic lie believe that "desire is autonomous, unmediated, and will lead to personal fulfillment" but often discover "the truth of desires, namely that desire will never lead to self-fulfillment but only to alienation, despair, and spiritual death."[2] Romantic novels, then, are works that flatter romantic readers into believing that they are original in their thoughts, actions, and interpretations of the text. These works "reflect the presence of a mediator without ever revealing it"[3]—that is, they keep the mimetic process hidden from the reader and sustain the romantic lie of "spontaneous desire."[4] Romanesque novels, by contrast, are novelistic. The novelistic reveals what is hidden in a novel by exposing the mechanisms of mediated desire. In these novels characters undergo a radical conversion—a "novelistic conversion"—as they confront the true nature of desire. Such characters begin with the naïve belief that they are autonomous and independent, but as they are disabused of this false autonomy and confront their fundamental interdependence on others, they are humbled. Conversion involves "giving up one's dearest illusions," Girard explains. "[I]t is always victory over desire, victory over Promethean pride."[5]

Part of the romantic lie is to be beguiled by the Satan figure, the "father of lies from the beginning." Each of the doctors discussed in this chapter tries to make the myth of the self-made man, the man-made-god, his story. Each man fails. Rather than perfect a new creation and become like God, each unleashes a monstrosity into the world: Frankenstein reanimates a corpse that then goes on a killing spree; Jekyll lets a violent pervert loose in London; and Banner unleashes a green monster that wants to kill everybody.

Girard helps us to see these dynamics and uncovers the way of atonement through his insight into the scapegoat. Scapegoating always fails, as these tragedies demonstrate, and in the end, each doctor must atone for what he has done. Atonement—literally, being at-one with oneself—requires that he vanquish his monster, which means vanquishing his pride. True peace and wholeness come not through violence but through forgiveness. The logic of prideful self-assertion must give way to the logic of forgiveness.

Popular culture texts have a reputation as low brow because they tend to be romantic instead of novelistic. They tend to portray heroes as existing unto themselves and triumphing thanks to their originality and guts. Yet, the failure of so many pop heroes to repudiate the romantic lie does not disqualify these texts from philosophical or theological discussion. Indeed, pop culture heroes offer us exceptional *negative* exemplars of Girard's theory of conversion. In the cases of the three doctors, we see what happens to people who fall for the ultimate romantic lie—that they can compete with God, create like God, and be like God. Like Frankenstein, Jekyll, and Banner, we might convince ourselves that we can control our desires for power only to discover that our desires control us. Then we will have a choice: Do we live the romantic lie and let our desires consume us? Or do we renounce our pride and ask others to help us order our desires?

DESIRE FOR GOD-LIKE POWER

Victor Frankenstein remains in our cultural consciousness not simply because he is the first character in modern science fiction, but because he embodies the archetype of the rebel angel so perfectly for our technological times. He is a proud man who admits to Walton, the captain of the ship that rescues him, that he has committed a great evil. Distraught by the death of his mother, Frankenstein coveted God's power to create new life and vanquish death:

> A new species would bless me as its creator and source; many happy and excellent natures would owe their being to me. No father could claim the gratitude of his child so completely as I should deserve theirs. Pursuing these reflections, I thought that if I could bestow animation upon lifeless matter, I might . . . renew life where death had apparently devoted the body to corruption.[6]

In his search for a god-like power, Frankenstein turns to alchemical and occultic science found in the works of Paracelsus and Cornelius Agrippa.[7] Frankenstein masters these dark arts and, late one evening, imparts life on a hulking collection of stitched together body parts. The monster, meant to be beautiful, is ravishingly ugly. Horrified at his "catastrophe," Frankenstein flees.[8] He abandons his monster, but it does not abandon him.

The threads of Greek myth, the Book of Genesis, and *Paradise Lost* that Shelley weaves into her novel play out as a series of Girardian imitations and reversals. The first she signals in the subtitle her novel: "The Modern Prometheus." The Greeks credited Prometheus with teaching humans to use fire, an advance that made human civilization possible. As punishment for defying the gods, Zeus bound Prometheus to a rock and tortured him for eternity. Victor Frankenstein is the modern Prometheus, the one who defies God and suffers for his transgression. But unlike the Titan, who in Aeschylus's plays civilizes humanity, Frankenstein hoards this knowledge and power for himself. He shares Prometheus's desire to defy God, but not the desire to civilize his creation.

Without direction from his creator, the monster seeks instruction in the world. His search for models offers a clear example of Girard's mediated desire—desire that is mediated to one person through another. In this case, the monster models himself after characters in the books he reads. They mediate his desire. The self-obsessed and suicidal Werther from Goethe's *Sorrows of Young Werther* provides one example. Through Werther, who he views as divine, the monster "wants to be loved in the way that Werther is loved and wants to be in love as Werther loves."[9] The monster also finds inspiration in Lucifer from *Paradise Lost* (a book he believes is "true history"). Like Lucifer, the monster rebels against his Creator and attacks his Creator through others (Lucifer attacks Adam and Eve; the monster kills Frankenstein's friends and family). On his own, the monster is no one and everyone: stitched together from many others. The characters mediate to the monster a sense of who he should be. They direct his desire not to a *what* (an honest man, perhaps) but the *who* he will be (Werther, or Lucifer).

Frankenstein, too, imitates Satanic figures. Most obviously, he models himself on Milton's Lucifer. He shares Lucifer's contempt for God and wishes to upset His order. More subtly, Frankenstein embodies Girard's understanding of Satan. Satan, Girard argued, is not a goateed devil, but the dark side of society. The Hebrew word for "Satan" is "the Accuser." It is Satan who accuses God in the Book of Job, and it is Satan—found in society as the mob—who accuses the innocent of crimes. This accusation begins the process of scapegoating.

In *Frankenstein*, the scapegoating ritual happens the moment that Frankenstein brings his monster to life. The monster is, at this point in the novel, entirely innocent. It was supposed to be beautiful—and it is, in the sense that it is miraculous—but Frankenstein views his creation as an abomination. Frankenstein flees, the monster pursues him, and Frankenstein's guilt at bringing the unholy thing into God's creation intensifies. He comes to believe that if he kills the creature, he will right his wrongs.

A pervasive line in *Frankenstein* scholarship is that Victor Frankenstein and the creature are the same person. Both grow up without a mother, educate themselves mostly through private reading, suffer loneliness and friendlessness, reject their creator, and ultimately fail in their pursuits.[10] To put it as Girard might, Frankenstein essentially duplicated himself when he created his monster. This mimetic doubling intensifies as the novel progresses, with the two rivals pursuing the single goal of undoing creation, a failing mission that devolves into a desire to destroy the other. For Frankenstein, his homicidal drive to erase the creature inverts into a suicidal crusade to eliminate himself and his lethal pride.

Like Lucifer, Frankenstein is destined to fail in his original desire to supplant God. Unlike God, who creates out of love and whose creations are beautiful, Frankenstein creates out of a desire to remake the natural order and ends up creating disorder and ugliness. Where God creates *ex nihilo*, Frankenstein creates by weaving together dead flesh. What is more, his creation never could have rivaled God's, since created works must always be inferior to their creator. Humanity sits below God; humanity's creations must necessarily sit below humanity.

Ultimately, Frankenstein fails as Creator because he does not understand love. When God sees that Adam is lonely, He creates for him a companion, Eve. He does this because he loves Adam. But when the monster tells Frankenstein that he is lonely, Frankenstein creates, and then spitefully destroys, a bride for the monster. In this way, Shelley's novel inverts Genesis: fallen man creates a fallen creature; sees its presence as a rupture in creation; and heals the rupture by destroying it. Where God says in Genesis that his work is "good," Frankenstein realizes that his work is "bad." And where the Christian God seeks out his creation, in the novel, the creature must seek out the creator. When Frankenstein finally does search for his creation, it is to kill it.

Frankenstein sought power, not "happiness in tranquility."[11] In the end, his misdirected desire for god-like power destroyed him, much like it destroyed Henry Jekyll.

A SURRENDER TO DESIRE

On the surface, Dr. Henry Jekyll conducts himself like a perfect Victorian gentleman. But there is more to the man. Like Frankenstein, the ambitious Jekyll hoped to remake creation. He admits in a letter to his lawyer Gabriel Utterson that he sought to improve his humanity by performing "a miracle"[12] that would separate the evil aspect of his being from his good. Once liberated from the "current of disordered sensual images" that ran through his mind, he hypothesized that he could finally live a virtuous life as the all-good Henry Jekyll.[13] He studied the occult and devised a green potion that transformed him into Edward Hyde, a dwarfish, ugly man who embodied all his desires. At night, Jekyll drank his potion so that he could, in the guise of Hyde, indulge his desires for sex and violence.

The real horror of the novel begins when Jekyll discovers the consuming power of disordered desire: the longer he spends as Hyde, and the more he indulges his dark desires, the more powerful these desires become. Hyde grows in stature and strength, from a dwarf to a man, until one morning Jekyll wakes to find himself trapped in the body of Hyde. Jekyll's desires overtake him, and he must now drink the potion to revert to Jekyll. He becomes, through errant desire, a monstrous double and interchangeable with Hyde.

For Girard, the monstrous double represents the moment when desires align to such an extent that the double and the monster come to share the same being, their differences "muddied and confused." "When violent hysteria reaches a peak the monstrous double looms up everywhere at once. The decisive act of violence is directed against this awesome vision of evil and at the same time sponsored by it."[14]

This is exactly what happens to Jekyll. In his last testament, Jekyll explains that the salts in his potion were contaminated by some unknown element, and he cannot reconstitute enough potion to maintain his appearance as Jekyll. In his final act, he directs a "decisive act of violence against this awesome vision of evil" and kills himself before transforming permanently into Hyde.

The story asks whether we can separate ourselves from our desires. Its answer: We cannot. As Padnick observes, *The Strange Case* is not a story about duality in the human person, as it is popularly understood; rather, it is a story about the unity of the person.[15] We are each products of our choices to do good or to do evil. Jekyll's powers were not creative—that is, he did not create a new person named Hyde. All that he did was to break his inhibitions. All he did was put on a mask. Hyde was the mask, and he wore it to "hide" from himself.

Mimetic desire and the scapegoating mechanism unfold in *The Strange Case* much as they do in *Frankenstein*. Jekyll wants God's power to remake human nature. Since God's power is inaccessible to Jekyll, Jekyll commits himself to the study of magic, much like Frankenstein did. And like Frankenstein, Jekyll fails. Instead of preserving himself as a virtuous man, he unleashes Hyde, an unrepentant deviant. Jekyll's desire culminates in violence: His transformation into Hyde is a violent self-effacement, and Hyde's crimes are violence against others.

With Hyde's violence now threatening Jekyll's own life and security—not to mention his conscience—Jekyll seeks to scapegoat his crimes. Here we see one of the story's most interesting turns. Jekyll accuses Hyde for the disorder and violence. At first glance, this accusation seems correct. After all, Hyde *did* commit the crimes. On a closer inspection, however, we see how Hyde is scapegoated. Indeed, Jekyll created Hyde *as* a scapegoat. The plan all along was to isolate Jekyll's desires from his conscience so that, his desires "housed" in a "separate identit[y],"[16] he would no longer feel guilt about his sins. In fact, he would not even know what he was doing when he "wore the semblance of Edward Hyde."[17] In a sense, Jekyll wanted to maintain his innocence—and ignorance—of the crimes his dark side committed. He wanted to be able to make an accusation against the guilty party with unimpeachable righteousness. Or to put it another way, he wanted a criminal party that he could justly destroy.

Jekyll's plan to scapegoat Hyde is diabolical—Satanic, even—and it is *his* plan, not Hyde's. Hyde is guilty, no doubt, but so is Jekyll. The problem, from a Girardian perspective, is that Jekyll does not truly understand the unity of his person and the consequences of the actions he committed as Hyde—and if he does understand, he cannot fully own up to his guilt. Girard argued that to overcome self-centeredness—the romantic lie—we must, as do characters in great novels, draw more deeply into ourselves and to know ourselves to the point that we can see others in ourselves.[18] Jekyll cannot overcome himself. He speaks of Hyde as another, even when he speaks of Hyde's experiences from a first-person perspective. Jekyll maintains a Self-Other distance between himself and Hyde to the point that he speculates that if Hyde dies on the scaffold, such a death would concern "another than myself."[19]

Nobody and nothing can compete with God, who is all good, and only the proudest and most foolish believe they can create as God creates. The dark arts—the weak alternative that Frankenstein and Jekyll seize—will always bring destruction since they lack the virile, creative power of God's goodness. *The Strange Case* makes this point emphatically: Jekyll's science was entirely ineffectual; it was only an accident of contaminated salts that brought about his transformation. The man, who boasted to his colleague Lanyon that establishment science would have to recognize Hyde as their "superior,"[20] proved to be a personal and professional failure. His act of atonement—suicide—looks as much like an evasion of justice as it does a desire to strike down Hyde before the deviant can hurt more people.

In the end, Jekyll's story is one about surrender. Jekyll surrendered to his self-centered desires. Jekyll's self-centeredness is, as Girard described, not the "one-sided egotism" that we commonly associate with selfish people. Instead, Jekyll's self-centeredness led him to believe that he was two people: himself, the good man; and another, the evil one. He gave into "an impulse in two contradictory directions which always ends up tearing the individual apart."[21]

To Jekyll's horror, he discovered that a surrender to even the slightest of his desires led to him becoming subject to and enslaved by desire. In a real sense, he chose who he would be—not the good Dr. Jekyll but the cruel Mr. Hyde. This choice came early in the novel, exactly at the point when Jekyll decided to invent a potion to separate his conscience from actions. Once he chose to cede his will to his desire, his fall became impossible to arrest, like a tumble down a greased pipe. For he had already ceded his will to his desires. Dr. Bruce Banner, a reimagining of Jekyll, learned this lesson too: Once the demon is free, it is hard to control.

EVIL—MORE OR LESS

The Incredible Hulk made his comic book debut in 1962. Stan Lee, who with Jack Kirby created the character, meant for the Hulk to retell *The Strange Case* for the Nuclear Age.[22] The many iterations of the Hulk over the last fifty years, from comic books to big budget films, give us new ways of understanding the tragedy of Henry Jekyll.

In the first and most popular iteration of the character, Dr. Bruce Banner is a military scientist who builds a weapon of mass destruction: the gamma bomb. As the bomb test begins, Banner runs onto the testing ground to save the life of a teenager who has wandered onto the test site. The bomb explodes, exposing Banner to gamma rays that transform him into the beast called the Hulk.

The Banner/Hulk character developed over the years, but the stories never ventured far from the Jekyll/Hyde storyline about a man's battle to control his passions. In early storylines, Banner transforms into the Hulk when he becomes enraged. By the 1990s, the character morphed into the cynical Grey Hulk, a direct parallel of Hyde. Grey Hulk indulged in sex and violence and played the hero only when it suited him—or when he disliked his enemy, either out of vanity or spite. This storyline progressed and eventually readers learned the source of Banner's rage: he had an abusive father. Unconsciously, Banner imitated his father and grew up to become a duplicate of his father, a monster who took his anger out on others.

The Immortal Hulk, a 2018 reboot of the character written by Al Ewing, breaks from the duality of earlier versions of the character and meditates on what Banner would be if he and the Hulk consciously shared the same goal. The answer is evil—more or less. Readers learn that the gamma rays that Banner had been exposed to were, in fact, emanations from Hell. Banner the scientist becomes Banner the alchemist; the Hulk, once an expression of Banner's fears, is now animated by evil. More dramatically, Banner is shown to have had a plan for his gamma bomb. As the Hulk, he accuses humanity's leaders of endangering life on the planet with nuclear bombs and environmental degradation. So, he says, he will destroy the planet and start over.[23]

Ewing's reenvisioning of the Hulk makes the character a more conscious imitation of Jekyll. Like Jekyll, Banner desires a godly power to remake creation. Like Jekyll, he devises a green potion that—entirely by accident, as it turns out—physically transforms him into a monster composed entirely of his most wicked desires. Both Banner and Jekyll exhibit contempt for their professional rivals and lord their power over others. And both men—Jekyll and Ewing's Hulk—scapegoat their crimes. Jekyll blames Hyde, who is himself. Hulk accuses humanity and its imperfect leadership for being "puny humans"—as if we could be anything other than puny and human. (Ewing's version complicates the version of the Hulk popularized in serials from the 1970s. In that version, Banner, having admitted to himself that he is the monster, casts himself out of society, as much to protect civilization as to punish himself. Hated and alone, he tries to develop a cure that will banish the monster forever. Ewing's version turns on humanity and sees his power—and himself—as the solution, not the problem, for humanity.)

The Luciferian desire of Ewing's Hulk to destroy Creation sets up a storyline about redemption: Can Banner/Hulk, classically presented as a superhero, gain control over his desires, or will he succumb to dark desires like Henry Jekyll did? In one sense, it all depends on who mediates the Hulk's desire. In Ewing's vision, David Banner, Bruce Banner's violent, wife-beating father, played this role. His need to assert control through violence is duplicated in his son, a man who lacks self-control. Girard teaches that scapegoating produces a fragile, temporary peace. Eventually, violence will return until one party vanquishes the other. Jekyll can destroy Hyde, and Hulk can destroy the planet (but not his father, who the comic reveals to exist now in Hell), but peace will come only when they order their desires. What they need is what we each probably need: a better model for living.

A TRAGEDY TOLD AGAIN AND AGAIN

The stories of the three doctors are tragic because each discovers, in the moment when he must confront himself, that he has become evil. In his pursuit of power—to recreate himself as the most powerful being—he realizes that he can be judged a failure and condemned as evil. It is a judgment that is not meaningless for these men, but is, in fact, a source of great shame. Frankenstein discovers that he will be remembered as a man ruled by vanity. Jekyll discovers in his final moments that he committed his crimes and he, and not another, will be condemned as a vain, bloodthirsty pervert. Various iterations of Banner, too, feel shame at his constant childish boasting that "Hulk is the strongest one there is!" Each of these three stories tell of a prideful genius who wishes to remake creation; unwittingly brings violence into the world; and blames others for his crimes before finally atoning in some way.

The similarities of these characters are no accident. Instead of being wholly innovative or creating characters out of nothing, Lee imitated Stevenson, Stevenson consciously imitated Shelley, and Shelley, in the preface to her novel, admits to imitating Shakespeare, Milton, and the Greeks.[24] Lee acknowledged his imitation of Stevenson and stated that in writing superhero comic books he wanted to create nondenominational "religious" texts that Levitz says constitutes "modern mythmaking."[25] This statement turns out to be important in helping us to understand why writers so often return to the tragedy of the proud genius.

According to Girard, myths conceal cultural guilt. Ancient myths, he argued, were once true stories that recorded the ritual executions of innocent victims as performed by ancient societies. Over time, these testimonies became myths as society purged the societal guilt from the stories either by sublimating the violence in the fantasy, or by turning the innocent victims into guilty parties deserving of punishment. A Girardian study of myth attempts to "deconstruct" the stories so that what is hidden in myth—and unconscious to society—becomes a conscious truth.[26] By this logic, the stories of the three doctors recapitulate the same myth. We can understand this recapitulation as part of the artist's work in breaking open truths concealed in the stories. To put it in more Girardian terms, the modern retelling of myths points backwards to ancient violence—violence that we, today, risk committing against innocents.

The stories of the three doctors return us to the story of the first sin. Each desires godly power and considers himself a worthy opponent to God and His order. Their sin is pride—the original sin, "the most intellectual of the vices . . . the one vice that is simply thought."[27] Original sin is popularly understood as a punishment—that God cursed Adam and all of humanity was tainted by the first father's sin. But this is not quite right. God cursed the snake and the ground but did not curse Adam and Eve. He let them have what the tree gave them: knowledge of evil. Our knowledge of evil is an undeniable aspect of our human nature. It is the route through which violence enters the world, as when we delude ourselves that we can control our most monstrous desires.

This is what happens to the three doctors. Each man becomes captive to his desire, of which the "ultimate meaning . . . is death."[28] Through their scientific and alchemical experiments, each doctor indulges "the deceptive divinity of pride,"[29] learns the meaning of evil by becoming evil, and accuses another for the evil he perpetrated. Blame the monster in the woods or the wicked man in the shadows, they say, but do not blame me.

It is here that Girard can help us. In our daily lives, his mimetic theory warns us that we must think carefully about who we choose as our role models. Who should I, or my children, imitate, and why? These should be conscious questions (although as Girard might insist, imitative desire always operates pre-consciously). As any adult who has looked back on his life with regret can attest, the right model can change the course of a life. We might, in our middle years, come to realize that the celebrity's desire for limitless indulgence, the rock star's celebration of violent death, or the radical philosopher's longing for transgression, had warped our desires. We might even arrive at an understanding of Self that Girard and many others, including people like St. Augustine, arrived at—that the Self is not a monad, nor is it a fiction dissipated in the cosmos, but is a dynamic process animated by desire and through relations with others. To be is to be relational, and to live well is to turn from a self-centered person into an other-centered person. "Since we are made for covenant, for communion we can never retreat within our walls of defensiveness.... Only in 'another' can one truly live again."[30] In searching for a better model for our lives, we might discover that the dutiful father and the nurturing mother were the ones who found the thing that we desired all along—and who we wish to be.

RENOUNCING PRIDE

Classical Christian theology teaches that salvation is external to each of us, but the choice to let salvation in belongs entirely to us. "[T]he bolt on the door that seals off the way into the open air is not located outside, but inside, the person," writes Josef Pieper. "It is the stiff-necked will of the damned person himself, a will that turns away from God, which has closed the gates of hell in on itself."[31] The quality of being broken means that we cannot fix ourselves alone. In the same way that we cannot see our own faces without a mirror or a friend to look at us, we cannot climb from a pit without somebody to throw down a rope. "We don't want a Saviour if it turns out that we can manage just fine on our own."[32] But the moments that define us are often the moments when we cannot manage on our own.

Pride brings tragedy. Rather than asking for help, each doctor battles his monster alone, even though others could have helped destroy the monster. Frankenstein's friend Clerval could have helped him kill the monster. Utterson and Lanyon presumably could have helped Jekyll contain his desires. Others try to help Banner, but only in later parts of the serials; mostly, Banner counts on his own genius to cure himself. If Girard is correct, in this the three doctors act against their natures as relational creatures. They try to cling to the romantic lie that they can succeed alone and to varying degrees resist embracing the novelistic truth that requires them to renounce their pride. Each one, in effect, closes himself off from the Other, and, in so doing, inadvertently locks himself in with the evil he wants to oppose. He "turns in on himself" (*incurvatus se*), which is Augustine's notion of sin. It is only in opening oneself to the Holy Other that desire is redeemed and healed.

According to Girard, well-wrought stories point toward a singular, novelistic truth. In great novels heroes realize the negative influence of their models and renounce them and their desire. "Repudiation of the mediator implies renunciation of divinity, and this means renouncing pride."[33] Of the three works, *Frankenstein* comes closest to achieving Girard's novelistic unity. By the end of the novel, Frankenstein is repulsed by himself, his monster, and his own pride. He feels so strongly that he warns Walton, who he knows covets fame, of the dangers of pride. Even though Frankenstein tries through the novel to distance himself from his pride (and the violence it caused), in the end he dies trying to save humanity from the threat posed by his monster. If he could kill his monster—which would be like killing himself—Frankenstein would vanquish pride and return Nature to the state that God had intended for it.

The Strange Case is ambivalent about novelistic unity. It is true that Jekyll, who as Hyde boasted that he was a "prodigy to stagger the unbelief of Satan,"[34] expresses his remorse to God.[35] It is also true that he sacrifices himself to stop his monster's rampage. And we cannot deny that the man is ashamed of himself. He admits in his final testament that he has nothing to be proud of. Even his prowess as a scientist is nullified when he realizes that his miraculous potion was an accident. But we also see that Jekyll never fully takes ownership of the crimes he committed as Hyde. Until the end he continues to treat Hyde as both himself and as Other. His suicide reads not so much as an act of atonement as it does an escape.

Banner, trapped in a never-ending comic serial, atones in various ways—often by becoming a reluctant hero—only to see his life begin again in yet another series reboot where he will, inevitably, discover again the folly of playing God. Ewing's Hulk, part of an ongoing serial, has yet to renounce his pride, making him an antagonist rather than the hero who overcomes his desire. In this iteration, Banner remains trapped in the romantic lie.

"For the soul, loving its own power, slips onwards from the whole, which is a commonweal, to a part, which can belong specially to itself," writes St. Augustine. "And this slipping is initiated by the apostatizing pride, which is called the beginning of sin."[36] The first sin of the first couple drives home a point that echoes across literature. Pride destroys, and the path to liberation is not by power. While pop culture can often teach how not to live, we might eventually wonder how we should live and who is worthy of imitation. In this respect, we can look again to Girard for instruction. Famously, Girard returned to Catholicism after discovering the mimetic structures underlying human activity and the emancipatory role Jesus played in human history. By dying an innocent victim of the mob, Jesus exposed the scapegoating process and for all time made the scapegoating of innocents a transparently evil process of rivalry, accusation, and destruction.

Even those disinclined to embrace Christianity can see the value of religious discipline in daily life, if discipline is understood not as a punishment but as a way of orienting one's desires toward what is good. Most religious fasting, for example, is a practice in self-discipline, one that attempts to direct appetite upwards to God, rather than downwards to our stomachs. Similarly, seeking a model life through scripture can help to break destructive desires.

The Decalogue's commandments to worship God before all other things, to honor one's parents, to deny the desire to covet—these imperatives humble the penitent who understands these commandments as a means for triumphing over the desire to self-worship. Once we renounce pride and reject the models whose desires will destroy us, love for the other becomes possible.

If, on our own, we cannot reject the models and desires that lead to ruin, we must ask others for help, or give ourselves to a discipline that can liberate us, or a model by whose imitation we might discover freedom. The choice is one between the Crucified, who rejects violence and "the will to annihilate,"[37] or Dionysus, who relishes violence and casts brokenness onto somebody else, who must be destroyed. That is the same as letting the monster loose on the world.

NOTES

1. René Girard, *Deceit, Desire, and the Novel* (Baltimore: Johns Hopkins University Press, 1976).

2. Robert Doran, "René Girard's Concept of Conversion and the 'Via Negativa': Revisiting *Deceit, Desire, and the Novel*," *Religion & Literature* 42, no. 3 (Autumn 2011): 171.

3. Girard, *Deceit*, 17.

4. Girard, *Deceit*, 16.

5. Girard, *Deceit*, 300.

6. Mary Shelley, *Frankenstein: The 1818 Text* (New York: Penguin, 2018), 42.

7. Michael Rose, "Frankenstein. By Mary Shelley. A validation of family, marriage, & natural human values," *New Oxford Review* 86, no. 4 (July–August 2019), https://www.newoxfordreview.org/documents/frankenstein-by-mary-shelley/

8. Shelley, *Frankenstein*, p. 45.

9. Astrida Orle Tantillo, "*Werther, Frankenstein* and Girardian Mediate Desire," *Studia Neophilologica* 80, no. 2 (2008): 178.

10. Anthony Backes, "Revisiting *Frankenstein*: A Study in Reading and Education," *English Journal* 83, no. 4 (April 1994).

11. Shelley, *Frankenstein*, 211.

12. Robert Louis Stevenson, *The Strange Case of Dr. Jekyll and Mr. Hyde* (Mineola, NY: Dover Publications, 1991), 43.

13. Ibid, 44.

14. René Girard, *Violence and the Sacred* (New York: Bloomsbury Academic, 2013), 161.

15. Steven Padnick, "What everybody gets wrong about Jekyll and Hyde," *Tor*, June 22, 2012, https://www.tor.com/2012/06/22/what-everybody-gets-wrong-about-jekyll-and-hyde/.

16. Stevenson, *The Strange Case*, 43.

17. Ibid, 45.

18. Girard, *Deceit,* 298.
19. Stevenson, *The Strange Case*, 54.
20. Ibid, p. 40.
21. Girard, *Deceit,* 298.
22. Sean Howe, *Marvel Comics: The Untold Story* (New York: HarperCollins, 2012).
23. Al Ewing, *The Immortal Hulk* 1, no. 15 (May 2019).
24. Shelley, *Frankenstein*, 3.
25. Ricker, Aaron Ricker, "The Third Side of the Coin: Constructing Superhero Comics Culture as Religious Myth," *Arc 43* (2015), 96.
26. René Girard, *The Girard Reader,* ed. James G. Williams (New York: Crossroad Publishing, 1996), 137.
27. James V. Schall, *A Line Through the Human Heart: On Sinning and Being Forgiven* (Kettering, OH: Angelico Press, 2016), 11.
28. Girard, *Deceit*, 290.
29. Girard, *Deceit*, 307.
30. David Vincent Meconi, *On Self-harm, Narcissism, Atonement, and the Vulnerable Christ* (New York: Bloomsbury Academic, 2020), 32–34.
31. Josef Pieper, *The Concept of Sin*, trans. Edward T. Oakes (South Bend: St. Augustine's Press, 2001), 90.
32. Miles Hollingworth, *St. Augustine of Hippo: An Intellectual Biography* (Toronto: Oxford University Press, 2013), 147.
33. Girard, *Deceit*, 294.
34. Stevenson, *The Strange Case*, 40.
35. Ibid, p. 50.
36. St. Augustine as qtd. in Hollingworth, *St. Augustine*, 160.
37. Girard, *The Girard Reader*, 250.

BIBLIOGRAPHY

Backes, Anthony. "Revisiting Frankenstein: A Study in Reading and Education." *English Journal 83*, no. 4 (1994): 33–36.

Doran, Robert. "René Girard's Concept of Conversion and the 'Via Negativa': Revisiting Deceit, Desire, and the Novel." *Religion & Literature 42*, no. 3 (Autumn 2011): 170–179. https://www.jstor.org/stable/23347096.

Ewing, Al. *The Immortal Hulk*. New York: Marvel, 2019.

Girard, René. *Deceit, Desire, and the Novel*. Baltimore: Johns Hopkins University Press, 1976.

———. *The Girard Reader*. Edited by James G. Williams. New York: Crossroad Publishing, 1996.

———. *Violence and the Sacred*. New York: Bloomsbury Academic, 2013.

Hollingworth, Miles. *St. Augustine of Hippo: An Intellectual Biography*. Toronto: Oxford University Press, 2013.

Howe, Sean. *Marvel Comics: The Untold Story*. New York: HarperCollins, 2012.

Meconi, David Vincent. *On Self-harm, Narcissism, Atonement, and the Vulnerable Christ*. New York: Bloomsbury Academic, 2020.
Padnick, Steven. "What everybody gets wrong about Jekyll and Hyde." *Tor*, June 22, 2012. https://www.tor.com/2012/06/22/what-everybody-gets-wrong-about-jekyll-and-hyde/.
Pieper, Josef. *The Concept of Sin*. Translated by Edward T. Oakes. South Bend, Indiana: St. Augustine's Press, 2001.
Rose, Michael S. "Frankenstein. By Mary Shelley. A validation of family, marriage, & natural human values." *New Oxford Review*, July–August, 2019. https://www.newoxfordreview.org/documents/frankenstein-by-mary-shelley/#
Ricker, Aaron. "The Third Side of the Coin: Constructing Superhero Comics Culture as Religious Myth." *Arc 43* (2015): 91–105.
Schall, James V. *A Line through the Human Heart: On Sinning and Being Forgiven*. Kettering, OH: Angelico Press, 2016.
Shelley, Mary. *Frankenstein: The 1818 Text*. New York: Penguin, 2018.
Stevenson, Robert Louis. *The Strange Case of Dr. Jekyll and Mr. Hyde*. Mineola, New York: Dover Publications, 1991.
Tantillo, Astrida Orle. "Werther, Frankenstein and Girardian Mediated Desire." *Studia Neophilologica 80*, no. 2 (2008): 177–187. DOI: 10.1080/00393270802082986.

Chapter 13

Subtweeting in the End Times
Social Media and the Escalation to Extremes

Justin Lee

On the occasion of René Girard's induction into the Académie Française, Michel Serres lamented our cultural obsession with violence. The media represent and multiply human sacrifice "with a frenzy such that these repetitions return our culture to melancholic barbarism. . . . The most advanced technologies thrust our culture back to the archaic age of sacrificial polytheism."[1] Speaking in 2005, Serres couldn't have known how radically social media would accelerate our return to barbarism. Facebook wasn't yet publicly accessible. YouTube was only a month old; Reddit wouldn't be launched for another four months, Twitter for a full year. In time, however, each platform would bear out René Girard's mimetic theory in ways both terrifying and absurd.

While nearly all manner of mimetic phenomena are demonstrated on social media, this paper focuses on the scapegoat mechanism, the multiplication of victims, and the escalation to extremes within the post-Christian context.[2] I discuss findings in neuroscience and social psychology in order to argue that computer mediated communication (CMC) accelerates the "escalation to extremes" by blurring the boundaries between our digital and embodied lives, attenuating empathy, disinhibiting our behavior, and lowering barriers to violence. The pathologies of CMC demonstrate that the "absolute war" Carl von Clausewitz deemed to be only theoretical is now becoming realizable, and on a planetary scale. I conclude by reflecting on this apocalyptic reality in light of Girard's insights in *Battling to the End*.

According to Girard, once the lie of victimage has been revealed to a community, that community must either accept the gospel of Christ, with its radical rejection of violence, or else suffer undoing at the hands of unresolvable mimetic crises. The gospel's exposure of the mythical lie is an apocalypse—in both the lexical sense of an "unveiling" and the colloquial sense of an "end of the world." "If unanimous victimization reconciles and reorders societies in direct proportion to its concealment," writes Girard, "then it must lose its effectiveness in direct proportion to its revelation."[3] But the need for peace, for the restoration of difference, remains. Thus: "The more radical the crisis of the sacrificial system becomes, the more men will be tempted to multiply victims in order to accede, finally, to the same effects."[4]

The United States is following Europe in its post-Christian shift,[5] but this doesn't mean that either has shed the concern for victims that the Christian faith first made universal. Rather, it has been involuted into an instrument of power. "The current process of spiritual demagoguery and rhetorical overkill has transformed the concern for victims into a totalitarian command and a permanent inquisition," writes Girard. "We are living through a caricatural 'ultra-Christianity' that tries to escape from the Judeo-Christian orbit by 'radicalizing' the concern for victims in an anti-Christian manner."[6] He had in mind progressive identity politics, which under the star of "intersectionality" privileges those marginalized by previous generations; but the insight is equally applicable to the renascent identitarianism of the Right, which privileges the white working class. For both sides of the aisle, concern for victims has devolved into a competition of mimetic rivalries: "The victims most interesting to us are always those who allow us to condemn our neighbors."[7]

THE TWITTER HATE MACHINE

The propensity towards multiplying victims was demonstrated in the months following Brett Kavanaugh's confirmation to the Supreme Court. What began as choreographed outrage—Senate Democrats conspired with activists and news media to maximize the impact of Christine Blasey Ford's allegation that Kavanaugh sexually assaulted her[8]—mushroomed into a nation-wide mimetic crisis, replete with copycat allegations, attempts by conservatives to offload the allegations onto a different scapegoat, the staging of testimony to recall Clarence Thomas's confirmation hearings, and threats of violence against, and a near-brawl among, U.S. senators.[9] Conservatives polarized against progressives, and vice-versa, deepening unanimity within each coalition while national unanimity proved impossible. Democrats spent their fury and achieved reunification—enabling their victories in the 2018 midterm elections. But simmering underneath that solidarity was the knowledge that it had been bought with a scapegoat. Such knowledge fractures unity and threatens to plunge the community back into crisis, thus priming the search for new victims.

On the weekend of January 19, 2019, Twitter was flooded with outrage at the MAGA-hatted students of the all-male Covington Catholic High School.[10] A viral video appeared to show the boys surrounding and taunting a Native American elder, Nathan Phillips, as he beat a ceremonial drum. For many, the idea of teenagers disrupting the inaugural Indigenous Peoples March with shouts of "Build the wall!" encapsulated the "spirit of Trumpism."

It was a despairing spectacle, or so it seemed, but it also provided schadenfreude for many commentators eager to see the teenagers doxxed and tarred by their bigoted folly. "Have you ever seen a more punchable face?" religion writer and former CNN host Reza Aslan tweeted of one of the Covington boys. "Look at the shit-eating grins on all those young white slugs' faces," tweeted a writer for *Vulture*, "Just perverse pleasure at wielding a false dominion they've been taught their whole life was their divine right. Fucking die." Comedian Kathy Griffin tweeted: "Name these kids. I want NAMES. Shame them. If you think these fuckers wouldn't dox you in a heartbeat, think again." Public figure after public figure participated in the shaming. Covington Catholic High School promised disciplinary proceedings. Even the school's diocese condemned the boys. For a few brief hours, erstwhile political enemies were united by gleeful denunciation.

But then new footage began to spread across Twitter. In none of the videos of the incident will one hear anyone chanting "Build the wall!" Nor will one see students "swarm" Phillips and his compatriots. Rather, one sees a group of teenage boys chanting their school's fight song as they wait on steps near the Lincoln Memorial for their bus to arrive. One sees Phillips, accompanied by a troupe of activists, their phones out and filming, insert himself into the boys' midst while drumming and chanting. The boys attempt to participate in his chanting—ineptly and raucously. The mood shifts when Phillips approaches a student and beats his drum inches from the kid's face. Multiple videos show that the kid never moved from where he was standing prior to being approached by Phillips.[11]

Even after the full story was widely known, progressives were still publishing articles with titles like "The Little Brett Kavanaughs from Covington Catholic High."[12] Kathy Griffin, among others, claimed the school had a history of embracing white supremacy—this deduced from a photo of a basketball player making the "OK" hand signal, which has been appropriated by white supremacists.[13] The photo antedated that usage, and the gesture signifies a three-pointer; all of which journalists would have known were they not so inebriated by mimesis.

Unanimity was aided by the homophily of mainstream news organizations (e.g., the *New York Times*, the *Washington Post*, CNN, NPR, NBC News),[14] which skew overwhelmingly progressive.[15] Exculpatory footage was available the night of the incident, but progressives ignored or never saw it because of their social networks' ideological homogeneity. The narrative proved too useful to abandon: not only were the Covington boys Trump supporters, they were in D.C. for the March for Life. Commentators seized on the opportunity to smear the anti-abortion movement as racist.[16]

The episode also demonstrates how easily the boundary between physical and digital can blur. The violent rhetoric of prominent progressives was soon mirrored by credible threats of violence against the boys.[17] And, emboldened by the outpouring of support, Phillips attempted a sequel the following evening when, accompanied by a large crowd, he tried to force his way into the Basilica of the National Shrine of the Immaculate Conception during the celebration of mass. He failed, rebuffed by security guards who barricaded the cathedral's doors.[18]

Scapegoating is itself mimetically reproduced. In the culture wars, progressives and conservatives fixate on each other and become "mimetic doubles"—rivals undifferentiated by their conflict. Even as the progressive Left multiplies its victims after each failed scapegoating, the conservative and libertarian Right pursues its own victims and succumbs to the same failures and multiplications.

Shortly after the Covington Catholic scandal, Republicans found their scapegoat in Ilhan Omar (D-MN), a first-term congresswoman with a history of making anti-Semitic remarks. Omar had resurrected the slander of divided loyalty during a town hall meeting, decrying American Jews who "push for allegiance to a foreign country [Israel]."[19] While Omar deserved censure, Republicans pilloried her as a study in why Muslim refugees should be denied access to the United States. Weeks later, after another gaffe, she received hundreds of death threats via Twitter.[20] Omar's scapegoating impulses led to her own scapegoating, and would do so again in July when she introduced a resolution defending the boycott, divestment, and sanctions movement.[21] Rather than censure Omar, Democratic Party leadership embraced her. John Podhoretz lamented that "the Democratic Party decided that it had to choose between Jews and intersectionality and chose the latter."[22]

Intersectionality requires one to choose against the Jews because solidarity within the progressive coalition depends upon scapegoating.[23] Any community characterized by the radicalized concern for victims has reembraced the mythical lie—its survival depends on the production of new victims. Because each member group of the coalition has its own favored scapegoats, harmony within the coalition depends on tolerance by each group of the victimage practices of the others. It is cruelly ironic that those who pride themselves on being "woke" are no less prone than others of being seduced by mythic darkness.

The Right, insofar as its character ceases to be defined by orthodox Christian values, also derives solidarity from scapegoating. Following Ilhan Omar's comments, some questioned whether her Muslim faith implies an opposition to the Constitution.[24] The mimesis is patent: Omar accuses Jews of divided loyalty; the Right mimics her by accusing Muslims of the same. Naturally, President Trump *saw* in the radicalism of Ilhan Omar and other junior members of Congress an opportunity to ride the victimage mechanism to reelection.[25] Because they are guilty of advocating pernicious ideologies, they are vulnerable to the charge that they are guilty of infinitely more.

The Kavanaugh, Covington, and Omar scandals each transformed Twitter into a mimetic hellscape. It's difficult to imagine they would have provoked such venom absent the amplifying and contorting power of social media. Why is social media such a uniquely toxic environment? Why do we behave in ways online we would never dream of behaving "in real life"? The answer is that our brains are ill-equipped to navigate online spaces and incapable of reflexively observing the norms of offline existence.

MIMETIC BRAINS AND ONLINE DISINHIBITION

Girard's theory of mimetic desire is perhaps the only theory derived from close readings of literary texts to be validated by the hard sciences. Findings in developmental psychology and cognitive neuroscience have shown that interpersonal reciprocity and mirrored neural activity profoundly shape human development.[26] French neuropsychiatrist Jean-Michel Oughourlian, first to recognize therapeutic utility in Girard's ideas, wasn't surprised when Giacomo Rizzolatti's 1996 discovery of "mirror neurons" revealed a neurological structure undergirding imitation. Vittorio Gallese, one of Rizzolatti's collaborators, summarized the operation of mirror neurons: "The same neural circuits underpinning our own actions, intentions, emotions, and sensations also underpin our capacity to recognize and identify with the actions, intentions, emotions, and sensations of others."[27] Alongside Andrew Meltzoff's studies of imitative behavior in infants, the discovery of mirror neurons established mimesis as central to human development.

Oughourlian examines the work of Rizzolatti, Gallese, and Meltzoff at length in *The Mimetic Brain*. "To express this mirroring activity," he writes, "Gallese forges the expression embodied simulation: the mimetic neuronal system of the one who is watching reflects like a mirror, automatically reproducing the neuronal activity of the brain of the person who is acting."[28] This transforms "the other into 'another self,' thereby establishing the groundwork for empathy." Interestingly, "the contemplation of an object triggers no mirror activity . . . our brain reflects only the brain of those who are like us."[29] Absent crucial sensory information, embodied simulation will be deficient, and faculties dependent upon simulation will be impaired. Despite our euphemisms about the "information superhighway," when it comes to the data that matter most to human behavior, the internet is a stunningly impoverished place.

Many commentators single out "trolls" as the source of toxicity. According to one study, the archetypal troll "is male, high in trait psychopathy and sadism, and has low affective empathy." Crucially, trolls "cognitively understand the emotional distress they cause through their trolling behavior without empathizing with their victim's emotional suffering."[30] That suffering, however, is usually a by-product of trolling rather than its raison d'être, which is ostensibly anarchic humor. While trolls may target emotionally reactive individuals "for the lolz," it makes little difference to their victims.

But focusing on one class of bad actors obscures the more important fact that we are the problem. In a study of behavior in online comment sections, researchers at Stanford and Cornell found that everyone can become a troll. "[N]egative mood and the surrounding discussion context prompt ordinary users to engage in trolling behavior," which then spreads to others. Their findings, in sum: trolling, like laughter, is contagious.[31]

Why do so many of us behave online in ways we reject in embodied life? The answer is that online environments have a uniquely disinhibitory effect on human behavior.

John Suler, who established the framework for investigations into online disinhibition, distinguishes benign from toxic disinhibition.[32] Benign disinhibition often manifests as self-disclosure in excess of what one might volunteer offline. While not unproblematic, "oversharing" is often performed in service of self-actualization—an attempt, in Girardian terms, to differentiate oneself amidst flattened distinctions. Toxic disinhibition manifests in antisocial behaviors one would otherwise eschew offline. Suler identified six factors contributing to online disinhibition: dissociative anonymity, invisibility, asynchronicity, solipsistic introjection, dissociative imagination, and minimization of status and authority. While each factor has implications for mimetic theory, I will focus on invisibility and minimization of authority.

Most of our online activity is invisible to others. One may peruse a crush's social media profile without evidencing one's presence. And even when one does interact with others, the encounter is less rich in information than a face-to-face interaction. Absent social cues, it is difficult to modulate our behavior to observe norms.[33] One lacks the information vital for reflexive empathic responses. For example, in offline encounters eye contact serves an important inhibitory function; but in even the most media rich online interactions, eye contact is impossible.[34]

In embodied life, we constantly assess our status vis-à-vis others around us, and we adjust our behavior according to our perceived position within a hierarchy. Online, however, the information by which we assess one another's relative authority is limited. "The absence of those cues in the text environments of cyberspace," writes Suler, "reduces the impact of their authority."[35] The flattening of distinctions has troubling consequences—undifferentiation greases the tracks for rivalry.

We are vulnerable to "emotional contagion" online. One study found that users are more affected by the aggressive behavior of others than by anonymity online, and while both contexts of perceived homogeneity or heterogeneity generated social influence, subjects became more aggressive online in response to the aggression of those perceived as other.[36] Another study found that Facebook users became angrier or more upbeat in response to the quantity of negative or positive stories in their newsfeed, with negative newsfeeds having a stronger effect on mood than positive. "Emotional contagion" spreads like a virus.[37]

As of 2019, the average internet user spends nearly seven hours online each day—and, of that, over two hours on social media.[38] The inundation of social and consumer choices is exhausting and depletes self-control;[39] this amplifies the already strong disinhibiting effect of CMC. Thus, internet use in general and social media use in particular increase our vulnerability to the darker effects of mimetic desire.

BLURRING BOUNDARIES AND IRL VIOLENCE

Toxic online disinhibition has serious real-world consequences, such as "cyberbanging"—inner-city gang rivalries transposed onto social media. Ben Austen explains the phenomenon: when a "Facebook driller" insults someone in a rival gang, the insult spreads virally throughout the neighborhood, and the target retaliates with lethal violence to save face.[40]

Violent rhetoric, reflexively produced, yields actual violence. As Austen reports, 80 percent of fights within Chicago public schools started online. The norms of gang culture guarantee violent reciprocity. In *LikeWar: The Weaponization of Social Media*, P.W. Singer and Emerson T. Brooking note that this dynamic accelerates the escalation to extremes. "If someone is fronted and doesn't reply . . . the gang as a whole . . . loses status. The outcome is that anyone can start a feud online, but everyone has a collective responsibility to make sure it gets consummated in the real world."[41]

Boundary-blurring violence isn't always merely reactive. Mexican drug cartels "edit graphic executions into shareable music videos and battle in dueling Instagram posts."[42] Mara Salvatrucha (MS-13), the infamous El Salvadoran drug gang, has embraced an ISIS-inspired, social media-driven "franchise model," with imitative chapters spread around the world. "The result," explain Singer and Brooking, "is a cycle of confrontation in which the distinction between online and offline criminal worlds has essentially become blurred."[43]

The effects of this global phenomenon range from the interpersonal to the geopolitical. In 2017, "a surge of Facebook rumor-mongering helped fuel genocide against [Myanmar's] Rohingya Muslim minority."[44] The Chinese Communist Party likewise facilitates the scapegoating of its own Muslim minority using a combination of digital propaganda and surveillance to identify candidates for forced deconversion in concentration camps.[45] In contexts where interminable conflict has attenuated empathy for out-groups,[46] online disinhibition can trigger violent persecution. Or worse: when Pakistan's defense minister read a fabricated threat of Israeli nuclear attack, he promised retaliation on Twitter.[47]

IMITATING THE MACHINES

Toxic online disinhibition occurs spontaneously, but it can also be enhanced and guided by artificial means. For example, Russian botnets—networks of automated social accounts—influenced both Brexit and the 2016 US election. "On Twitter alone, researchers discovered roughly 400,000 bot accounts that fought to sway the outcome of the race—two-thirds of them in favor of Donald Trump."[48] "In the final month and a half before the election, Twitter concluded that Russian-generated propaganda had been delivered to users 454.7 million times."[49]

Bots and "sockpuppets"—fake accounts controlled by actual humans—have influenced more than elections. On 4chan, the notorious pasteboard site popular with alt-right trolls, Russian sockpuppets amplified the influence of racist users by imitating their worst content. "The hateful fakes were mimicking real people, but then real people began to mimic the hateful fakes."[50] But with respect to human-bot interaction, mimesis is a two-way street. In 2016, Microsoft opened a Twitter account for a "neural network powered chatbot" designed to learn from other users. Trolls pounced and the chatbot was soon espousing racism, misogyny, and Holocaust denial.[51] Mimetic desire is more dangerous online than off because mimesis is more easily manipulated to produce artificial crises.

Irrespective of amplification, disinformation and extremism spread faster online than vetted sources and moderate voices. Pew Research Center found that "the more unyieldingly hyperpartisan a member of Congress is . . . the more Twitter followers he or she draws."[52] Often, Russian sockpuppets and botnets amplify a message after it has caught fire organically. The #Pizzagate conspiracy theory, for example, was promoted by far-Right fringe outlets before being co-opted by Russian sockpuppets. "When polled after the election, nearly half of Trump voters affirmed their belief that the Clinton campaign had participated in pedophilia, human trafficking, and satanic ritual abuse."[53] One would-be vigilante stormed D.C.'s Comet Ping Pong pizzeria with an AR-15 in an attempt to free child sex slaves he believed were imprisoned in a secret room.

Boundary-blurring isn't merely a domestic issue. As the authors of *LikeWar* put it, "internet conflicts now merge seamlessly with those of flesh and blood."[54] This interplay has produced dire geopolitical consequences, from the Islamic State's social media mastery[55] to Russia's manipulation of the narrative on their annexation of Crimea.[56] Somewhat paradoxically, social media provides a crucial platform for the lies of victimage that emerge to resolve mimetic crises even as it produces those crises by intensifying mimetic rivalries.

The IDF's 2012 campaign against Hamas terror sites is instructive. The IDF spread videos of drones destroying targets across social media and Hamas responded with propaganda of their own—images of obliterated homes and dead children with the hashtag #GazaUnderFire.[57] The IDF adapted in real time, suspending bombing in response to pro-Hamas sympathy on Twitter, while Hamas placed women and children in harm's way—in order to document their suffering—as they violently provoked further bombing.[58] This mimetic oscillation demonstrates Girard's contention in *Battling to the End* that "reciprocal action both provokes and suspends the escalation to extremes."[59]

MIMETIC APOCALYPSE

Girard emphasized the centrality of the gospel's apocalypticism, but for a period of his career he believed that knowledge of the mythical lie would itself suffice to dispel violence. In his final two decades, however, he embraced what from a worldly perspective must appear as pessimism: "Christ took away humanity's sacrificial crutches and left us before a terrible choice: either believe in violence, or not; Christianity is nonbelief."[60] Those who believe in violence have embraced unresolvable mimetic crisis; and the world has rejected Christ. We are thus living in the end times.

Battling to the End clarifies how mimetic reciprocity intensifies by scrutinizing the thought of Prussian general Carl von Clausewitz, who first theorized the tit-for-tat structure of the duel recapitulated in war. For Clausewitz, reciprocal action provokes the trend to extremes "when both adversaries behave in the same way, and respond immediately by each modeling his tactics, strategy and policy on those of the other."[61] If normal complications of war preclude immediacy, however, reciprocal action can suspend the trend to extremes and reintroduce differences amidst undifferentiation. But if reciprocal action "promotes and accelerates the trend to extremes, the 'friction' of space and time disappear, and the situation strangely resembles what I call the 'sacrificial crisis' in my theory of archaic societies."[62]

This dangerous immediacy is readily achievable in the digital age. As we have seen, social media has the effect of collapsing time and space and abolishing distinctions: anyone anywhere in the world can become a mimetic rival; at any moment one's old tweets might be dredged up, decontextualized, and spark outrage in the eternal "now" of the "extremely online." This is the "asynchronicity" Suler identified as a cause of online disinhibition. "When a society breaks down, time sequences shorten," Girard wrote in *The Scapegoat*. "The reciprocity of negative rather than positive exchanges becomes foreshortened as it becomes more visible. . ."[63] Even when reciprocity suspends escalation, "the reduction of a conflict is only apparent, and leaves open the possibility of its even more violent return."[64]

Clausewitz understood "absolute war" as a theoretical terminus to escalation; theoretical because it required a "continuity" precluded by the chaos of war. Such continuity would "drive everything to extremes. Not only would such ceaseless activity arouse men's feelings and inject them with more passion and elemental strength, but events would follow more closely on each other, and be governed by a stricter causal chain."[65] This state is realized within the flattened perceptual horizon of CMC, and increasingly pertains in embodied life. Absent our "sacrificial crutches," humanity will guarantee that mimetic crisis becomes global.

A grim vision, to be sure. But is it, at the last, pessimistic?

"More than ever," writes Girard, "I am convinced that history has meaning, and that its meaning is terrifying." And yet he gives Hölderlin the last word:

> But where danger threatens
> That which saves from it also grows.

Only Christ can save us from our violence, and it is the promise of the gospel that he will indeed do so. Girard anticipates Christ's return, that "great and terrible Day of the Lord" when unrestrained human violence burns itself to embers and Christ is made all-in-all. In the interval, "We can all participate in the divinity of Christ so long as we renounce our own violence."[66] Humanity cannot be saved by human effort, which always entails negative reciprocity, but we are nevertheless commanded to act. "We have to fight to the end," writes Girard, "even when we think it is 'vain.'"[67]

That fight is a fight for the truth. Girard was convinced that when Christians lose their "sense of eschatology" they cease to influence worldly events.[68] "Battling to the End" means imitating Christ, escaping from the "hidden logic [of the duel] by means of a better one, that of love, of positive reciprocity."[69]

Such an escape requires more than simply unmasking the logic of the duel. Truth must be lived as well as spoken. This means renouncing the *lex talionis* and embracing the otherworldly justice of Christ's kingdom. Even more, it means renouncing all solidarity rooted in victimage, and instead rooting one's identity in Christ through fellowship with his mystical body. Finally, the fight for the truth requires rightly identifying our enemy. As St. Paul wrote in Ephesians, "we do not wrestle against flesh and blood, but against the rulers, against the authorities, against the cosmic powers over this present darkness, against the spiritual forces of evil in the heavenly places." For Girard, our enemy is Satan, the "Accuser," who is the process of mimetic rivalry itself. In a rivalrous imitation of Christ, Satan "presents himself as a model for our desires, and he is certainly easier to imitate than Christ, for he counsels us to abandon ourselves to all our inclinations in defiance of morality and its prohibitions"—in order to deprive us "of everything that protects us from rivalistic imitation."[70] To fight for the truth is to obey Christ, cultivating habits which make for peace and excising those practices that make us vulnerable to negative mimesis. For most if not all of us, this will include radically altering how we use social media.

NOTES

1. Michel Serres, "Receiving René Girard into the Académie Française," trans. William A. Johnsen, in *For René Girard: Essays in Friendship and in Truth*, ed. Sandor Goodhart, Jörden Jörgensen, Tom Ryba, and James G. Williams (East Lansing: Michigan State University Press, 2009), 10–12.

2. A "post-Christian" society is one whose moral imagination is no longer tethered to the grammar of orthodox Christian faith and practice. The post-Christian is less characterized by secularity than by Tara Isabella Burton's category of "Remixed religion" in *Strange Rites: New Religions for a Godless World* (New York: PublicAffairs, 2020).

3. René Girard, "Are the Gospels Mythical?" *First Things*, April 1996.

4. René Girard, *Things Hidden since the Foundation of the World*, trans. Stephen Bann and Michael Metteer (Redwood City: Stanford University Press, 1987), 34.

5. Michael Lipka, "A closer look at America's rapidly growing religious 'nones,'" *Pew Research Center*, May 13, 2015.

6. René Girard, *I See Satan Fall Like Lightning*, Translated by James G. Williams (Maryknoll: Orbis Books, 2001), 178–179.

7. Girard, *I See Satan Fall Like Lightning*, 164.

8. Mollie Hemingway and Carrie Severino, *Justice on Trial: The Kavanaugh Confirmation and the Future of the Supreme Court* (Washington, D.C.: Regnery Publishing, 2019), Chapter Three.

9. Hemingway and Severino, Justice on Trial.

10. Material on the Covington controversy has been adapted from: Justin Lee, "Did the Boys of Covington Catholic 'Mob' a Native American Elder?" *Arc Digital*, January 20th 2019.

11. For video links, see Justin Lee, "Did the Boys of Covington Catholic 'Mob' a Native American Elder?"

12. Raouf Halaby, "The Little Brett Kavanaughs from Covington Catholic High," *Counter Punch*, January 22, 2019

13. Douglas Ernst, "Kathy Griffin deletes 'Nazi sign' smear from stream of Covington Catholic tweets," *Washington Times*, January 22, 2019.

14. Soave, Robby, "A Year Ago, the Media Mangled the Covington Catholic Story. What Happened Next Was Even Worse," *Reason*, January 21, 2020.

15. Dave Levinthal and Michael Beckel, "Journalists shower Hillary Clinton with campaign cash," *Columbia Journalism Review*, October 17, 2017.

16. Frank, Gillian, "The Deep Ties Between the Catholic Anti-Abortion Movement and Racial Segregation," *Jezebel*, January 22, 2019.

17. Katelyn Caralle, "Covington student: 'People have threatened our lives' after confrontation with Native American protester," *Washington Examiner*, January 23, 2019.

18. Ed Condon, "Nathan Phillips rally protesters attempted to disrupt Mass at DC's National Shrine," *Catholic News Agency*, January 22, 2019.

19. Alana Abramson, "'I Believe in My Work.' How Rep. Ilhan Omar Rose From Refugee to Trump's Top Target," *Time*, July 18, 2019.

20. Michael Brice-Saddler, "He easily found hundreds of death threats against Rep. Ilhan Omar. He wants Twitter to stop them," *Washington Post*, April 16, 2019.

21. Bryant Harris, "Ilhan Omar seizes spotlight to push pro-BDS resolution," *Al-Monitor*, July 16, 2019.

22. John Podhoretz, "The Democrats and Anti-Semitism," *Commentary*, March 7, 2019.

23. See Justin Lee, "Coalitions of Hate: Ilhan Omar, Donald Trump and the allure of scapegoating," *Religion and Ethics*, from which a portion of this section has been adapted.

24. Schwartz, Ian. "Pirro: Ilhan Omar Wears a Hijab, Her Adherence to Islamic Doctrine Antithetical to Constitution." *Real Clear Politics*, March 11, 2019.

25. Julie Hirschfeld Davis, Maggie Haberman and Michael Crowley, "Trump Disavows 'Send Her Back' Chant After Pressure From G.O.P." *New York Times*, July 19, 2019.

26. Garrels, Scott R., "Imitation, Mirror Neurons, and Mimetic Desire: Convergence between the Mimetic Theory of Rene Girard and empirical research on imitation," *Contagion: Journal of Violence, Mimesis, and Culture* 12–13 (2006), 49.

27. Vittorio Gallese, "The Two Sides of Mimesis," in Oughourlian, *The Mimetic Brain*, 27.

28. Jean-Michel Oughourlian, *The Mimetic Brain*, trans. Trevor Cribben Merrill (East Lansing: Michigan State University, 2016), 27.

29. Jean-Michel Oughourlian, *The Mimetic Brain*, 27.

30. Natalie Sest, Evita March, "Constructing the cyber-troll: Psychopathy, sadism, and empathy," *Personality and Individual Differences* 119 (2017), 72.

31. Justin Cheng, Michael Bernstein, Cristian Danescu-Niculescu-Mizil, Jure Leskovec, "Anyone Can Become a Troll: Causes of Trolling Behavior in Online Discussions," *CSCW Conf Comput Support Coop Work* (Feb.–Mar. 2017).

32. John Suler, "The Online Disinhibition Effect," *Cyberpsychology & Behavior* 7, no. 3 (2004), 1.

33. Birgit J. Voggeser, Ranjit K. Singh and Anja S. Göritz, "Self-control in Online Discussions: Disinhibited Online Behavior as a Failure to Recognize Social Cues," *Frontiers in Psychology* (January 2018).

34. Noam Lapidot-Lefler, Azy Barak, "Effects of anonymity, invisibility, and lack of eye contact on toxic online disinhibition," *Computers in Human Behavior* 28, no. 2 (March 2012).

35. Suler, "The Online Disinhibition Effect," 324.

36. Leonie Rösner and Nicole C. Krämer, "Verbal Venting in the Social Web: Effects of Anonymity and Group Norms on Aggressive Language Use in Online Comments," *Social Media + Society* 2, no. 3 (August 2016).

37. Adam D.L. Kramer, Jamie E. Guillory, and Jeffrey T. Hancock, "Experimental Evidence of Massive-Scale Emotional Contagion Through Social Networks," *PNAS* 111, no. 24 (2014), in Singer and Brooking, *LikeWar*, 162.

38. Simon Kemp, "Digital 2019: Global Internet Use Accelerates," *We Are Social*, January 30, 2019.

39. K.D. Vohs, R.F. Baumeister, B.J. Schmeichel, J.M. Twenge, N.M. Nelson, and D.M. Tice, "Making choices impairs subsequent self-control: A limited-resource account of decision making, self-regulation, and active initiative," *Journal of Personality and Social Psychology* 94, no. 5 (2008).

40. Ben Austen, "Public Enemies: Social Media Is Fueling Gang Wars in Chicago," *Wired*, September 17, 2013.

41. P.W. Singer and Emerson T. Brooking. *LikeWar: The Weaponization of Social Media* (New York: Houghton Mifflin Harcourt, 2018), 13.

42. Singer and Brooking, *LikeWar*, 14.

43. Singer and Brooking, *LikeWar*, 14.

44. Singer and Brooking, *LikeWar*, 136.

45. Austin Ramzy and Chris Buckley, "'Absolutely No Mercy': Leaked Files Expose How China Organized Mass Detentions of Muslims," *New York Times*, November 16, 2019.

46. Jonathan Levy et al., "Adolescents growing up amidst intractable conflict attenuate brain response to pain of outgroup," *Proceedings of the National Academy of Sciences of the United States of America* 113, no. 48 (November 2016): 13696–13701.

47. Singer and Brooking, *LikeWar*, 135.

48. Singer and Brooking, *LikeWar*, 143.

49. Singer and Brooking, *LikeWar*, 144.

50. Singer and Brooking, *LikeWar*, 147.

51. Singer and Brooking, *LikeWar*, 252.

52. Singer and Brooking, *LikeWar*, 160.

53. Catherine Rampell, "Americans—especially but not exclusively Trump voters—believe crazy, wrong things," The Washington Post, December 28, 2016, in Singer and Brooking, *LikeWar*, 128.

54. Singer and Brooking, *LikeWar*, 193.

55. Singer and Brooking, *LikeWar*, 150–154.

56. Singer and Brooking, *LikeWar*, 204–205.

57. Singer and Brooking, *LikeWar*, 193–195.

58. Singer and Brooking, *LikeWar*, 196.

59. René Girard, *Battling to the End: Conversations with Benoît Chantre* (East Lansing: University of Michigan Press, 2009), 13.

60. René Girard, *Battling to the End*, 21.

61. René Girard, *Battling to the End*, 13.

62. René Girard, *Battling to the End*, 13.

63. Rene Girard, *The Scapegoat*, trans. Yvonne Freccero (Baltimore: Johns Hopkins University Press, 1986), 13, in Haven, 239.

64. René Girard, *Battling to the End*, 13.

65. Carl von Clausewitz, *On War*, in René Girard, *Battling to the End*, 13–14.

66. René Girard, *Battling to the End*, xvi.

67. René Girard, *Battling to the End*, 74.

68. René Girard, *Battling to the End*, 64.

69. René Girard, *Battling to the End*, 63.

70. René Girard, *I See Satan Fall Like Lightning*, 32.

BIBLIOGRAPHY

Abramson, Alana. " 'I Believe in My Work.' How Rep. Ilhan Omar Rose from Refugee to Trump's Top Target." *Time*, July 18, 2019. https://time.com/5628844/ilhan-omar-profile/

Austen, Ben. "Public Enemies: Social Media Is Fueling Gang Wars in Chicago." *Wired*, September 17, 2013. https://www.wired.com/2013/09/gangs-of-social-media/

Brice-Saddler, Michael. "He easily found hundreds of death threats against Rep. Ilhan Omar. He wants Twitter to stop them." *Washington Post*, April 16, 2019. https://www.washingtonpost.com/technology/2019/04/16/he-easily-found-hundreds-death-threats-against-rep-ilhan-omar-he-wants-twitter-stop-them/

Burton, Tara Isabella. *Strange Rites: New Religions for a Godless World* (New York: PublicAffairs, 2020).

Caralle, Katelyn. "Covington student: 'People have threatened our lives' after confrontation with Native American protester." *Washington Examiner*, January 23, 2019. https://www.washingtonexaminer.com/news/covington-student-people-have-threatened-our-lives-after-confrontation-with-native-american-protester

Cheng, Justin, Michael Bernstein, Cristian Danescu-Niculescu-Mizil, Jure Leskovec. "Anyone Can Become a Troll: Causes of Trolling Behavior in Online Discussions." CSCW Conf Comput Support Coop Work (Feb.–Mar. 2017): 1217–1230. https://doi.org/10.1145/2998181.2998213

Condon, Ed. "Nathan Phillips rally protesters attempted to disrupt Mass at DC's National Shrine." Catholic News Agency, January 22, 2019. https://www.catholicnewsagency.com/news/nathan-phillips-rally-attempted-to-disrupt-mass-at-dcs-national-shrine-91038

Ernst, Douglas, "Kathy Griffin deletes 'Nazi sign' smear from stream of Covington Catholic tweets," *Washington Times*, January 22, 2019. https://www.washingtontimes.com/news/2019/jan/22/kathy-griffin-deletes-nazi-sign-smear-from-stream-/

Frank, Gillian. "The Deep Ties Between the Catholic Anti-Abortion Movement and Racial Segregation." *Jezebel*, January 22, 2019. https://theattic.jezebel.com/the-deep-ties-between-the-catholic-anti-abortion-moveme-1831950706

Garrels, Scott R. "Imitation, Mirror Neurons, and Mimetic Desire: Convergence between the Mimetic Theory of Rene Girard and empirical research on imitation." *Contagion: Journal of Violence, Mimesis, and Culture* 12–13 (2006): 47–86.

Girard, René. "Are the Gospels Mythical?" *First Things*, April 1996. https://www.firstthings.com/article/1996/04/are-the-gospels-mythical

———. *Battling to the End: Conversations with Benoît Chantre*. East Lansing: University of Michigan Press, 2009.

———. *I See Satan Fall Like Lightning*. Translated by James G. Williams. Maryknoll: Orbis Books, 2001.

———. *The Scapegoat*. translated by Yvonne Freccero. Baltimore: Johns Hopkins University Press, 1986.

———. *Things Hidden since the Foundation of the World*. Translated by Stephen Bann and Michael Metteer. Redwood City: Stanford University Press, 1987.

Halaby, Raouf. "The Little Brett Kavanaughs from Covington Catholic High." *Counter Punch*, January 22, 2019. https://www.counterpunch.org/2019/01/22/the-little-brett-kavanaughs-from-covington-catholic-high/

Harris, Bryant. "Ilhan Omar seizes spotlight to push pro-BDS resolution." *Al-Monitor*, July 16, 2019. https://www.al-monitor.com/pulse/originals/2019/07/ilham-omar-pro-bds-legislation-trump-israel.html

Haven, Cynthia L. *Evolution of Desire*. East Lansing: Michigan State University Press, 2018.

Hemingway, Mollie and Carrie Severino. *Justice on Trial: The Kavanaugh Confirmation and the Future of the Supreme Court*. Washington, D.C.: Regnery Publishing, 2019.

Hickok, Gregory. *The Myth of Mirror Neurons: The Real Neuroscience of Communication and Cognition*. New York: W.W. Norton, 2014.

Horkheimer, Max and Theodor W. Adorno. *Dialectic of Enlightenment*. Edited by Gunzelin Schmid Noerr, Translated by Edmund Jephcott. Redwood City: Stanford University Press, 2007.

Kemp, Simon. "Digital 2019: Global Internet Use Accelerates." *We Are Social*, January 30, 2019. https://wearesocial.com/blog/2019/01/digital-2019-global-internet-use-accelerates

Kramer, Adam D.L., Jamie E. Guillory, and Jeffrey T. Hancock, "Experimental Evidence of Massive-Scale Emotional Contagion Through Social Networks," *PNAS* 111, no. 24 (2014): 8788–90. https://doi.org/10.1073/pnas.1320040111; quoted in LW 162.

Lapidot-Lefler, Noam, and Azy Barak. "Effects of anonymity, invisibility, and lack of eye contact on toxic online disinhibition." *Computers in Human Behavior* 28, no. 2 (March 2012): 434–443. https://doi.org/10.1016/j.chb.2011.10.014

Lee, Justin. "Coalitions of Hate: Ilhan Omar, Donald Trump and the allure of scapegoating." *Religion and Ethics*, July 23, 2019. https://www.abc.net.au/religion/ilhan-omar-donald-trump-and-the-allure-of-scapegoating/11339746

———."Did the Boys of Covington Catholic 'Mob' a Native American Elder?" *Arc Digital*, January 20, 2019.

Levinthal, Dave, and Michael Beckel. "Journalists shower Hillary Clinton with campaign cash." *Columbia Journalism Review*, October 17, 2017. https://www.cjr.org/covering_the_election/campaign_donations_journalists.php

Levy, Jonathan, Abraham Goldstein, Moran Influs, Shafiq Masalha, Orna Zagoory-Sharon and Ruth Feldman. "Adolescents growing up amidst intractable conflict attenuate brain response to pain of outgroup." *Proceedings of the National Academy of Sciences of the United States of America* 113, no. 48 (November 2016): 13696–13701. https://doi.org/10.1073/pnas.1612903113

Lipka, Michael, "A closer look at America's rapidly growing religious 'nones.'" Pew Research Center, May 13, 2015. https://www.pewresearch.org/fact-tank/2015/05/13/a-closer-look-at-americas-rapidly-growing-religious-nones/

Oughourlian, Jean-Michel. *The Mimetic Brain*. Translated by Trevor Cribben Merrill. East Lansing: Michigan State University Press, 2016.

Phillips, Whitney, and Ryan M. Milner. *The Ambivalent Internet: Mischief, Oddity, and Antagonism Online*. Boston: Polity, 2017.

Podhoretz, John. "The Democrats and Anti-Semitism." *Commentary*, March 7, 2019. https://www.commentarymagazine.com/politics-ideas/the-democrats-and-anti-semitism/

Radulova, Lillian. " 'I need to get a new mugshot': Suspect arrested after he taunts police over wanted picture on Facebook." *Daily Mail Australia*, 19 October 2014. https://www.dailymail.co.uk/news/article-2798802/if-good-finding-comebacks-man-23-mocks-new-zealand-police-social-media-appeal-public-arrest.html

Rampell, Catherine. "Americans—especially but not exclusively Trump voters—believe crazy, wrong things." *Washington Post*, December 28, 2016.

Ramzy, Austin, and Chris Buckley. "'Absolutely No Mercy': Leaked Files Expose How China Organized Mass Detentions of Muslims." *New York Times*, November 16, 2019. https://www.nytimes.com/interactive/2019/11/16/world/asia/china-xinjiang-documents.html

Rösner, Leonie, and Nicole C. Krämer. "Verbal Venting in the Social Web: Effects of Anonymity and Group Norms on Aggressive Language Use in Online Comments." *Social Media + Society* 2, no. 3 (August 2016). https://doi.org/10.1177/2056305116664220

Schwartz, Ian. "Pirro: Ilhan Omar Wears A Hijab, Her Adherence To Islamic Doctrine Antithetical To Constitution." *Real Clear Politics*, March 11, 2019. https://www.realclearpolitics.com/video/2019/03/11/pirro_ilhan_omar_wears_a_hijab_her_adherence_to_islamic_doctrine_antithetical_to_constitution.html

Serres, Michel. "Receiving René Girard into the Académie Française." Translated by William A. Johnsen. In *For René Girard: Essays in Friendship and in Truth*, edited by Sandor Goodhart, Jörden Jörgensen, Tom Ryba, and James G. Williams, 1–18. East Lansing: Michigan State University Press, 2009.

Sest, Natalie, and Evita March. "Constructing the cyber-troll: Psychopathy, sadism, and empathy." *Personality and Individual Differences* 119 (2017): 69–72. https://doi.org/10.1016/j.paid.2017.06.038

Sidner, Sara. "Native American elder Nathan Phillips, in his own words." CNN, March 12, 2019. https://www.cnn.com/2019/01/21/us/nathan-phillips-maga-teens-interview/index.html

Singer, P.W., and Emerson T. Brooking. *LikeWar: The Weaponization of Social Media*. New York: Houghton Mifflin Harcourt, 2018.

Soave, Robby. "A Year Ago, the Media Mangled the Covington Catholic Story. What Happened Next Was Even Worse." *Reason*, January 21, 2020. https://reason.com/2020/01/21/covington-catholic-media-nick-sandmann-lincoln-memorial/

Suler, John. "The Online Disinhibition Effect." *Cyberpsychology & Behavior* 7, no. 3 (2004). https://doi.org/10.1089/1094931041291295

Viebeck, Elise. "In Minnesota, Rep. Ilhan Omar's comments cause pain and confusion." *Washington Post*, March 10, 2019. https://www.washingtonpost.com/politics/in-minnesota-rep-ilhan-omars-comments-cause-pain-and-confusion/2019/03/10/ff3f3700-41cb-11e9-9361-301ffb5bd5e6_story.html?utm_term=.25282dbc4c78

Voggeser, Birgit J., Ranjit K. Singh. and Anja S. Göritz. "Self-control in Online Discussions: Disinhibited Online Behavior as a Failure to Recognize Social Cues." *Frontiers in Psychology* (January 2018). https://doi.org/10.3389/fpsyg.2017.02372

Vohs, K. D., Baumeister, R. F., Schmeichel, B. J., Twenge, J. M., Nelson, N. M., & Tice, D. M. "Making choices impairs subsequent self-control: A limited-resource account of decision making, self-regulation, and active initiative." *Journal of Personality and Social Psychology* 94, no. 5 (2008): 883–898. https://doi.org/10.1037/0022-3514.94.5.883

Woodson Jr., Cleve R., Antonio Olivo, and Joe Helm. "'It was getting ugly' Native American drummer speaks on his encounter with MAGA-hat-wearing teens." *Washington Post*, January 22, 2019. https://www.washingtonpost.com/nation/2019/01/20/it-was-getting-ugly-native-american-drummer-speaks-maga-hat-wearing-teens-who-surrounded-him/

Chapter 14

Starving for Beauty
On Anorexia and Mimetic Desire

Anna Scanlon

Many of us have heard some variation of the following joke: a guy walks into a restaurant and instead of asking for a menu, he asks to see the head chef. When a portly figure walks out, the customer nods, satisfied, and orders the chef's special. The waiter, curious, asks why he wanted to see the chef first to which the customer responds with the well-known line: "I never trust a skinny cook." It's hard to use media now without seeing the current trends in food competitions like the *Great British Bake Off* and *Chopped*; recipes and fad diets like keto that promote a "healthier" lifestyle; and celebrity chefs like Gordon Ramsay who look even healthier than the food they promote. But what you don't see a lot of anymore are the portly chefs, the ones you can be *certain* taste-tested their dishes before sending them out. Instead, we're graced with ethereal figures, recipes that taste "just like" whatever they're mimicking for fewer calories, and literal tons of baked goods that we can only assume the crew eats as the cooks don't. We have, as a culture, become voyeuristic when it comes to the pleasures of food.

So what has lead us to this impasse? Why are we so invested in cooking food that mimics the real thing with half the calories? And what happens when what we see on TV begins to create reality, instead of the other way around? Drawing on the work of René Girard, I believe we can determine not only where this mimesis arises, but in part what might be done to combat the notion of ascetic eating shown by the media, a style which, if mimicked inaccurately, may lead to a full-blown Eating Disorder (ED).

Girard first introduced the connection between his theory of contemporary culture and anorexia at a conference in 1995. He presented articulately the issue many college-age students were facing at the time, when eating disorders were "reaching epidemic proportions."[1] Since Girard first presented his findings, Western understandings of EDs have stabilized some, as have treatment options for people suffering from these illnesses.[2] However, even as the Western world comes to terms with disordered eating patterns and the population these affect, the Eastern world is experiencing an increase in diagnoses, no doubt in part due to the global distribution of the Westernized ideal.[3] Girard's research still proves useful today, not because he furnishes a full representation of eating disorders, but because he *does* provide a useful explanation of the mimetic devices operating behind these EDs.

As Girard revised his lecture for publication in the journal *Contagion* a year after the conference, he acknowledged several key points which in turn became the focus of this research and work on emerging patterns of eating disorders. First, Girard notes that he would use female pronouns to refer to those diagnosed with an ED because at the time "nine out of ten sufferers [were] women."[4] However, he does clarify that "some undergraduates at Stanford tell me that the epidemic is spreading to male students."[5] Today, researchers studying the spread of eating disorders know these undergraduates are right and that EDs are also diagnosed in men.[6] Therefore, scholars interested in Girard's notions of mimetic rivalry and anorexia must expand their research into the larger relationship between gender and EDs.[7]

Secondly, Girard addresses the ways in which some blame the Christian church for EDs, articulating why this scapegoating is problematic.[8] He explains, "Puritanical and tyrannical as our ancestors may have been, their religious and ethical principles could be disregarded with impunity" when assigning blame.[9] However, just as scholars must study the modern gender dynamics of eating disorder diagnoses, they should push further than Girard did. It is not enough to acknowledge that EDs are not the sole fault of religious fasting practices. Researchers of these illnesses must also reject the notion that they are connected to any form of organized spiritual practice. Instead, it would be prudent to consider the ways in which spiritual practices can assist in mitigating or in curing disordered eating.

Finally, Girard is focused on a Western-centric view not uncommon from scholars in his era, writing exclusively about the presence of EDs in the West. Girard cogently ascribes these disorders to mimesis: "Westerners are always forced into action, and when they no longer imitated heroes and saints they are drawn into the infernal circle of mimetic futility."[10] However, modern understandings of the increase of globalization and the influence of that Western mimetic futility have spread globally and eating disorders are on the rise as a result, at least in part due to the influence of Western media.[11] In fact, in a 2018 study from Budapest, the researchers discovered that due to the mixed messages of the media, disordered eating diagnoses are increasing throughout the world.[12] They specifically articulate that as these disorders are on the rise, so, too, are cooking shows "on every platform."[13] It is not hard, therefore, to see a correlation between the three: globalization, media, and EDs. Additionally, the rise of diagnosed eating disorders in areas like Japan further supports the claim that globalization has led to increased pressures to fit the thin ideal. While the authors of an early-2000s study note that cultural ideals in Japan play a part, they cannot completely reject the idea that exposure to Western beauty standards has further exacerbated the drive for thinness.[14]

While Girard doesn't give a full account of the relationship between EDs and spirituality, gender, and region, he does acknowledge the borders of his work, providing us with a structure to build upon. Thus, in studying the spread of EDs and the influence of mimesis on said disorders, this chapter must acknowledge three key points which expand Girard's examination. First, eating disorders are not exclusive to females. Secondly, ascetic Christian practices aren't to blame for the spread of EDs, but neither are other faith and spiritual customs. In fact, spiritually-based assistance may help in mitigating the detrimental effects of an eating disorder. Finally, and thirdly, EDs are not Western-exclusive diagnoses as they spread due to the process of globalization which makes negative portrayals of food in Western media more accessible.[15]

GENDER: THE ATYPICAL ANOREXIC

As mentioned, Girard's text—even with the 2003 updates—is outdated with regard to understanding the gendered dynamics of EDs. His notions about women and diagnoses of disordered eating—which largely ignore bulimia and obesity—are proof of this point.[16] For example, Girard writes "Many women would like to be anorexics,"[17] but fails to follow this hasty generalization with evidence, leaving readers to believe his logical fallacy is factual. He compounds this gender-biased error with a further one, explaining that "Anorexia strikes the best and the brightest among our young women. The typical victim is well educated, talented, ambitious, eager for perfection."[18] Readers are thus led to consider only those women which meet Girard's profile as anorexic, instead of looking more broadly at the wider spectrum of those affected including other genders, the poor, or the undereducated.

The above point is made not to argue that diagnoses of anorexia are the same across genders but rather to stake the general claim that EDs are found among a variety of gendered, global populations. In an interview after his initial presentation, Girard himself admits that in terms of diagnoses among the sexes, the distinction in numbers is growing less and less pronounced.[19] However, while anyone can be diagnosed with an ED, the gendered biases persist for different reasons. Ahlich et al. expand on this notion of causation, articulating that while researchers and diagnosticians assume the typical male sufferer is athletic—a parallel to Girard's own specific assumptions about the typical female sufferer—the association between eating disorders, body talk, and males did not differ greatly between athletes and nonathletes.[20] Unfortunately, despite the fact that the typical sufferer doesn't actually exist among any gendered demographic, inaccurate and incomplete notions of what the anorexic looks like—and who they are—remain, making diagnoses and treatments difficult. In fact, because the anorexic body is often assumed to have a typical presentation depending on one's sex, those who are both anorexic and atypical strive to fall in line with the idealized figure, feeding into what Girard proclaims is the mimetic rivalry phenomenon.

Girard describes this phenomenon specifically in relation to his gendered perceptions of anorexia nervosa, using the case of Elizabeth of Austria (Sisi) the wife of Emperor Franz Joseph to illustrate mimetic rivalry. He suggests that Sisi used disordered eating to find her own identity in a time when women were generally seen first as a daughter, then as a wife, and finally, as a mother. Sisi ultimately became the opponent of Napoleon III's wife, Empress Eugenie of France.[21] While she and her contemporary existed before media as we define it today, they were still held up as the beauty ideal of their time.[22] Girard posits that, as a result of this idealization, the competition between these two women started "a pattern of mimetic rivalry among the numerous aristocratic ladies who had nothing better to do than look up to Sisi and Eugenie and copy their behavior down to the last detail."[23] The women, in an effort to outdo one another, crafted bigger and bigger feasts, showing off with food they won't eat, much like the fantasy of the modern television chef, baker, or cook.[24] Ultimately, Girard sums up this desire toward thinness as entertainment, explaining that "[m]imetic desire aims at the absolute slenderness of the radiant being some other person always is in our eyes but we ourselves never are, at least in our own eyes."[25] Neither woman is satisfied with her offerings, both in terms of figures and food, but each will keep trying. Girard ends his examination with the reflection that while these mimetic underpinnings are clear to him in cases of anorexia, medical minds are slower to catch on.

However, in treating and diagnosing anorexia, medical practitioners are perhaps not slowly catching on, but rather more aware of the nuanced nature of EDs, particularly as these disorders spread among regions, faith practices, and genders. Undoubtedly hampered by the medical gaze, medical practitioners are nevertheless aware of not only the nuances of mimetic rivalry and the influences that the above can have on disordered eating among the sexes, but also carry knowledge of the more-complicated psychological underpinnings of an ED diagnosis that Girard's work does not have.[26] Mattias Strand, who approaches Girard's work from this psychological standpoint, notes that Girard's response remains outside the purview of healthcare.[27] Strand is quick to follow this point up, however, with the idea that because of Girard's renown in other circles, his work is still worthy of critical attention, as we examine it here.[28]

RELIGION: ASCETIC ANOREXICS

Gender is not the only influence Girard is not able to fully consider in his brief treatise. As mentioned, Girard does not devote his limited space to considering the relationship, or what he deems the lack thereof, between spirituality, religion, and EDs. He focuses exclusively on the mimetic rival as in Sisi and Eugenie's cases instead, explaining that "our modernist and postmodernist teachers will keep blaming the dead prohibitions until doomsday, but their students, some day, should finally question this dogma."[29] While Girard is indubitably right to question those who blame religious ascetic practices—"the dead prohibitions"—for the increase in eating disorders across the globe due to their longevity as compared to the recent rise in EDs, he misses an important means of addressing and diverting mimetic rivalry: that of treating the disease and removing the rival.

Girard is not entirely incorrect. We cannot uncritically assign religious practices as the cause of EDs. He decries the problematic notion that religious asceticism is to blame as it represents what he quotes as "an early form of anorexia," instead arguing that genuine religious asceticism exists and it is only when one wants to be praised for their ascetic practices that a problem arises.[30] It is this search for praise and validation, he clarifies, that breeds mimetic rivalry and escalates the competition for who is the most holy (and thin).[31]

Vandereycken and van Deth, authors Girard cites, carefully examine the connection between religious asceticism and anorexia. They explain the rise of religious asceticism, noting that it began with the practice of fasting—particularly abstaining from certain foods, wine, and sexual relations—and became a way to perfect one's spiritual life by denying food which "only benefits the body and harms the soul."[32] However, Vandereycken and van Deth also point out that by the sixteenth century, fasting was no longer connected exclusively to Christian ascetic practices but some saw it as indicative of "bewitchment and demonic possession."[33] They explain that "fasting became increasingly alienated from its traditionally religious background," clearly indicating that while initially disordered eating may have had a connection to religion, EDs became associated with other factors including family structure and globalization, as Girard articulates.[34]

Instead of looking at spirituality as the prevailing cause of eating disorders, scholars should connect with how spiritual practices might *help* those suffering from such a diagnosis. Many studies focus on the ways in which spirituality and religion can work to combat disordered eating as part of treatment. Developing evidence suggests that while there may be a correlation between religion, other spiritual practices, and the etiology of eating disorders, religion and spirituality also play an important role in treatment and recovery.[35] In fact, in studies of people with eating disorders, researchers reported that a statistically significant portion of the people studied and interviewed shared that religion and/or spirituality were critical in supporting their treatment for an eating disorder.[36]

So why doesn't Girard consider the connection between eating disorder prevention, the subduing of the mimetic rival, and religion? Others who have explored *Anorexia and Mimetic Desire* have hinted at this disconnect, including Strand who notes that "Girard argues that the rejection of what may rightly have been seen as oppressive cultural edicts came with a price: increased mimetic rivalry."[37] While Strand does not offer any further insight into Girard's omission, I suggest that if, as Girard insists, mimetic rivalry arises in part from the decay of religious institutions leading to more internal rivalry, couldn't this same rivalry be ended with the restoration of these same unions? The scholarship inclines us towards this interpretation.[38]

In fact, across many faith-based practices, there has been a high association of body satisfaction and religious customs. For example, among Australian Muslim women, "a greater extent of religiosity was associated with less body dissatisfaction."[39] This contentedness is not limited to that area of the world, either. Muslim women living in America, for example, experienced less of a drive towards thinness, despite the overwhelming presence of media pushing for that ideal.[40] Furthermore, these correlations are not found exclusively in Muslim women. Among college students who identified as Christian, positive body image was correlated with a positive relationships with God.[41] Additionally, in studies of young women from Belize, researchers found that since these women saw their bodies as gifts from God there existed a profound lack of eating disorders despite globalization.[42]

These points are not to say that religious persons are never diagnosed with an ED. However, even when body dissatisfaction has been noticed among people who identify as spiritual or religious, a return to faith-based practices and customs assisted the patients. For example, in a study conducted among Christian and Jewish women with eating disorders, returning to religious and spiritual beliefs played a significant part in the patients' recovery.[43] In the second study conducted by the same group, researchers surveyed Christian, Jewish, Buddhist and Atheist women and found that many of the participants felt their religion or spirituality was the catalyst to seek eating disorder treatment and to ultimately recover.[44] Therefore, while we can no longer blame religion for the increase in eating disorders, we should be looking to faith and spirituality as a means of treating the rivalry before it spreads further.[45]

REGION: AREA-BASED ANOREXIA

If, as Girard posits and this research insists, we cannot uncritically blame religious practices and we also cannot look specifically to one gender for causes of eating disorders, we must then ask ourselves, what is contributing to the spread of EDs across the globe? One answer is globalization. While Girard presents a mostly Western-centric view of EDs, modern research has proven they are a global health concern.[46] But how did EDs become a significant global health issue? Research indicates the spread of EDs is due to several changes in societal dynamics, including shifts in family structures and the processes of urbanization and globalization. Girard supports these points about these changing dynamics, articulating that EDs "are caused by the destruction of the family and other safeguards [including faith practices] against the forces of mimetic fragmentation and competition, unleashed by the end of prohibitions."[47] Thus, even though there is disagreement about the role of religion in eating disorders and the impact these diagnoses have on gender, consensus seems clear that they are on the rise due to shifting social expectations. A recent article on Korean cooking shows addresses this point, noting that female broadcast jockeys (BJs) often try to both eat and stay thin as they attempt to appeal to a broader audience.[48]

Eating disorders have arguably increased due to the process of globalization—linked to Girard's own theories of contagion—wherein specifically Western notions of the thin ideal have spread to other countries, continents, and cultures.[49] The continent of Africa, for example, has seen a sharp rise in eating disorders as Western advertisements, television, and practices arrived in the region. In fact, in the limited amount of studies done on the connection between eating disorders and Africa, two main predictors for the development of an ED were student status and exposure to media.[50] Additionally, even if one isn't initially exposed to the thin ideals of Western culture, if they move to a more industrialized nation than the one they lived in previously, they are at risk as they come into contact with the body-thin ideals of that developed nation.[51]

However, as Girard only applies a Western-centric examination to the spread of eating disorders, developing nations are largely not on his radar.

Most of his examples come from Europe, as in the case of Napoleon's wife, with a few from America, as Girard was teaching at Stanford. His text introduces the idea of anorexia and mimetic desire but just as with religion and gender, it is up to modern scholars to examine the larger scope of region as eating disorders spread due to television shows, fashion magazines, and media in general.[52]

Scholars, medical personnel, and everyone else interested in ED treatment and prevention must pair their growing consciousness with the fact that treatments should vary as needed in the same ways that presentation of the EDs diverge. In part, because eating disorders in developing regions like Africa are still relatively underresearched phenomenon, scholars do not have evidence to make generalized statements about what treatments would work best globally. While religion and spirituality can and should be considered in the treatment process, the specific religion or spiritual practices of each culture are the ones which must be used regionally. Additionally, because body concerns are seen differently across the globe, despite some shared languages, practices, or beliefs, "these variables must be considered in research protocols and/or interventions for body weight concerns."[53] Therefore, the treatment options offered for eating disorders should take into account that the factors contributing to EDs are global and myriad.

CONCLUSION

Eating disorders and their contributing dynamics are far more nuanced than Girard's initial audiences might believe. As the (pop) cultural examples explain, mimetic rivalry for the perfect form is not limited to sex, region, or religion, but rather is promoted by a pervasive combination of factors occurring within a global society, illustrated above by just one facet: cooking shows. Girard's three assumptions must be questioned: Gender is not a cut-and-dry indication of whether or not a patient is susceptible to an eating disorder, religion cannot be scapegoated as the cause of an ED, and region does not protect one from contracting the illness. It is also clear more research still needs to be done. The studies cited in this chapter must be replicated in order to determine if their results are truly significant or outliers. Further, scholars should conduct additional examinations of EDs in developing regions as more and more Western content is shared with them. Additionally, religion and spirituality must be included in discussions of treatment options. When Girard rejects blaming the "doomsday prohibitions," he also removes from consideration the ways in which religion can *help* those diagnosed with an ED or symptoms of disordered eating. However, as indicated by the studies examining the many faith practices mentioned, religion and spiritual practices assist in mitigating the negative factors of an ED such as body dissatisfaction.[54]

As Girard indicates, eating disorders have a beginning—one which logically can be seen as stemming from mimetic rivalry—a development and an end. Scholars, spiritual advisors, and medical practitioners have become acquainted with the beginning, are working on the middle, but have yet to see to see the end. However, as we study treatments, explore spirituality, regulate media, and examine patterns of EDs further, the end will hopefully come sooner, and we may return to enjoying food for food's sake.

NOTES

1. Girard, René, *Anorexia and Mimetic Desire* (Lansing, MI: Michigan State University Press, 2013), 1.

2. Richards, P. Scott, Carrie L. Caoili, Sabree A. Crowton, Michael E. Berrett, Randy K. Hardman, Russell N. Jackson, and Peter W. Sanders, "An Exploration of the Role of Religion and Spirituality in the Treatment and Recovery of Patients with Eating Disorders," *Spirituality in Clinical Practice* 5, no. 2 (2018): 89.

3. Hay, Phillipa & Stephen Touyz, "Editorial: Globalisation and the *Journal of Eating Disorders*," *Journal of Eating Disorders* 4, no. 1 (2016): 1.

4. Girard, *Anorexia and Mimetic Desire*, 1.

5. Ibid.

6. Ahlich, Erica, Emily Choquette, and Diana Rancourt, "Body Talk, Athletic Identity, and Eating Disorder Symptoms in Men," *Psychology of Men & Masculinities* 20, no. 3 (2019) explain that "It long was assumed that only 10% of eating disorder cases occurred in men; however, data suggest this number may be closer to 25% (Hudson, Hiripi, Pope, & Kessler, 2007)." They further articulate that due to gender biases in medicine, men presenting the same symptoms as women who have an eating disorder are less likely to be so diagnosed, therefore "25% may still be a conservative estimate," 347.

7. It is important to note that nonbinary individuals are also experiencing an increase in diagnoses of EDs with little assistance in the way of treatment. Sydney Hildebrandt, author of "Link Found Between Eating Disorders and Gender Identity; For Non-Binary Patients Seeking Treatment, Health-Care Services Woefully Fall Short," *The Toronto Star*, June 29, 2018, explains "Eating disorder rates are rising among transgender individuals, according to a 2015 study by the Children's Hospital of Eastern Ontario (CHEO) Research Institute. This research suggests they are more likely to develop an eating disorder if they experience gender dysphoria, the feeling of conflict when one's biological makeup does not match their internal gender identity," E1.

8. Girard coined a specific definition of scapegoating used across many of his texts. In the foreword to an interview between Girard and Rebecca Adams from the University of Notre Dame, she describes the term as the "victimage mechanism."

Girard expands on this notion during the interview, providing the example of Joan of Arc, seen as a demon by those who wished to undermine her cause, creating a scapegoat on which to blame their concerns. For more on Scapegoating Theory, see also Girard's text, *The Scapegoat* (Baltimore, MD: Johns Hopkins UP, 1986).

9. Girard, *Anorexia and Mimetic Desire*, 17.

10. Girard, *Anorexia and Mimetic Desire*, 15.

11. Hay and Touyz, "Editorial," 1.

12. Forgács, Atilla, Bóna Enikő, Csikos Tímea, and Helga Metercsik in their study "Media Messages and Eating Disorders: Taste and Price of a Message," *Central and Eastern Europe | Journal of the Corvinus University of Budapest* 40, no 3 (2018) explain that "[f]ood-related media messages are multilayered and contradictory on many levels," 401.

13. Ibid, 406.

14. Pike, Kathleen M., and Amy Borovoy, "The Rise of Eating Disorders in Japan: Issues of Culture and Limitations of the Model of 'Westernization,'" *Culture, Medicine & Psychiatry* 28, no. 4 (2004), 524.

15. This point is a key one to consider. There is inarguably a connection between media and eating disorders, evidence of which can be found in a novel poster presentation by Francisco-Natanauan, Pia, Eric Sigel, and Jeanelle Sheeder at the Children's Hospital of Colorado (2013). Francisco-Natanauan et al., "Media Use of Adolescent Women with Eating Disorders: Is There More to It Than What Meets the Senses?," Journal of Adolescent Health 52, no. 2 (2013) determined that "Women with ED watch cooking shows and visit food websites twice as often as women without ED," thus promoting the connection between access to cooking-based media and diagnosed EDs, S42.

16. A claim Girard justifies by articulating that most of us resort at some point or another to a "mild form of bulimia," 10.

17. Ibid.

18. Ibid, 9.

19. Ibid, 50.

20. Ahlich, Choquette, & Rancourt, "Body Talk," 350. Body talk, as defined by Ahlich et al. is the means through which men express concerns about their body type and is measured in 16 different ways by the Male Body Talk Scale, 349.

21. Girard, *Anorexia and Mimetic Desire*, 26.

22. Ibid.

23. Ibid, 27.

24. Ibid.

25. Ibid, 17.

26. A term another philosophical Frenchman, Michel Foucault, coined in *Birth of the Clinic* (New York, NY: Pantheon Books, 1973) to refer to medical professionals'— doctors in particular—tendency to look at the patient as representative of his or her symptoms instead of looking at the patient as a human with more than just a disease diagnosis, a notion which calls to mind Girard's claim that "our eating disorders are discussed exclusively in medical terms, as if they had nothing to do with the culture at large and its recent evolution," 35.

27. Strand, Mattias, "René Girard and the Mimetic Nature of Eating Disorders," *Culture, Medicine & Psychiatry* 42, no. 3 (2018), 557.

28. Ibid. 557.

29. Girard, *Anorexia and Mimetic Desire*, 14.

30. Ibid, 34.

31. Ibid.

32. Vandereycken, William and Ron van Deth, *From Fasting Saints to Anorexic Girls: A History of Self-Starvation* (London: Athlone Press, 2019) 17-8.

33. Ibid, 31.

34. Ibid. Perhaps the most literary example of Girard's point here comes from Marya Hornbacher's *Wasted: A Memoir of Anorexia and Bulimia* (New York: HarperPerennial, 1999), in which Hornbacher grapples with her own struggle with eating disorders, noting first that "we needed religion, salvation, something to fill the anxious hollow in our chests. Many of us sought it in food and thinness" (118) and later articulating further that "Many of us came from less-than-grounded families. We were living inside a pressure cooker, competition tough, stakes very high, the certainty of our futures nonexistent," 119.

35. While Richards et al., "Exploration," 88, articulate the above point, others are not so quick to contribute religious practices to eating disorder etiology, acknowledging that while the notion of this connection persisted into the 1990s, no evidence was ever produced to reach a clear consensus on the relationship (Strand, "René Girard," 563).

36. Richards et al., "Exploration," 100.

37. Strand, 559.

38. Girard himself seems inclined to consider this idea that without these unions, we don't have the values to teach our children what to and what not to hold dear, articulating early in his text that "The anorexic pattern of behavior makes sense within the context not of our nominal values but of what we silently teach our children when we stop chattering about values" (*Anorexia and Mimetic Desire*, 7). By removing the presence of the church and the values present therein, we remove the chance to talk with our children about healthy life choices, a fact seen shortly in Anderson-Fye's work with ED trends in Belize.

39. Wilhelm, Leonie, Andrea S. Hartmann, Julia C. Becker, Melahat KiAi, Manuel Waldorf, and Silja Vocks, "Body Covering and Body Image: A Comparison of Veiled and Unveiled Muslim Women, Christian Women, and Atheist Women Regarding Body Checking, Body Dissatisfaction, and Eating Disorder Symptoms," *Journal of Religion and Health* 57, no. 5 (2018), 1810.

40. Ibid.

41. Ibid, 1809.

42. Anderson-Fye, Eileen, "A 'Coca-Cola' Shape: Cultural Change, Body Image, and Eating Disorders in San Andrés, Belize" in *Culture, Medicine, and Psychiatry: An International Journal of Cross-Cultural Health Research* 28, no. 4 (2004), 2004), 570. Fye also points out that while the notion of the body as a gift from God tends to persist among the families employed in more traditional roles throughout Belize, the same cannot be said of all young people working in that country. In fact, there

has been an increase in disordered eating behavior among women employed by the tourism industry. The implication here being that globalization plays into their world view and shifts their perceptions of their own bodies, 563.

43. Richards et al., "Exploration," 91.

44. Ibid, 95.

45. A quick scan of published cookbooks reveals texts that are directly linked with spirituality, including *Cooking with the Saints* (2019) by Alexander Greeley and Fernando Flores, *The Lifegiving Table: Nurturing Faith through Feasting, One Meal at a Time* (2017) by Sally Clarkson, and *Cooking with Spirits for the Spirit: A Meditative Approach to Cooking* (2012) by Janet Hall Svisdahl among many others. Texts like these, which have a vested interest in holistic health could provide another resource for those suffering from an ED.

46. Hay & Touyz, "Editorial," 1; Girard explains, "Westerners are always forced into action, and when they no longer imitate heroes and saints they are drawn into the infernal circle of mimetic futility," 15.

47. Girard, *Anorexia and Mimetic Desire*, 19.

48. Rhee, Jooyeon, "Gender Politics in Food Escape: Korean Masculinity in TV Cooking Shows in South Korea" *Journal of Popular Film & Television* 47, no. 1 (2019) explains "It is especially discomforting to see how female BJs try to overperform their ability to eat when many eating disorders, such as binging and bulimia, often stem from social pressure to stay thin," 63.

49. Hay & Touyz, "Editorial," 1.

50. van Hoeken, Daphne, Jonathan K. Burns, & Hans W. Hoek, "Epidemiology of Eating Disorders in Africa" in *Current Opinion in Psychiatry* 29, no. 6 (2016) specify further that "the exposure to western cultures, particularly in highly educated persons, is rising, and with it the risk for developing an eating disorder," 376.

51. Eddy, Kamryn T., Moira Hennessey, and Heather Thompson-Brenner, "Eating Pathology in East African Women: The Role of Media Exposure and Globalization" *Journal of Nervous and Mental Disease* 195, no. 3 (2007), 197.

52. Girard himself notes in an interview included at the end of *Anorexia and Mimetic Desire* that there were even, for a time, lawsuits brought against media outlets and fashion designers due to the "acute consciousness of the problem in American society," 46. However, in so doing, Girard once again keeps the problem in a strictly Western context, not looking at its influence further afield.

53. da Silva, Roberto Wanderson et al., "Body Weight Concerns: cross-national study and identification of factors related to eating disorders" in PLoS *One* 12, no. 7 (2017), 11.

54. In fact, many books address the spiritual side to recovery from EDs including Sheryle Cruse's *Thin Enough: My Spiritual Journey Through the Living Death of an Eating Disorder* (2006), Rabbi Dovid Goldwasser's *Starving Souls: A Spiritual Guide to Understanding Eating Disorders: Anorexia, Bulimia, Binging* (2010), Mark E. Shaw's *Eating Disorders: Hope for Hungering Souls* (2014), and Emma White's *The Spirituality of Anorexia: A Goddess Feminist Thealogy* (2018). As the above texts indicate, spiritual and religious practices recognize the important role they can play

in recovery for those suffering from an ED. Unfortunately, popular culture is slower to catch on.

BIBLIOGRAPHY

Adams, Rebecca, and René Girard. "Violence, Difference, Sacrifice: A Conversation with René Girard." *Religion & Literature* 25, no. 2 (July 1993): 9–33. https://www.jstor.org/ stable/40059554.

Ahlich, Erica, Emily M. Choquette, and Diana Rancourt. "Body Talk, Athletic Identity, and Eating Disorder Symptoms in Men." *Psychology of Men & Masculinities* 20, no. 3 (July 2019): 347–55. doi:10.1037/men0000168.supp.

Anderson-Fye, Eileen P. "A 'Coca-Cola' Shape: Cultural Change, Body Image, and Eating Disorders in San Andrés, Belize." *Culture, Medicine, and Psychiatry: An International Journal of Cross-Cultural Health Research* 28, no. 4 (December 2004): 561–95. doi:10.1007/s11013-004-1068-4.

Clarkson, Sally. *The Lifegiving Table: Nurturing Faith through Feasting One Meal at a Time*. Carol Stream, IL: Tyndale House Publishers, 2017.

Cruse, Sheryle. *Thin Enough: My Spiritual Journey Through the Living Death of an Eating Disorder*. New York, NY: PWxyz, LLC, 2005.

da Silva, Wanderson Robert, Moema De Souza Santana, João Maroco, Benvindo Felismino Samuel Maloa, and Juliana Alvares Duarte Bonini Campos. "Body Weight Concerns: Cross-National Study and Identification of Factors Related to Eating Disorders." *PLoS ONE* 12, no. 7 (July 7, 2017): 1–16. doi:10.1371/journal.pone.0180125.

Eddy, Kamryn T., Moira Hennessey, and Heather Thompson-Brenner. "Eating Pathology in East African Women: The Role of Media Exposure and Globalization." *Journal of Nervous and Mental Disease* 195, no. 3 (March 2007): 196–202. doi:10.1097/01.nmd.0000243922.49394.7d.

Forgács, Attila, Enikő Bóna, Tímea Csíkos, and Helga Metercsik. "Media Messages and Eating Disorders: Taste and Price of a Message." *Society and Economy. Central and Eastern Europe | Journal of the Corvinus University of Budapest* 40, no. 39 (2018): 401–415. doi: 10.1556/204.2018.40.3.7.

Foucault, Michel. *The Birth of the Clinic: An Archaeology of Medical Perception*. [1st American ed.]. New York: Pantheon Books, 1973.

Francisco-Natanauan, Pia, Eric Sigel, and Jeanelle Sheeder. "Media Use of Adolescent Women With Eating Disorders: Is There More to It Than What Meets the Senses?" *Journal of Adolescent Health* 52, no. 2 (2013): S42. https://doi.org/10.1016 /j.jadohealth.2012.10.100

Girard, René. *Anorexia and Mimetic Desire*. Edited by Mark R. Anspach. Lansing, MI: Michigan State University Press, 2013.

Goldwasser, Dovid. *Starving Souls: A Spiritual Guide to Understanding Eating Disorders: Anorexia, Bulimia, Binging*. Brooklyn, NY: KTAV Publishing House, 2010.

Greeley, Alexander, and Fernando Flores. *Cooking with the Saints*. Manchester, NH: Sophia Institute Press, 2019.

Hay, Phillipa and Stephen Touyz. "Editorial: Globalisation and the Journal of Eating Disorders." *Journal of Eating Disorders* 4, no. 1 (2016): 1. doi:10.1186/s40337-016-0099-x.

Hildebrandt, Sydney. "Link Found Between Eating Disorders and Gender Identity; For Non-Binary Patients Seeking Treatment, Health-Care Services Woefully Fall Short." *Toronto Star*, June 29, 2018. https://link.gale.com/apps/doc/A544711229/STND? u=uiuc_iwu &sid=STND&xid=4a548165

Hornbacher, Marya. 2005. *Wasted: A Memoir of Anorexia and Bulimia*. New York, NY: HarperPerrenial, 1999.

Pike, Kathleen M, and Amy Borovoy. "The Rise of Eating Disorders in Japan: Issues of Culture and Limitations of the Model of 'Westernization.'" *Culture, Medicine and Psychiatry* 28, no. 4 (December 2004): 493–531. doi: 10.1007/s11013-004-1066-6.

Rhee, Jooyeon. "Gender Politics in Food Escape: Korean Masculinity in TV Cooking Shows in South Korea." *Journal of Popular Film & Television* 47, no. 1 (January 2019): 56–64. doi:10.1080/01956051.2019.1563445.

Richards, P. Scott, Carrie L. Caoili, Sabree A. Crowton, Michael E. Berrett, Randy K. Hardman, Russell N. Jackson, and Peter W. Sanders. "An Exploration of the Role of Religion and Spirituality in the Treatment and Recovery of Patients with Eating Disorders." *Spirituality in Clinical Practice* 5, no. 2 (June 2018): 88–103. doi:10.1037/scp0000159.

Shaw, Mark. *Eating Disorders: Hope for Hungering Souls*. Bemidji, MN, Focus Publishing, 2014.

Strand, Mattias. "René Girard and the Mimetic Nature of Eating Disorders." *Culture, Medicine & Psychiatry* 42, no. 3 (2018): 552–83. doi:10.1007/s11013-018-9574-y.

Svisdahl, Janet Hall. *Cooking with Spirits for the Spirit: A Meditative Approach to Cooking*. Bloomington, IN, iUniverse, 2012.

Vandereycken, William, and Ron van Deth. *From Fasting Saints to Anorexic Girls: A History of Self-Starvation*. London: Athlone Press, 2019.

van Hoeken, Daphne, Jonathan K. Burns, and Hans W. Hoek. "Epidemiology of Eating Disorders in Africa." *Current Opinion in Psychiatry* 29, no. 6 (November 2016): 372. https://i-share-iwu.primo.exlibrisgroup.com/permalink/01CARLI_IWU/ba3o89/cdi_proquest_ miscellaneous_1824545329

White, Emma. *The Spirituality of Anorexia: A Goddess Feminist Theology*. Oxfordshire, UK, Routledge, 2018.

Wilhelm, Leonie, Andrea S. Hartmann, Julia C. Becker, Melahat KiAi, Manuel Waldorf, and Silja Vocks. "Body Covering and Body Image: A Comparison of Veiled and Unveiled Muslim Women, Christian Women, and Atheist Women Regarding Body Checking, Body Dissatisfaction, and Eating Disorder Symptoms." *Journal of Religion and Health* 57, no. 5 (2018): 1808. doi:10.1007/s10943-018-0585-3.

Chapter 15

From #MeToo to #WeToo

Mimetic Ecclesiology and the Possibility of Structural Reform

T. Derrick Witherington

Since the birth of the #MeToo Movement, our society has grown progressively more attentive to the voices of women who report having been sexually abused or harassed. The Catholic Church has also had its own #MeToo moment, though the cycles of abuse and inappropriateness uncovered extend to minor children and young men as well. Interestingly, in the uncovering of these cycles of abuse—in contexts not just limited to the Church—social and mass media has served to lead the offensive, casting light on systems of oppression. This, in turn, has forced the affected institutions to a process of reckoning and reform lest they lose all credibility in the eyes of the broader public.

In this chapter, I will be examining how this has worked itself out in the response of the Catholic Church to the sex-abuse crisis. In order to frame these considerations in a Girardian way, I will be following James Alison's reflections on the nature of the Church as systematized by Grant Kaplan. As we will see, the question before us will be whether or not the "mimetic ecclesiology" advocated by Alison is able to be "interrupted" by critique in such a way that new horizons of possibilities can become possible for moving forward. In framing our critique we suggest Lieven Boeve's model of "interruption" as a necessary element in any contemporary ecclesiology. The chapter concludes by pointing toward what kind of Church structures are required if the Church is to maintain relevance to contemporary men and women, a relevance that is achieved by admitting that the voices of #MeToo have led the Church to a #WeToo moment of admitting how its structures may have contributed to the perpetuation of abuse.

THE CHARACTERISTICS OF MIMETIC ECCLESIOLOGY

Grant Kaplan, in his *René Girard, Unlikely Apologist: Mimetic Theory and Fundamental Theology*,[1] devotes a chapter to laying out and evaluating what a mimetic ecclesiology would look like. Kaplan masterfully weaves together a tapestry depicting the characteristics of a Girardian-influenced fundamental ecclesiology which he helpfully summarizes under seven headings. The themes treated here represent a very systematic and highly readable account of what an Alisonian fundamental ecclesiology would look like. As we will see, this framework is indebted and related to Alison's reflections on sin, grace, and forgiveness.

The first theme highlighted by Kaplan is the utter gratuity of the forgiveness granted by Christ. The risen Christ's appearance to the disciples is seen as not only a free grace, but as itself being *graced forgiveness*. Christ's first words of *peace* to the disciples gathered in the upper room are seen as not a demand for restorative justice or retribution so much as an invitation *to see aright*, to see that the previous way of proceeding and conceptualizing the way God and the world works was flawed and limited. In Kaplan's words, "one discovers this truth in recognizing the entirely wrong way that one has been going about things."[2] Not only, in other words, are the disciples challenged to see that Jesus has not been limited and defeated by death, they are shocked to learn that Jesus does not accuse them as being accomplices in his death by abandoning him. The initial fear of the disciples in the upper room was undoubtedly related to their belief that they would be demanded to make atonement for their act of betrayal, an assumption which turns out to be a part "of an idolatrous order of things which had previously been confused with the worship of the true God."[3] Indeed, as Alison notes, the Resurrection "happened as forgiveness" which "allows for a reimagination of a relationship not rooted in reciprocity."[4]

The second theme, flowing from the first, is that this reimagination of relationship implies the creation of a community or "church" rooted in this new idea of divine-human relationality. Such a community is not founded on a strict distinction between who is "in" and who is "out" by means of fabricating complex rules and structures to delineate this. The church, indeed, is called to witness to "the unity of humanity that the Holy Spirit creates out of the risen victim, the unity which subverts all other unities."[5] All members of the ecclesial community are equally "forgiven *as* sinners," and, thereby, "enabled to experience this grace in such a way that makes grace the coefficient in front of any account of human goodness."[6] Being forgiven by the risen Christ enables Christians to live together in a new way by means of showing a new pattern of human relationship not based on reciprocity and vengeance. In this way, Alison notes, "the coming into being of the Church is not an add-on, but what the whole project was about."[7]

The leads to the third theme, namely, the need of an ecclesial apologetic which is not defensive. The need for an undefensive ecclesiology is meant to counterbalance early modern forms of ecclesial apologetic which were formulated to defend the Catholic Church from external critique. While rightfully pointing out that the ecclesiology of the Second Vatican Council has moved away from this model, Kaplan maintains that Girard's conceptions of being and belonging serve to further enhance this. Going back to the way Jesus "founds" the church in the peace and forgiveness bestowed after the Resurrection, Kaplan notes that "the Church allows one to belong in a way that throws into question earlier ways of belonging."[8] The Revelation of *God's peace* is, in the final analysis, creative and constitutive of a new historical, linguistic, representational community, which is simultaneously seen to have been originary: what humans were always meant to be."[9] Being in and belonging to the Church, then, enables a revolution in the way human beings conceptualize these things. Insofar as the peace and forgiveness given by Christ levels the playing field by emphasizing that all have been equally forgiven as sinners, the community "forgiven sinners" is called to witness to the universal/catholic faith which, by its very nature, has no over against."[10] Ultimately, Kaplan notes, "the new community called "Church" demands that believers settle into a belonging without exclusion." [11]

In order to ground the claims made to this point, Kaplan notes Alison's recourse to scriptural texts, particularly the vision of Cornelius in Acts 10 which is identified as a major impetus for allowing the baptism of non-Jewish people. Alison, in fact, identifies Acts 10:28[12] as "an extraordinary anthropological earthquake" insofar as it serves to break down the exclusionary walls which had been incorrectly erected around the early Christian church. This Biblical Revelation is seen as calling "into question such patterns of identity seeking" which serve to build walls that diminish humanity's fundamental oneness in Christ.[13]

Kaplan then identifies Alison's advocation of indifference when it comes to a Christian's attitude vis à vis the institutional Church. Alison notes that such an attitude "is of vital importance for fundamental ecclesiology" insofar as it, in Kaplan's words, "permits believers to *be in* and *belong to* the Church in a new way."[14] For Alison, Jesus always maintained an indifferent view of the Temple rather than one of anger or hatred, and this should be seen as enabling Christians to "relate indifferently to supposedly sacred structures."[15]

For Alison, it is incorrect to conceive of the Church as a temple in the first place, for

> It is the constant opening up of our intellects and imaginations toward the engaging in a new form of shepherding, leading people away from being trapped in sacred structures and forms of behaviour run by stumbling blocks.[16]

Noting that, for many readers, this description will not match their experience of the Church, he maintains that such indifference is a sign of spiritual maturity. If we lack this, this means that we have "not left the Temple at all" and are, instead, still "locked in to the centre of mimetic fascination, with its draw and is repulsion, and our sense of being good and bad will be utterly dependent on it."[17] This amounts to a kind of moral failure, then, for this indicates that one has not yet been "converted" from his/her mimetic fascination with the church, wishing to derive his/her moral worth and justification not from God's free gift of grace and forgiveness, but from a human institution.

This leads directly to Kaplan's sixth theme, namely, that we can only completely work through a false notion of being and belonging to the church if we maintain a constant connection to the Christ who upends the mimetic logic of cold institutionalism. This connection is to be maintained through Eucharistic worship which is seen as being the mechanism for turning this logic on its head. To quote Alison, "there is not true worship except in the presence of the true victim, because it is only from the victim that the voice which can undo the lies will come."[18] Insofar as this process takes time and patience, it requires a constant practice and posture which Kaplan classifies as "Eucharistic abiding." By means of the constant celebration of the Eucharist, we are pulled "out of a force field of Romantic self-regard and into a remembering of our being forgiven by the innocent victim."[19] Ultimately, "it is only by *abiding* that we can experience the slow process of coming to understand how we are caught up in unhealthy being and belonging," a process which also entails our owning up to our past sins of regarding the Church mimetically.[20]

This notion of Eucharistic or sacramental abiding in the Church has, of course, a very biographical resonance for Alison. As a gay man and a priest, he has had to navigate the narrows of being a part of, arguably, one of the most simultaneously homophobic and homoerotic institutions on earth on the one hand and his accepting of himself as a gay man on the other. As one reads Alison's writings, particularly *Faith Beyond Resentment*, one can sense the long struggle that Alison has had to undergo to reconcile these aspects of his identity. Unlike many others in his situation who have chosen to leave the institutional church, he chooses to "abide," a decision related to his maintaining that the Church has a fundamental role to play in teaching people how to enter into a new way of being and belonging. Indeed, he notes, "during the slow drip-drip of regular participation at Sunday Mass," the real "nonresentful presence" of the Risen Lord becomes present in the gathered community who "keeps alive the dynamic of enabling us to find ourselves within a catholic story."[21] In the final analysis, then, Alison seems to privilege the locally gathered Eucharistic community over a centrally organized Magisterium. In Kaplan's words, "Alison suggests imagining the Church as the group of people—however haltingly or invisibly—not totally opposed to receiving the graces needed to abide peacefully with another."[22]

The final theme Kaplan highlights in presenting Alison's ecclesiology is the Church's call to portray a "victimless sacred" which enables people "to receive an identity without resentment."[23] In order to get to this point, Christians should slowly unlearn a patriarchal view of the church and substitute a more fraternal one. This would represent a new way of belonging which "requires a letting-go of the need for human approval, because such approval can never mediate the graced sense of approval that comes from God."[24] Focusing on the need to be approved by the ecclesiastical father-figure, then, represents a failure to do one's part in realizing the new form of ecclesial community based on a proper sense of being and belonging.

The Church is, ultimately, "a dwelling place for lifelong therapy," a place where individual Christians can confess their past patterns of sinful being and belonging.[25] Reconciliation and penance as "a place where one can slowly 'cook' in therapy" is the place where one is "loved into a more relaxed way of being and belonging."[26] As a result of this long and patient process, believers are led to accepting a new mode of identity in the Church, a true "faith beyond resentment."

QUESTIONING ELEMENTS OF ALISON'S FUNDAMENTAL ECCLESIOLOGY

Let us briefly summarize the seven themes or "marks" of a fundamental ecclesiology deduced from Alison's theology. First, the Church is "founded" in the free gift of graced forgiveness and friendship offered by the Risen Christ. This freely given forgiveness serves to teach and invite the followers of the Risen One into a new kind of community which is itself founded on this forgiveness instead of vengeance. This leads to the formulation of an undefensive and inclusive ecclesiology, a move which is itself grounded in and justified by Alison's reading of Scripture. Christians are called to cultivate a sense of indifference toward the Church in its institutionality which represents being and belonging in the Church in a nonmimetic fashion. Moreover, Alison advocates a Eucharistic/liturgical abiding in the Church as a means of bringing about this nonmimetic form of community. All in all, the Church is called to model a victimless sacred which gives people the means to grow into spiritual maturity which is characterized as a faith beyond anger and resentment.

While I would agree that moving to a space of a spiritually mature "faith beyond resentment" should be the goal, I question whether such an ecclesiology bypasses or downplays the important role that justified anger can play in reforming church structures. While Jesus did forgive the disciples, this same Jesus also wielded a whip and drove out the money changers from the Temple. Far from being "indifferent," it seems that Jesus harbored a justified and righteous zeal for the Temple and Jerusalem, going so far as to weep over the former's upcoming destruction. Furthermore, the relaxed Eucharistic abiding in the church Alison advocates seems rather unconvincing when the same church sings each evening that God "has showed strength with His arm," and "has put down the mighty from their seat and exalted the humble and weak." While the ultimate sign of this strength and exaltation is nothing other than the Cross and the grace and forgiveness streaming from it, sometimes for this efficacious grace and forgiveness to be fully appropriated and habituated, we who are the "hands and feet of Christ" are commissioned to model the latter's zeal: driving out the contemporary money changers from the Temple. Far from being indifferent or apathetic to the structures of the visible church, we must allow "zeal for the *house*" to motivate us in deconstructing structures which continue the mimetic logic Alison so rightly criticizes.

Indeed, as I read Alison, I cannot help but be a bit struck at his criticism of structures and Magisterium on the one hand and his unfailing trust in and reliance on the Eucharistic liturgy on the other. The liturgy and Eucharist seem, for Alison, to create a space where the new sense of being and belonging are "really" present by virtue of the "real presence" of the Crucified and Risen One in the consecrated bread and wine. This real presence seems, then, to hover above the Church in its institutionality rather than being inextricably caught up in it. Following Louis-Marie Chauvet's analysis that one can never completely separate the human and divine elements in the celebration of the sacraments, it seems to me a bit naïve to think that just because the Eucharist is celebrated that it automatically ensures that a "victimless sacred" is enacted.[27] While there are certainly parishes which strive to model this, there are equally many, it seems, which have no interest in exploring such a thing. While pointing out the moral fault of such mimetic logic, Alison does not provide a systemic means to overcome it which focuses on structures and institutions more than individual conversions.[28] While it is true that institutions are only "converted" insofar as its individual members are, it is equally true that sometimes people need a rude awakening to see the forest for the trees. For some, perhaps, the Sermon on the Mount was less effective than the crisp cracking of a whip.

THE INTERRUPTION OF THE OTHER AND FUNDAMENTAL ECCLESIOLOGY

For Alison, it was his experience as a gay priest and reading of Girard which gave him the heuristic tool by which to see the mimetic structures in place in the institutional church which made gay people into a scapegoat. Probably as a result of many sleepless nights and intense discernment, he eventually came into a place of mutual acceptance of himself as a gay man and of the Church—though the institutionality of the latter was to be regarded with a healthy dose of indifference. Through this, Alison was able to reconcile his dual identity and so was able to create a space for himself to "survive" within the Church.[29] While I cannot question elements of his discernment, I do feel compelled to question whether such a model would be useful for others who are contextualized differently. As indicated above, the Eucharist can become itself a tool in the mimetic logic Alison claims it is free from. As the Eucharist is itself mediated through institutionality (approved liturgical books, scriptural formulae which have been accepted as canonical, confected by validly ordained male priests), if the Eucharist is to enact a realty free of mimetic logic, so too is the Church called to do this. While Alison would agree with this sentiment, I find that he does not adequately account for what the Bible calls "hardness of heart" (whether personally or collectively) as well as the means for beginning to break this. While, it is true, that the "drip-drip" of the regular celebration of the Eucharist might eventually wear this down, what about structures that would preserve the Eucharist as a "prize for the perfect" rather than as a means to healing?

In short, what is needed is a means of breaking open structures which are closed off to recognizing the mimetic logic they have become very comfortable with. What is needed is a "whip" to wake such individuals and institutions up from their comfortable bourgeois complacency. In order to devise such a model, I make use of the category of "interruption" as developed by the Belgian theologian, Lieven Boeve.

In his book, *God Interrupts History: Theology in a Time of Upheaval*, Boeve notes that the category of interruption is able to hold together the internal continuity of ecclesial narratives while, at the same time, inserting an element of newness ("discontinuity") into them which must also be accounted for.[30] For, as Boeve notes, "what is interrupted does not simply continue as though nothing has happened."[31] Even though interruptions don't destroy the narrative, they "intensely halt the narrative sequence" and, thus, "draw attention to [the narrative's] narrative character and force an opening toward the other in the narrative."[32] The other halts the narrative by his/her testimony which forces the workaday functioning of the narrative to halt and reconsider the appropriate way of proceeding. The moment of interruption prompts a *crisis of discernment* which is itself caused by the *conflict of interpretations* precipitated by the interruption. It is, in many ways, akin to how Paul Ricoeur describes the creation of new metaphors in *The Rule of Metaphor.* Even after a new metaphor is used, some time elapses before it is accepted that it serves to reveal new shades of meaning to the thing being described.[33] Nevertheless, the conflict of interpretations does not cease until some resolution comes: the narrative cannot simply continue on as if nothing has happened.

In coming to give theological justification for interruption, Boeve provides a reading of the entire history of God's interaction with God's people as occurring in the mode of interruption. Concretely, Boeve points to "the call of Abraham, the Exodus tradition, the figure of the Prophet, the Pilgrim, the Suffering Servant, Mount Tabor, the Resurrection, and so forth."[34] All of these narratives point to the fact that "in the concreteness of particular histories, the God professed by Christians repeatedly breaks open the narratives of human beings and communities, including narratives about Godself."[35] It is Jesus of Nazareth who, for Boeve, is the interrupter *par excellence*, for his narrative continually refuses to become "closed," a fact made very poignantly by the Paschal Mystery.[36] Whereas the religious and secular powers of the age wanted to definitively close Jesus' narrative by killing him, Jesus's followers experienced it (and continue to experience it) "as newly and radically opened by God in the Resurrection."[37] Whenever personal or collective narratives become closed and inward-looking, "God nevertheless still breaks them open."[38] To put this another way, Jesus interrupted the closed narrative of how God was "supposed" to work, even to the point of being killed and then rising from the dead. As followers of Christ, we are called to engage in an *imitatio Christi* whereby we, likewise, interrupt personal and collective narratives which have become closed. As Jesus was quite critical towards his own religious tradition, our following of Christ shouldn't be fearful of interrupting ecclesial narratives which have become closed. As a result of this interruption, all should be welcomed to a place of discernment where the experiences and narratives of all parties are honored and respected.

THE CRITICAL ROLE OF THE SEXUALLY ABUSED OTHER

Returning to the issue prompting this reflection, how can we conceptualize the sexually abused other as exercising the interruptive role described in the previous section? Moreover, how might this serve to augment and strengthen Alison's fundamental ecclesiology as we described it earlier in this chapter?

Looking at the way the #MeToo Movement gained traction and popularity, it goes without saying that it has served to interrupt several narratives ranging from politics, show business, to the Church. The modality of this interruption did not come only from persons embedded within each of these respective narratives—it was aided by means of the social and mass media which both propagated and further investigated elements of this phenomenon. When it comes to the uncovering of patterns of sexual abuse in the Catholic Church, the role of mass media as well as local states' attorney generals cannot be downplayed.[39] It seems highly unlikely that the victims of abuse would ever have received justice had the "other" of the "secular mass media" not interrupted the surety and "business as usual" formalism of ecclesial structures which had become more concerned with self-preservation than with advocating for victims, and then questioning how elements of church culture and procedure worked to ensure that abusers were left unpunished for so long.

While the United States Conference of Catholic Bishops did, with great fanfare, in 2002 release the *Dallas Charter* which was seen as groundbreaking in reforming this broken system, the emperor was revealed to wearing no clothes in June 2018. On June 20 of that year, Theodore Cardinal McCarrick, former Archbishop of Washington, D.C., and unofficial "face" of American Catholicism, was removed from ministry after it was revealed that he had engaged in years of abuse with minors and seminarians. The fallout from this seems yet to have fully worked itself through insofar as questions of who knew what and when have yet to be fully owned up to. More "interruptions" seem needed, then, to prompt the reforms necessary for ensuring that patterns of abuse are not allowed to continue.

While structural and institutional reasons could be given for the perdurance of abusive patterns, one of the fundamental reasons seems to be an ingrained ecclesial double-speak when it comes to questions of sexual morality. The fact that the majority of abuse victims were young postpubescent men reveals that this is not a matter of pedophilia so much as it is one of repressed and dysfunctionally expressed homosexuality.[40] Moreover, it could be argued that the official ecclesial responses which have focused on the "pedophilia crisis" rather than the sexual abuse carried out by gay men in the priesthood serve to buttress an ideological distortion. For, if all "clerical sexual abuse" is equated with pedophilia, then "homosexuality" becomes just a depraved halfway house on the highway to Hell.[41] This, implicitly, serves to buttress and confirm the Catechism's portrayal of "homosexual acts" as being "intrinsically disordered" and "closed to the gift of life."[42] In this way, implicitly, gay men become the scapegoat of the official ecclesial response to clerical sex abuse.

Much of what was described in the preceding paragraph would be shared by Alison. However, I question whether or not the appropriate posture of homosexual persons and their allies in the Church should be simply to "learn to relax," stick around, ignore the dysfunctional elements in the Church, and attempt to foster a mature "faith beyond resentment." Perhaps (at least some) of these individuals are called to interrupt on behalf of God, to call the institutional Church to account and so prevent the continual creation of new scapegoats? While it is unhealthy to remain angry and resentful in the face of realities one is powerless to change, it is a moral fault to ignore systems of injustice which are clearly visible. This moral fault is founded in the fact that any *imitatio Christi* always involves calling out systems and institutions which are so closed in their own self-preservation that they unwittingly create scapegoats. To fail at doing this could even be seen as reflecting self-interest and privilege more than a healthy spirituality.

While not the place to fully elaborate on the practical contours of this interruption, it bears identifying at least a couple of characteristics. To start, it must always take the form of a dialogue, and a dialogue implies two things. First, both parties in the dialogue must be willing to be vulnerable enough to learn from each other and so arrive at new shades of meaning. Secondly and relatedly, that both parties accept that they have something to learn from the other. In this way, one could point to the work of James Martin as representing an important inroad in this regard.[43]

A second important thing to note about this interruption is that it is not a purely "human" endeavor. God's grace must be invited into this process if it is to have any hope of succeeding. I would echo Alison's reliance on the Eucharist in providing the "drip-drip" necessary to open hearts and make grace fully operative. However, I would also maintain that for those on the margins of the Church, access to the Eucharist can be difficult, especially if they feel excluded from or threatened in their parishes. Without opening onto a full explication of sacramental theology here, I would, with Alison, simply point out the important role played by marginal Catholic communities as well as the open-table Eucharistic fellowship done by other (small "c") catholic churches.[44] While the sacraments of the visible (big "C") Catholic Church are the ordinary means of grace, they are not the *only* means. The Holy Spirit is operative in the whole of Creation, from those Catholics who find themselves at an Episcopal church on Sunday mornings to the drag queen entertaining crowds at the local gay bar. If we believe that the whole of Creation "is groaning" awaiting a future glory, it seems disingenuous to villainize those on the margins of the Church or even those who choose to leave for other Christian communions. Perhaps, their "dialogical interruptions" will be complemented by the marginal contexts out of which they are interrupting, nourished—in the first example I gave above—by the Eucharist and a local church community.

Contemporary society continues to grow more and more weary of institutions that fail to live up to their promised claims. If the Church is to serve as a moral guide and beacon in society, it must clean house and face up to its institutional shortcomings. Only in this way can the Church function as sign of hope and salvation to the world. To put this another way, the ecclesial "we" must more prophetically include the hard truths brought to the surface by means of the sexual abuse crisis. Only then will the Church be able to say #WeToo, and "we're willing to take the necessary steps to reform the structures which allowed abuse to occur."

NOTES

1. Grant Kaplan, "Imagining a Mimetic Ecclesiology" in *René Girard, Unlikely Apologist: Mimetic Theory and Fundamental Theology* (Notre Dame, IN: University of Notre Dame Press, 2016), 127–152.

2. Kaplan, 140–141.

3. James Alison, *Faith Beyond Resentment: Fragments Catholic and Gay* (New York: Crossroads, 2001), 32.

4. Kaplan, 141.

5. James Alison, *Knowing Jesus* (Springfield: Templegate, 1993), 91.

6. Kaplan, 142.

7. James Alison, *Jesus the Forgiving Victim: Listening for the Unheard Voice* (Glenview, IL: Doers, 2013), 309.

8. Ibid., 144.

9. James Alison, *The Joy of Being Wrong: Original Sin Through Easter Eyes* (New York: Crossroad, 1990), 88.

10. James Alison, *Knowing Jesus,* 90.

11. Kaplan, 144.

12. "He said to them: "You are well aware that it is against our law for a Jew to associate with or visit a Gentile. But God has shown me that I should not call anyone impure or unclean."

13. Kaplan, 145.

14. James Alison, *On Being Liked (New York: Herder and Herder, 2006),* 25.

15. Kaplan, 146–147.

16. Alison, *On Being Liked,* 125.

17. Ibid., 126.

18. James Alison, *Undergoing God: Dispatches from the Scene of a Break-In* (London: Continuum, 2006), 44.

19. Kaplan, 148.

20. *Ibid.*

21. Alison, *Faith Beyond Resentment*, 122.

22. Kaplan, 149.

23. Ibid., 150.

24. Ibid.

25. Kaplan, 151.

26. Ibid.

27. Cf.: Louis-Marie Chauvet, "La demande d'un 'rite de passage': Le Baptême des petits enfants" in *Le Corps, Chemin de Dieu: Les Sacrements* (Paris: Bayard, 2010), 353ff.

28. As Alison has pointed out elsewhere, the focus should be on small localized Eucharistic Communities, "small groups that are able to meet regularly around a Eucharist and not only share the liturgy but also invite Jesus into their midst as one who talks to them through the gospel of the day as well as through their own sharing of their experiences as they talk through the gospel among themselves." These communities, often made up of those whom the mainstream church excludes, should be seen as "the church of the confessors: those who held firm to their faith, and confessed it, in the midst of the great persecution." Alison, who was prompted to write these words after Pope Francis surprised him with a phone call validating his priestly ministry, seems convinced that such Eucharistic communities witness to "Pope Francis' expressed view that the peripheries will bring the gospel to the center." Without denigrating the importance of the peripheries and the prophetic witness they provide, it still strikes me as unlikely that such very small and covert communities will effect the changes in church teaching on sexuality which Alison advocates for. These communities serve an important role, to be sure, in providing Catholics on the margins with access to the sacraments, however, one needs to find a balance between pastoral boldness and the necessary and mediatorial role of institutions. (James Alison, "Father James Alison on How Pope Francis is Changing the Church." U.S. Catholic. March 3, 2020. https://uscatholic.org/articles/202003/father-james-alison-how-pope-francis-is-changing-church/).

29. Alison describes this in detail in a recent Commonweal article wherein he describes how his ministry always makes him vulnerable to being killed by the "wolf" of the "clerical closet" which is populated by individuals hiding the truth about themselves in order to advance their clerical careers. Here as elsewhere, he offers no tools for structural reform and instead offers a—quite powerful—personal testimony about how he is willing to risk his own good standing in order to live authentically. Personal testimony is important, as is pastoral boldness: but more is needed in order to ensure that future generations of priests do not suffer in the same way as Alison has. (James Alison. "Facing Down the Wolf." Commonweal. June 2020. http://www.commonwealmagazine.org/print/41212).

30. Cf.: Lieven Boeve, *God Interrupts History: Theology in a Time of Upheaval* (London: Continuum, 2007).

31. Boeve, *God Interrupts History*, 42.

32. Ibid.

33. Cf.: Paul Ricoeur, *The Rule of Metaphor: The Creation of Meaning in Language*, Robert Czerny trans. (London: Routledge, 2003) and T. Derrick Witherington, "Praying in the Breach: Worshipping Through the End of Metaphysics," *Horizons* 45, no. 2 (2018).

34. Boeve, Interrupting Tradition, 106.

35. Boeve, *God Interrupts History*, 46.
36. Boeve, *Interrupting Tradition*, 106.
37. Boeve, *God Interrupts History*, 46.
38. Ibid., 47.
39. Alison would not deny this either, especially insofar as he was interviewed and named by Frederic Martel's 2019 bombshell of a book, *In the Closet of the Vatican: Power, Homosexuality, Hypocrisy*. Cf.: James Alison. "Welcome to my World (notes on the reception of bombshell)." James Alison Online. February 2019. http://www.jamesalison.com/welcome-to-my-world/.
40. It should be noted, however, that alt-right Catholic groups have seized on this fact as a means to further intensify their homophobic villainization of the LGBTQ+ community (i.e., https://www.churchmilitant.com/news/article/qa-on-clergy-sex-abuse-scandal). While it should already be clear, I here emphasize that this is not my purpose: more than seeking to expunge gay men from the priesthood (the so-called gay lobby), I would see the "coming out" of gay men in the priesthood as a means to prompt serious ecclesial discernment around questions of sexuality, not to mention that an "outed" system would serve to disarm those who use it to abuse the vulnerable.
41. For more analysis as well as relevant statistics, see Karen J. Terry "Child sexual abuse within the Catholic Church: a review of global perspectives, *International Journal of Comparative and Applied Criminal Justice*, 39, no. 2 (2015), 139–154 and Gerard J. McGlone "Prevalence and Incidence of Roman Catholic Clerical Sex Offenders," *Sexual Addiction & Compulsivity*, 10, nos. 2–3 (2003), 111–121.
42. *Catechism of the Catholic Church*, #2357.
43. Cf.: James Martin, SJ, *Building a Bridge: How the Catholic Church and the LGBT Community Can Enter into a Relationship of Respect, Compassion, and Sensitivity* (New York: Harper One, 2018).
44. Cf.: James Alison, *How Pope Francis Is Changing the Church*.

BIBLIOGRAPHY

Alison, James. "Facing Down the Wolf." *Commonweal*. June 2020. http://www.commonwealmagazine.org/print/41212.

———. *Faith Beyond Resentment: Fragments Catholic and Gay*. New York: Crossroads, 2001.

———. "Father James Alison on How Pope Francis Is Changing the Church." *U.S. Catholic*. March 3, 2020. https://uscatholic.org/articles/202003/father-james-alison-how-pope-francis-is-changing-church/.

———. *Jesus the Forgiving Victim: Listening for the Unheard Voice*. Glenview, IL: Doers, 2013.

———. *The Joy of Being Wrong: Original Sin through Easter Eyes*. New York: Crossroad, 1990.

———. *Knowing Jesus*. Springfield: Templegate, 1993.

———. *On Being Liked*. New York: Herder and Herder, 2006.

———. *Undergoing God: Dispatches from the Scene of a Break-In.* London: Continuum, 2006.

———. "Welcome to my World . . . (notes on the reception of bombshell)." *James Alison Online.* February 2019. http://www.jamesalison.com/welcome-to-my-world/.

Boeve, Lieven. *God Interrupts History: Theology in a Time of Upheaval.* London: Continuum, 2007.

Catechism of the Catholic Church, 2nd ed. Washington DC: United States Conference of Catholic Bishops, 2019.

Chauvet, Louis-Marie. "La demande d'un 'rite de passage': Le Baptême des petits enfants" in *Le Corps, Chemin de Dieu: Les Sacrements.* Paris: Bayard, 2010.

Kaplan, Grant. "Imagining a Mimetic Ecclesiology" in *René Girard, Unlikely Apologist: Mimetic Theory and Fundamental Theology.* Notre Dame, IN: University of Notre Dame Press, 2016.

Martin, James. *Building a Bridge: How the Catholic Church and the LGBT Community Can Enter into a Relationship of Respect, Compassion, and Sensitivity.* New York: Harper One, 2018.

McGlone, Gerard J. "Prevalence and Incidence of Roman Catholic Clerical Sex Offenders." *Sexual Addiction & Compulsivity* 10, nos. 2–3 (2003), 111–121.

Ricoeur, Paul. *The Rule of Metaphor: The Creation of Meaning in Language.* Translated by Robert Czerny. London: Routledge, 2003.

Terry, Karen J. "Child Sexual Abuse within the Catholic Church: A Review of Global Perspectives." *International Journal of Comparative and Applied Criminal Justice* 39, no. 2 (2015), 139–154.

Witherington, T. Derrick. "Praying in the Breach: Worshipping through the End of Metaphysics." *Horizons* 45, no. 2 (2018), 317–346.

Index

The 100, 89–100

Abrams, J. J., 27, 29, 36
Alison, James, 54, 56, 67–68, 80, 84–85, 217–23, 225–26
anagnorisis, 61–62, 65
anosognosia, 73, 75, 78, 80
Anselm of Canterbury, 85
anthropology, xviii–xix, 156
anti-semitism, 141
apocalypse, xxi–xxii, 45, 88–89, 184
archaic world, 129, 133–36
Aristotle, 61–62, 136
Atonement, 170, 175
Augustine, 27, 35, 76, 179–80
Avengers, 155–57

Barthes, Roland, 28–29
Boeve, Lieven, 223–24; "Interruption," 223–24

The Brothers Karamazov, 92

Bruce Banner / The Hulk, 169–71, 175–77, 179–80

Campbell, Joseph, 13, 15, 28
catharsis, 123–124

the church, 58–59, 64, 217–27
contagion, 18, 27, 48, 68, 74, 88, 91, 189
conversion, x, xx, 79, 87, 92–98, 109–10, 168–69
Cowdell, Scott, 151
Covington Catholic High School, 185–87
crisis, 20; sacrificial crisis, 156–58, 163–65

the cross, xviii–xxi, 58–60, 65–67, 136–38; crucifixion, xviii, 57–60

Dante Alighieri, 72, 128
Dionysius, xxi–xxii, 179
desire: borrowed, xii; metaphysical, xiii, 76, 156; mimetic, x–xxiii, 30, 73, 106–9; triangular, xi, xxiii, 75–76, 107, 142
double-bind, 17, 73
Dr. Doom, 153, 155–63; von Doom, Victor, 169–70; God-Doom, 158–59

Eagleton, Terry, 30
ecclesiology, 217–27
Eisner, Will, 141–49
eros, 107–9

eternal return, 163–65
Eucharist, 220–23, 226, 228

Fight Club, 60–61
Flash Gordon, 29, 33
forgiveness, 94–95, 134–35, 218–22
Frankenstein, 169–75, 177–80

globalization, 204–5, 208–9
Gordon, Andrew, 27–28
Gospel, xviii, xxi–xxii, 21–22, 52, 64–68, 94–95, 135, 186, 194–95
grace, 9–11, 63–64, 84–85, 95, 97, 218–22

The Great British Baking Show, 203

hedonic adaptation, 74, 76
hermeneutics, 96, 100
hero, 13–16, 53–54
Hickman, Jonathan, 155–67
Hoarders, 73–85
Hobbes, Thomas, 30
homosexuality, 225
honor, 115–16, 121, 133

imitation, 5–6, 30, 73–76, 174–75, 178–79, 193
interdividual, xii, xiv, 4

jealousy, 17, 22, 44–45, 111
Jedi, 16–20, 22–24, 29–30
Jesus Christ, xiv, xvi, xviii–xxiii, 21–23, 45, 47, 49, 52–53, 57, 59, 64–68, 82, 93, 103, 107, 134–36, 138, 162, 216–17, 220, 222
Johnson, Rian, 30
Judaism, 141–42
Jung, Carl, 28

kairotic, 63–64

The Karate Kid, 105–18,
The Karate Kid, Part II, 112–13

Kant, Immanuel, 129; *Philosophy of Law*, 131
Kaplan, Grant, xxi, 95, 158, 217–21
katechon, 97–98
Kearney, Richard, 32

Lamb of God, xviii, 23, 58, 126, 135
lament, 83, 142, 149
Lefebure, Leo, 118–19
Leviticus, 124–25
Lucas, George, 28, 29, 35
Lucifer, 170

McSweeney, Terence, 34–35
mediation: external, x, xiii–xiv, xxiii, 4–5, 21–22; internal, x, xiii–xv, 5, 107, 140
metaphysical desire. *See* desire
midrash, 142–43
mimetic desire. *See* desire
mimetic doubles, 6, 15, 18, 31, 34, 188
mimetic rivalry, xv–xxiii, 5–6, 18, 30, 45, 99, 107, 114, 124, 142, 195, 204, 206–11
model, xi, xiii–xiv, 4–6, 17, 73–76, 105–8, 112–13, 117, 141, 146, 159–60, 175–76, 177–79, 193, 220–21
model-obstacle, xiv, 17, 74, 110, 114, 163
monster, 168–72
Moses, 149–50
mythology: Girard's critique of, xviii–xix, 58–62, 65–66; myths, 27–28, 31, 34, 35; monomyth, 13, 28

National Socialism, 30, 33
New Testament, 143
Nietzsche, Friedrich, xxi, 93
Nozick, Robert, 131–33
novelistic truth, xx–xxi, 75, 93, 167–68, 177–78

Oedipus, 14–17
ontological sickness, xxiii, 6, 71, 74, 79–80

Paradise Lost, 169–70

the passion, 13, 48, 53, 57, 68, 133

penal substitution, 126, 135–36
priesthood, 223, 227
protest against God, 140, 142–50
pseudo-Dionysius, 79, 84–85
    resurrection, xviii–xix, 24, 5–59, 63, 58, 216–17, 222
        Richards, Reed, 155–56, 162, 165

ritual 14, 29, 31, 131–32, 170
rivalry, xv–xvi, 5–6, 8, 10–11, 15–20, 23–23, 30, 35, 45, 80, 90, 105–8, 111–13, 134, 140–41, 159, 202, 204–8
Robinette, Brian, 77
romantic lie, xii, xx, 3, 11, 75, 167–69, 177–78

sacrifice, 13–16, 94, 97–98, 131–32, 135, 154–58, 163
Satan, xviii, 18–19, 43–53
scapegoat/scapegoating, x, xiv, xvi–xxii, 6–9, 15–16, 23, 27–36, 42, 51, 64, 95, 114, 134, 142, 144–45, 158–59, 170–81, 188–89, 223–26
Secret Wars, 155–66
sexual abuse, 224–27

Shakespeare, William: *The Tragedy of Hamlet, Prince of Denmark*, 124–26; *The Tragedy of Julius Caesar*, 134
Shelley, Mary, 169–77
skandalon, xviii
Sons of Anarchy, 123–36
Star Wars, 13–24, 27–36

The Strange Case of Dr. Jekyll & Mr. Hyde, 172–74

Sutter, Kurt, 123–26, 132, 135

Talmud, 142
triangular desire. *See* desire
tutelary beliefs, 107
twins, 18, 164

Ueshiba, Morihei, 111–12

victim/victims, xvi, xviii–xix, 20–23, 31–35, 47–48, 52–55, 57, 59, 62, 66–67, 93–98, 123–24, 156, 158–59, 216–18

The Village, 58–59, 61–62

violence, xvii–xxii, 6, 13–24, 29–36, 47–49, 87–91, 93–98, 113–16, 122–29, 140–44, 154–58, 161–64, 171–79, 189–92

About the Editors

Ryan G. Duns is a Jesuit priest and Assistant Professor of Theology at Marquette University. He holds a PhD in Systematic Theology from Boston College (2018). He is the author of *Spiritual Exercises for a Secular Age: Desmond's Quest for God* (Notre Dame Press, 2020). Ryan has published articles on René Girard, Karl Rahner, Jean-Luc Marion, Iris Murdoch, and the Irish philosopher William Desmond.

T. Derrick Witherington holds a PhD and STD in Systematic Theology from the Catholic University of Leuven, Belgium where he was an active member of the research unit Systematic Theology and the Study of Religion and the research groups Fundamental and Political Theology and Theology in a Postmodern Context, serving as secretary of the latter. Currently, he is the director of liturgy for Gesu Parish at Marquette University and adjunct lecturer of theology at Marquette University in Milwaukee, Wisconsin. His research interests include theological method, continental philosophy of religion, sacramental theology, and liturgy.

About the Contributors

Jordan Almanzar is professor of Greek and Latin studies at Magdalen College of the Liberal Arts in Warner, New Hampshire. He also teaches both languages online for Kolbe Academy. His interest in Girard became acute during his doctoral studies in Göttingen, Germany, where he completed a PhD in *History and Literature of Ancient Christianity* with a published dissertation entitled, *He Whom a Dream Hath Possessed: The Life and Works of the American John Knox*.

Brian Bajzek is visiting assistant professor of theology at Marquette University. He holds a PhD in theological studies from Regis College and University of Toronto (2018). His current work explores how the productive tensions inherent in intersubjectivity and otherness illuminate the intersection of theological anthropology and trinitarian theology. He has published in *The Heythrop Journal, International Philosophical Quarterly, Theological Studies*, and several edited volumes. He is also the director of the philosophy component of the International Institute for Method in Theology.

Matthew Brake is the series editor for Lexington's Theology and Pop Culture series. He has masters degrees in interdisciplinary studies and philosophy from George Mason University. He also has a Master of Divinity from Regent University. He has published numerous articles in the series *Kierkegaard Research: Sources, Reception, Resources*. He has chapters in *Deadpool and Philosophy*, *Wonder Woman and Philosophy*, and *Mr. Robot and Philosophy*. He also co-edits a series for Claremont Press on religion and comics with A. David Lewis.

Paolo Diego Bubbio (PhD, University of Turin, Italy) is associate professor of philosophy in the School of Humanities and Communication Arts at Western Sydney University, Australia. He is the author of *Sacrifice in the Post-Kantian Tradition: Perspectivism, Intersubjectivity, and Recognition* (State University of New York Press, 2014), *God and the Self in Hegel: Beyond Subjectivism* (State University of New York Press, 2017), and *Intellectual Sacrifice and Other Mimetic Paradoxes* (Michigan State University Press, 2018). He is also the coeditor of several collections of essays, including *Mimetic Theory and Film* (with Chris Fleming: Bloomsbury, 2019). His research is in post-Kantian philosophy, philosophy of religion, mimetic theory, and the intersections among these fields of inquiry. He has been researching and writing about mimetic theory for twenty-five years.

Erik Buys studied theology at the Catholic University of Leuven (Belgium) and currently teaches at a Jesuit High School (Sint-Jozefscollege, Aalst, Belgium). He published several books and articles in which he mainly explores the relevance of Judeo-Christian tradition in today's world, often using René Girard's mimetic theory as a starting point. Recent publications include the book *Geen vrede, maar een zwaard—Een christelijke provocatie in tijden van Facebook, IS en vluchtelingenstromen* (Averbode, 2017) and the article *El engaño, el deseo y la novela gráfica* on the graphic novel *Watchmen* for the Spanish Xiphias Gladius (Madrid, 2018), an academic journal dedicated to mimetic theory. Apart from being a member of the Dutch Girard Society, he is also an elected member of the Colloquium on Violence and Religion (COV&R). His blog, Mimetic Margins (https://mimeticmargins.com/), is dedicated to making mimetic theory and its implications known to a wider audience.

George A. Dunn has taught philosophy and religion in both the United States and the People's Republic of China. He is currently a special research fellow with the Institute for Globalizing Civilization at Zhejiang University in Hangzhou, China. He has published extensively on popular culture, as well as on Christianity, mimetic theory, ethics, philosophy of religion, and political philosophy. He is the editor of several books on philosophy and pop culture, including *The Philosophy of Christopher Nolan* (Lexington, 2017) and *Sons of Anarchy and Philosophy* (Wiley-Blackwell, 2013), both coedited with Jason T. Eberl. His latest book is *A New Politics for Philosophy: Essays on Plato, Nietzsche, and Strauss* (Lexington, 2021), coedited with Mango Telli.

Justin Lee is a lecturer in the English Department at the University of California, Irvine, where he earned an MFA in creative writing in 2014. His fiction and nonfiction have appeared in *First Things*, ABC's *Religion and Ethics*, *Spectator USA*, *The Independent*, *Vice*, *The Saturday Evening Post*, *Los Angeles Review of Books*, *ZYZZYVA*, and elsewhere. He is an associate editor at *Arc Digital*, co-host of the podcast *From Babylon, with Love*, and an active member of the Colloquium on Violence and Religion.

Daniel DeForest London is an Episcopal priest and rector of Christ Episcopal Church in Eureka, California. He earned his PhD in Christian spirituality at the Graduate Theological Union in Berkeley. He teaches courses on spirituality, ethics, and mysticism at the Church Divinity School of the Pacific and the Episcopal School for Deacons. He is the author of *Theodicy and Spirituality in the Fourth Gospel: A Girardian Perspective* published by Fortress Academic.

John C. McDowell is the academic dean at St Athanasius College and a professor in philosophy, systematic theology, and moral theology at the university, based in Melbourne. He has been the director of research and professor of theology at the University of Divinity; chair of theology and religion at the University of Newcastle, NSW; Meldrum lecturer in systematic theology at the University of Edinburgh; and doctoral student at Cambridge University. He has written several books and over sixty articles and book chapters, including the studies in popular culture: *The Politics of Big Fantasy: Studies in Cultural Suspicion* (Jefferson, NC: McFarland Press, 2014); *The Ideology of Identity Politics in George Lucas* (Jefferson, NC: McFarland Press, 2016); and *The Gospel According to Star Wars: Faith, Hope and the Force*, 2nd ed. (Louisville, Kentucky: Westminster John Knox Press, 1st ed. 2007, 2nd ed. 2017). Among other things, he is currently working on two further books on cinema: *Mimetic Theory and Disney's Star Wars* and *Reel Violence*.

Stephanie Perdew is an affiliate professor of Christian history at Garrett-Evangelical Theological Seminary in Evanston, Illinois, and the senior pastor of the First Congregational Church, United Church of Christ, in Wilmette, Illinois. She is the president of the Liturgical Conference, the editorial board for the journal *Liturgy*, and is the past editor of the *Proceedings* of the North American Academy of Liturgy. She is a co-author of *The Work of the People: What We Do in Worship and Why* (Rowman & Littlefield, 2006) and the co-editor of the volume "Inter-Religious Worship," *Liturgy* 26.3 (2011). A frequent presenter at interfaith events, she is a co-chair of the Jewish-Christian Interfaith Dialogue Group for Female Clergy in the Chicago area. Her research interests include the application of mimetic theory in congregational settings and liturgy; Jewish and Christian parting of the ways in early Christianity, and women's liturgical roles in the early church.

Robert Grant Price, PhD, lectures at the Institute of Communication, Culture, Information, and Technology at the University of Toronto Mississauga.

Anna Scanlon is the director of the Writing Center at Illinois Wesleyan University. She holds a PhD in English with a focus on the medical humanities from Marquette University. Her interest in Girard was sparked by her Uncle Dick, who sent her her first copy of *Anorexia and Mimetic Desire*. (Thanks, Uncle Dick!) Her current publications include "Everyday Reflective Practice" in *The Writing Center Journal* 37.2 and "Graduate Tutor Professional Development—and Leadership—in an Undergraduate Writing Center" in *Redefining Roles* from Utah State University Press.

Ryan Smock has taught higher-education philosophy, composition, and literature classes for ten years. During this time he has consistently received awards for "effective or highly effective" teaching from the Department of Education despite being legally blind and hard of hearing. He currently teaches at Mesa Community College, where his unfathomable love for applying philosophy to pop culture infuses and invigorates every lesson. His current projects include developing a podcast series for special needs parenting, constructing a blog that explores Girard's mimetics as they appear in video games, and writing his first novel.

www.ingramcontent.com/pod-product-compliance
Lightning Source LLC
Chambersburg PA
CBHW020114010526
44115CB00008B/822